# BIG BOOK OF INTERNET FILE TRANSFER RFCs

# BIG BOOK OF INTERNET FILE TRANSFER RFCs

Compiled by

**Pete Loshin**

**Morgan Kaufmann**

An Imprint of ACADEMIC PRESS
*A Harcourt Science and Technology Company*
San Diego   San Francisco   New York   Boston
London   Sydney   Tokyo

ACADEMIC PRESS

*A Harcourt Science and Technology Company*

525 B Street, Suite 1900, San Diego, CA 92101-4495 USA

http://www.academicpress.com

Academic Press

Harcourt Place, 32 Jamestown Rd., London NW1 7BY, UK

http://www.hbuk.co.uk/ap/

Morgan Kaufmann

*A Harcourt Science and Technology Company*

340 Pine Street, Sixth Floor, San Francisco, CA 94104-3205

http://www.mkp.com

Library of Congress Catalog Number: 99-69871

International Standard Book Number: 0-12-455845-3

Printed in the United States of America

00 01 02 03 IP 9 8 7 6 5 4 3 2 1

This book is dedicated to the members of the Internet Engineering Task Force.

# Table of Contents

Foreword    ix

Preface    xi

Introduction    xiii

RFC 906      Bootstrap Loading Using TFTP

RFC 949      FTP Unique-Named Store Command

RFC 959      File Transfer Protocol

RFC 1068     Background File Transfer Program (BFTP)

RFC 1350     The TFTP Protocol (Revision 2)

RFC 1415     FTP-FTAM Gateway Specification

RFC 1579     Firewall-Friendly FTP

RFC 1635     How to Use Anonymous FTP (FYI 24)

RFC 1639     FTP Operation Over Big Address Records (FOOBAR)

RFC 1785     TFTP Option Negotiation Analysis

RFC 1986     Experiments with a Simple File Transfer Protocol for Radio Links
             using Enhanced Trivial File Transfer Protocol (ETFTP)

RFC 2090     TFTP Multicast Option

RFC 2228     FTP Security Extensions

RFC 2347     TFTP Option Extension

RFC 2348    TFTP Blocksize Option

RFC 2349    TFTP Timeout Interval and Transfer Size Options

RFC 2389    Feature Negotiation Mechanism for the File Transfer Protocol

RFC 2428    FTP Extensions for IPv6 and NATs

RFC 2577    FTP Security Considerations

RFC 2585    Internet X.509 Public Key Infrastructure Operational Protocols: FTP and HTTP

RFC 2640    Internationalization of the File Transfer Protocol

Index

# Foreword

Today, it is hard to imagine the Internet without electronic mail or the downloading of material from a remote computer. Yet FTP lies at the foundation of each.

FTP originally stood for File Transfer Program, and it is one of the two oldest protocols in networking history. It antedates by several years both the Transmission Control Protocol (TCP) and the Internet Protocol (IP). Along with rlogin, it constituted teh entire repetoire of the ARPANET in 1969. By 1971,FTP had become the File Transfer Protocol (RFC 114) and the foundation for email (FTP mail, by Ray Tomlinson).

The FTP command is the user interface to the protocol, enabling file transfers to and from remote sites over the Internet. More importantly, FTP works across architectures: the source of the file and the destination of the file are not relevant to its successful transfer. And for a decade and a half, file transfers by FTP consituted over half the traffic on the ARPANET and the Internet.

Though it has but six "flags," it has over 50 commands. And it is far from simple. FTP has waxed in complexity with the Internet and its users. It's worth noting that there are several commands that are rarely (if ever) used anymore.

In the 1970s, there was an operating system called TENEX, which ran on the DEC-10. The TENEX file system was structured differently from those running on other computers. The tenex command set the "representation type" to that needed to talk to a TENEX machine.

This volume contains all the RFCs relevant to today's operation of FTP in a networked world. These RFCs date from Findlayson's RFC 906 (June 1, 1984) to Bill Curtin's RFC 2640 (July 1999).

RFC 906 can be seen arising from a series of early RFCs (114, 141, 171, 172); through RFC 412, Hicks' "User FTP Documentation" (27 November 1972); to RFC 783, TFTP (= Trivial File Transfer Protocol, K.R. Sollins, June 1981).

The increasing size of the Internet gave rise to a more hostile environment, and so we have RFC 1579, making FTP "firewall friendly," RFC 2090, involving multicasting, RFC 2228, detailing security extensions, as well as RFC 2577 on "Security Considerations."

The utility and the resilience of FTP over three decades is an example of just how important moving files is. This book puts all the important moving files is. This book puts all the important sources in one place, rendering the information readily accessible.

Peter H. Salus
Seattle, WA

# Preface

Most of the content in this book is available online, for free. As long as you know which RFCs you're looking for, you can find them (and more) in any number of RFC archives. In fact, if you don't know what you're looking for and just want to read the RFCs in this book, you can find them listed on my web site at Internet-Standard.com (along with RFCs in all the other books in the series, as well as RFCs on other selected topics).

So why should you buy this book? If you're like me, you probably find a book a more manageable tool for accessing information that is related and cross-referenced. Many of the RFCs here refer to each other; many of those refer to several different RFCs in this volume. Surely some readers will prefer to open related RFCs in multiple browser windows and then flip from one window to another. Personally, I prefer the option of physically flipping pages — it's faster, and that means I don't forget what I was looking for in the "other" RFC. Books have many other advantages over digital versions of the documents, such as portability (you can read them anywhere, as long as you have some light); adaptability (you can mark, highlight, and otherwise annotate the margins); and permanence (digital media can degrade over time and online resources are not always there when you need them).

However, the most important features of this book are these:

- An excellent, comprehensive, index. You may be able to easily search for terms in a single RFC with your browser or editor, but this book's index lets you search through all the related RFCs — something not always easy or even possible online.
- An introduction to the topic in general. Few, if any, Internet topics can be covered completely in a single RFC. If you're not familiar with the topic, the

introduction offers a context in which to read the RFCs. If you are familiar with the topic, the introduction will explain why RFCs were included (and in some cases, why some RFCs were not included). In any case, the introduction provides a framework in which to read the RFCs.

- Comprehensive and authoritative coverage of the topic.

That last feature is worth talking about a little more. "Doorstop" books (books big and fat enough to hold a big heavy door open) are all too common in the computer book industry. Publishers want fat books—800, 1200, or even 1500 pages long—for a number of reasons. None of those reasons make the books better buys for the consumer. And authors are hard-pressed to fill that many pages with useful information. So filler and fluff are common.

These books contain the most authoritative documentation possible of Internet specifications. Not all RFCs are standards, but all of the RFCs in this book are full Internet standards. This means that they define the way systems must work if they are to be connected to the Internet and considered Internet standards-compliant.

What this book does not contain are lame analogies that someone has cooked up trying to explain the painfully obvious, nor does it contain paper-wasting illustrations, lists, tables, or glossaries. All it has are the primary documents of the Internet, with a few pages of introductory material, and what we think is the best index possible for this material.

Finally, the RFCs included in this book were selected so as to provide the most complete reference about LDAP and the Internet in a reasonably sized book. Historic or marginally relevant RFCs have been left out, but everything else you need (and nothing else) has been included. If you need to know more about LDAP than what is in this book, you may need to get in touch with the people who wrote the RFCs.

# Introduction

The Internet Engineering Task Force (IETF) publishes a series of documents called Requests for Comments (RFC) that represent a sort of collective consciousness for the Internet community. These documents may also belong to other sets of documents such as the Internet standards (STD) series, the For Your Information (FYI) series, or the Best Current Practices (BCP) series. An RFC may contain a specification that is on the Standards track, meaning the protocol or mechanism described therein is intended for general standardized use and with a goal to someday attaining Standard status. Other RFCs may be Informational, describing something of interest to the Internet community but not necessarily a standard; still other RFCs may be designated Experimental, meaning they document work being done by cutting-edge researchers that is not currently intended for general use. And as RFCs become obsolete or irrelevant, they are relegated to Historic status.

This book includes the most important and relevant RFCs about Internet file transfer protocols. Some are on the Standards track, others may be Experimental or Informational. However, they all define Internet file transfer protocols, how they work, and how they are used both on and off the Internet.

After figuring out how to run terminal sessions with remote computers (with Telnet), early Internet researchers needed to build a mechanism for transferring files. The result was the File Transfer Protocol (FTP), and some relatives such as the Trivial File Transfer Protocol (TFTP) and the Simple File Transfer Protocol (SFTP). FTP and TFTP still have relevance as we enter the 21st century; SFTP and others have fallen by the wayside.

The importance of FTP and its sister protocols cannot be underestimated: for many years, FTP represented the single most important application for publishing data on the Internet. It still is used widely to disseminate software and other materials over the World Wide Web. More important, FTP is a seminal application and serves as a first step for learning how to make computers interoperate over an internetwork. Many of the mechanisms first devised for and implemented in FTP can be found in more modern protocols. If you understand how FTP works, you stand a very good chance of understanding how any Internet application protocol works.

## Why RFCs in a Book?

Containing, as it does, the fundamental standards for Internet hosts, this book is the definitive guide to the Internet host specifications. But all the RFCs are available for free, online. Why would anyone buy this book? For several reasons, listed in order of increasing importance:

- You may be able to read these specifications online, but if you want to read them while away from your computer, you must print them out. If you want to take notes, you must print them out. If you want to share them with coworkers, you must print them out. There is no denying the appeal of the printed page when working with complicated technical documents.
- This is a comprehensive collection of Internet file transfer RFCs. All the current RFCs are here — and only the current RFCs. You can flip from one specification to another, bookmark the important parts, and flip from one highlight to another instantly — much faster than is possible with a browser.
- Each RFC, as written, stands alone. Each defines some terms, but some use terms defined in predecessor documents. Putting them together, and in context, makes them that much more valuable.
- Nowhere else is this material collected together; nowhere has it ever been formally indexed in print. A high-quality index means that you no longer must search through dozens of different documents looking for the answer to a question — all answers are included in a single book, and you can search for a term in all the relevant documents in a single procedure.

## The RFCs

Included here are all current and relevant RFCs that describe or affect Internet file transfer, starting with RFC 906, "Bootstrap Loading Using TFTP," all the way through to RFC 2640, "Internationalization of the File Transfer Protocol."

Although the RFCs are included here in the order in which they were published, you would hardly read them in that order; though a reader interested in FTP would do well to begin with RFC 959, "File Transfer Protocol," a full Internet standard. However, the documents included in this volume represent different aspects of FTP and are written to different reader levels. RFC 1635, "How to Use Anonymous FTP," documents how anonymous FTP is used; RFC 2428, "FTP Extensions for IPv6 and NATs," describes how FTP is extended to work in IPv6 and with NATs (Network Address Translators). This book, therefore, is best used as a reference for understanding, implementing, adapting, deploying, and troubleshooting FTP.

Inasmuch as some of these RFCs are brief, the following summaries are presented for the purpose of guiding the reader rather than providing complete synopses of the documents.

### RFC 906, Bootstrap Loading Using TFTP

The Trivial File Transfer Protocol, defined in RFC 1350, is used where a very basic file transfer protocol makes sense: whenever systems with minimal resources must exchange information, for example. Bootstrap loading, especially of systems with little or no local storage, is one of those situations, and this RFC describes how TFTP can be used to boot a workstation, terminal, or other system from the network. Although not currently classified as an historical RFC, the current status of this specification is not clear. It is included here to illustrate how TFTP has been used.

### RFC 949, FTP Unique-Named Store Command

This is another RFC whose current status is not entirely clear, which describes an extension to FTP that can be used to generate a unique name for files automatically as they are stored on a system.

### RFC 959, File Transfer Protocol (FTP)

FTP is one of the few full Internet standard protocols. It is also the earliest example of a mass data transfer application, and provides the basis for most subsequent transfer applications including the Hypertext Transfer Protocol (HTTP). This specification explains how it works, including application protocol headers, negotiation of connections between client and server, and protocol response codes.

### RFC 1068, Background File Transfer Program (BFTP)

Another specification of uncertain standing, this RFC describes a mechanism by which FTP can be used as the basis of background file transfer services, using a third-party model. Rather than defining a new protocol, the authors show how the existing FTP can be adapted for use in new Internet service modes.

### RFC 1350, The TFTP Protocol (Revision 2)

FTP uses TCP for reliable and guaranteed service; however, at times such service is unnecessary and impractical. For down-and-dirty file transfers without such guarantees, the Trivial File Transfer Protocol (TFTP) is useful. Usually cited as a mechanism for booting network terminals, TFTP is sufficient when transfers are over networks that are themselves reliable. TFTP, like FTP, is also a full Internet standard as defined in this RFC.

### RFC 1415, FTP-FTAM Gateway Specification

The File Transfer, Access, and Management (FTAM) protocol defines how files are to be transferred within the OSI (Open Systems Interconnect) environment. As the "other" internetworking technology, OSI-IP interoperability was long considered an important goal. This specification describes an application that supports both OSI and IP and acts as a gateway between the two file transfer protocols. Although FTAM may not be important to many (if not most) readers, this Proposed Standard RFC demonstrates how to build a file transfer application gateway for FTP.

### RFC 1579, Firewall-Friendly FTP

This Informational RFC discusses how FTP behaves when it is passed through a network firewall, and suggests a change in the behavior of FTP clients that would make them "friendlier" to firewalls. Although no protocol changes are required to make this change, the author does outline some protocol changes that would be helpful in making FTP a safer protocol to pass through firewalls.

### RFC 1635, How to Use Anonymous FTP (FYI 24)

This document is part of the FYI (For Your Information) series of documents. Unlike Standards-track RFCs, this document is intended to explain how anonymous FTP works and how it can be used.

### RFC 1639, FTP Operation Over Big Address Records (FOOBAR)

This Experimental RFC describes how FTP could be modified to support longer network layer addresses than those provided by the IPv4 32-bit address space. Although the protocol defined here is not intended for general use, it does demonstrate how FTP (and other applications) could be deployed across next generation replacements for IPv4.

### RFC 1785, TFTP Option Negotiation Analysis

Internet application protocols often include options that permit clients to request specific features from servers; these should not affect normal operation of the protocol if the server does not support the options. There was some concern that TFTP servers that didn't support options might manifest abnormalities when clients used options, because they might respond unpredictably when clients attempted to negotiate the use of the options. This informational RFC summarizes the results of testing TFTP servers that don't support options with clients that do. The result: options do not adversely affect TFTP servers that don't support them.

### RFC 1986, Experiments with a Simple File Transfer Protocol for Radio Links Using Enhanced Trivial File Transfer Protocol (ETFTP)

This Experimental RFC describes a protocol called the Enhanced Trivial File Transfer Protocol (ETFTP). ETFTP is designed to allow users to tune transmission parameters to optimize for file transmissions over radio links, which can be low-speed, high-bit error rate channels. The goal of the research work represented in this RFC was to develop a protocol that enabled efficient file transfers over tactical (military) radio networks.

### RFC 2090, TFTP Multicast Option

This Experimental RFC describes a mechanism to add multicast capability to TFTP, so that when a file is transmitted it can be received by more than one system.

### RFC 2228, FTP Security Extensions

This RFC is a Proposed Standard, and it discusses the very important issue of network security as it relates to building and using FTP applications. Starting with an overview of the security issues inherent in FTP, this document goes on to define security extensions to FTP for user authentication as well as for server authentication, data integrity, and more.

### RFC 2347, TFTP Option Extension

This Proposed Standard RFC defines a mechanism that allows new features to be added to TFTP, and permits clients to query servers to determine what options the server supports.

### RFC 2348, TFTP Blocksize Option

TFTP, as originally defined, transmits data in 512-octet (byte) blocks. Though using a single block size simplifies implementation, doing so causes suboptimal utilization of bandwidth in networks that can support larger block sizes (e.g., Ethernet LANs can handle frames of up to 1,500 octets). This Proposed Standard RFC defines an option to allow clients and servers to negotiate an appropriate block size.

### RFC 2349, TFTP Timeout Interval and Transfer Size Options

This Proposed Standard RFC describes two options to TFTP. The timeout interval option allows servers and clients to negotiate a timeout interval (how long to wait after the last transmission before timing the session out). The transfer size option allows the receiving system to determine the size of the file being transferred before starting the transfer.

### RFC 2389, Feature Negotiation Mechanism for the File Transfer Protocol

This Proposed Standard RFC defines the mechanism by which new features can be added to FTP. Internet protocols occasionally add features, but still want to interoperate with older systems that don't support the new features. Negotiation mechanisms like this one are added to the specifications to allow clients to query servers to discover what optional or extended features they support.

### RFC 2428, FTP Extensions for IPv6 and NATs

Although the FTP Operation Over Big Address Records (FOOBAR) mechanism defined in RFC 1639 allows FTP to work with network layer protocols other than IPv4, it does not work well in a multiprotocol environment such as is expected as the transition from IPv4 to IPv6 is made. This Proposed Standard RFC describes two extensions that allow FTP clients and servers to negotiate the network protocol to be used in the exchange.

### RFC 2577, FTP Security Considerations

This informational RFC expands on the security issues raised in RFC 2228 as well as many others, providing a comprehensive discussion of FTP security.

### RFC 2585, Internet X.509 Public Key Infrastructure Operational Protocols: FTP and HTTP

The Internet Public Key Infrastructure (PKI) requires one or more mechanisms for distributing X.509 certificates and revocation lists. FTP and HTTP are defined here as the operational protocols for transmitting this data. This Proposed Standard RFC describes how FTP (and HTTP) are used for this purpose.

### RFC 2640, Internationalization of the File Transfer Protocol

As the Internet becomes more important internationally, Internet application protocols must be adapted for use in all languages — not just languages that can be supported with standard 7-bit ASCII characters. This Proposed Standard RFC describes how FTP can be internationalized in accordance with RFC 2277, "IETF Policy on Character Sets and Languages."

## Getting RFCs Online

We could waste several pages with pointers to different web sites and mailing lists where you can find out more about RFCs in general and Internet standards in particular. Let's just say, you can find plenty of online resources (including up-to-date pointers to all those online resources) at this web site:

*http://www.Internet-Standard.com*

You will also find pointers to all the RFCs published in this book, up-to-date information about new RFCs released after this book was published, and much more about this book, others in the series, and other books about Internet standards.

## Reading This Book

RFCs in this volume (and others in the series) are published in chronological order. This provides relatively little logical flow for the reader, inasmuch as attempting to start at the beginning and read (more or less) straight through would skip from topic to topic. However, readers seeking to understand the basics of Internet file transfer would do well to skip around the volume themselves, starting with the basic FTP specification in RFC 959.

Alternatively, you may prefer to simply use this volume as a reference, consulting it as needed for details about file transfer and its use and implementation on the Internet.

## For More Information

As editor of this series, I intend that this volume be used as a tool for network implementers and deployers. Please let me know if you find it useful — and please let me know if you know of a way to make it more useful. For more information about Internet standards in general, check out Internet-Standard.com; if you have a question or comment about this series, or if you've discovered a bug in the text, or just want to get in touch, email me at:

*pete@loshin.com*

Hearing from readers of material I've edited or written is usually the best part of my day; I'd love to hear what you think!

Bootstrap Loading using TFTP


Status of this Memo

   It is often convenient to be able to bootstrap a computer system from
   a communications network.  This RFC proposes the use of the IP TFTP
   protocol for bootstrap loading in this case.

   This RFC specifies a proposed protocol for the ARPA Internet
   community, and requests discussion and suggestions for improvements.


Introduction

   Many computer systems, such as diskless workstations, are
   bootstrapped by loading one or more code files across a network.
   Unfortunately, the protocol used to load these initial files has not
   been standardized - numerous methods have been employed by different
   computer manufacturers. This can make it difficult, for example, for
   an installation to support several different kinds of systems on a
   local-area network.  Each different booting mechanism that is used
   must be supported, for example by implementing a number of servers on
   one or more host machines.  This is in spite of the fact that these
   heterogeneous systems may be able to communicate freely (all using
   the same protocol) once they have been booted.

   We propose that TFTP (Trivial File Transfer Protocol) [6] be used as
   a standard protocol for bootstrap loading.  This protocol is
   well-suited for our purpose, being based on the standard Internet
   Protocol (IP) [4].  It is easily implemented, both in the machines to
   be booted, and in bootstrap servers elsewhere on the net.  (In
   addition, many popular operating systems already support TFTP
   servers.)  The fact that TFTP is a rather slow protocol is not a
   serious concern, due to the fact that it need be used only for the
   primary bootstrap.  A secondary bootstrap could use a faster
   protocol.

   This RFC describes how system to be booted (called the "booter"
   below) would use TFTP to load a desired code file.  It also describes
   an existing implementation (in ROM) for Ethernet.

   Note that we are specifying only the network protocols that would be
   used by the booting system.  We do not attempt to mandate the method
   by which a user actually boots a system (such as the format of a
   command typed at the console).  In addition, our proposal does not

presuppose the use of any particular data-link level network
architecture (although the example that we describe below uses
Ethernet).

Network Protocols used by the Booting System

To load a file, the booter sends a standard TFTP read request (RRQ)
packet, containing the name of the file to be loaded. The file name
should not assume any operating system dependent naming conventions
(file names containing only alphanumeric characters should suffice).
Thereafter, the system receives TFTP DATA packets, and sends TFTP ACK
and/or ERROR packets, in accordance with the TFTP specification [6].

TFTP is implemented using the User Datagram Protocol (UDP) [5], which
is in turn implemented using IP. Thus, the booter must be able to
receive IP datagrams containing up to 524 octets (excluding the IP
header), since TFTP DATA packets can be up to 516 octets long, and
UDP headers are 8 octets long. The booting machine is not required
to respond to incoming TFTP read or write requests.

We allow for the use of two additional protocols. These are ARP
(Address Resolution Protocol) [3], and RARP (Reverse Address
Resolution Protocol) [1]. The possible use of these protocols is
described below. The booter could also use other protocols (such as
for name lookup), but they should be IP-based, and an internet
standard.

The IP datagram containing the initial TFTP RRQ (and all other IP
datagrams sent by the booter) must of course contain both a source
internet address and a destination internet address in its IP header.
It is frequently the case, however, that the booter does not
initially know its own internet address, but only a lower-level (e.g.
Ethernet) address. The Reverse Address Resolution Protocol
(RARP) [1] may be used by the booter to find its internet address
(prior to sending the TFTP RRQ). RARP was motivated by Plummer's
Address Resolution Protocol (ARP) [3]. Unlike ARP, which is used to
find the 'hardware' address corresponding to a known higher-level
protocol (e.g. internet) address, RARP is used to determine a
higher-level protocol address, given a known hardware address. RARP
uses the same packet format as ARP, and like ARP, can be used for a
wide variety of data-link protocols.

ARP may also be used. If the destination internet address is known,
then an ARP request containing this address may be broadcast, to find
a corresponding hardware address to which to send the subsequent TFTP
RRQ. It may not matter if this request should fail, because the RRQ
can also be broadcast (at the data-link level). However, because
such an ARP request packet also contains the sender's (that is, the

booter's) internet and hardware addresses, this information is made
available to the rest of the local subnet, and could be useful for
routing, for instance.

If a single destination internet address is not known, then a special
'broadcast' internet address could be used as the destination address
in the TFTP RRQ, so that it will be received by all 'local' internet
hosts.  (At this time, however, no standard for internet broadcasting
has been officially adopted. [**])

An Example Implementation

The author has implemented TFTP booting as specified above.  The
resulting code resides in ROM.  (This implementation is for a
Motorola 68000 based workstation, booting over an Ethernet.)  A user
wishing to boot such a machine types a file name, and (optionally)
the internet address of the workstation, and/or the internet address
of a server machine from which the file is to be loaded.  The
bootstrap code proceeds as follows:

   (1) The workstation's Ethernet address is found (by querying the
   Ethernet interface).

   (2) If the internet address of the workstation was not given, then
   a RARP request is broadcast, in order to find it.  If this request
   fails (that is, times out), then the bootstrap fails.

   (3) If the internet address of a server host was given, then
   broadcast an ARP request to try to find a corresponding Ethernet
   address.  If this fails, or if a server internet address was not
   given, then the Ethernet broadcast address is used.

   (4) If the internet address of a server host was not given, then
   we use a special internet address that represents a broadcast on
   the "local subnet", as described in [2].  (This is not an internet
   standard.)

   (5) A TFTP RRQ for the requested file is sent to the Ethernet
   address found in step (3).  The source internet address is that
   found in step (2), and the destination internet address is that
   found in step (4).

Note that because several TFTP servers may, in general, reply to the
RRQ, we do not abort if a TFTP ERROR packet is received, because this
does not preclude the possibility of some other server replying later
with the first data packet of the requested file.  When the first
valid TFTP DATA packet is received in response to the RRQ, the source
internet and Ethernet addresses of this packet are used as the

destination addresses in subsequent TFTP ACK packets.  Should another
server later respond with a DATA packet, an ERROR packet is sent back
in response.

An implementation of TFTP booting can take up a lot of space if care
is not taken.  This can be a significant problem if the code is to
fit in a limited amount of ROM.  However, the implementation
described above consists of less than 4K bytes of code (not counting
the Ethernet device driver).

Acknowledgements

The ideas presented here are the result of discussions with several
other people, in particular Jeff Mogul.

References

[1]   Finlayson, R.,  Mann, T.,  Mogul, J.  & Theimer, M.,  "A Reverse
      Address Resolution Protocol", RFC 903  Stanford University,
      June 1984.

[2]   Mogul, J., "Internet Broadcasting",  Proposed RFC, January 1984.

[3]   Plummer, D., "An Ethernet Address Resolution Protocol",
      RFC 826,  MIT-LCS, November 1982.

[4]   Postel, J., ed., "Internet Protocol - DARPA Internet Program
      Protocol Specification", RFC 791, USC/Information Sciences
      Institute, September 1981.

[5]   Postel, J., "User Datagram Protocol", RFC 768 USC/Information
      Sciences Institute, August 1980.

[6]   Sollins, K., "The TFTP Protocol (Revision 2)", RFC 783, MIT/LCS,
      June 1981.

[**]  Editor's Note:  While there is no standard for an Internet wide
      broadcast or multicast address, it is strongly recommended that
      the "all ones" local part of the Internet address be used to
      indicate a broadcast in a particular network.  That is, in class
      A network 1 the broadcast address would be 1.255.255.255, in
      class B network 128.1 the broadcast address would be
      128.1.255.255, and in class C network 192.1.1 the broadcast
      address would be 192.1.1.255.

Network Working Group                                    Mike Padlipsky
Request for Comments: 949                                        Mitre
Semisupersedes RFC 505                                      July 1985

                    FTP UNIQUE-NAMED STORE COMMAND


STATUS OF THIS MEMO

    This RFC proposes an extension to the File Transfer Protocol for the
    ARPA-Internet community, and requests discussion and suggestions for
    improvements.  Distribution of this memo is unlimited.


DISCUSSION

    There are various contexts in which it would be desirable to have an
    FTP command that had the effect of the present STOR but rather than
    requiring the sender to specify a file name instead caused the
    resultant file to have a unique name relative to the current
    directory.  This would be useful for all sorts of "pool" directories;
    the directories that serve as queues for printer daemons come
    immediately to mind (so do fax and even cardpunch daemons' queues),
    although naturally the sort of printer queue that a local command has
    to manage the interface to isn't what's meant by "pool" in this
    context.

    If we accept the need for such an FTP extension, and that it should
    not be done with an "X" command because it needs to be relied on
    "everywhere," the interesting question then becomes how to mechanize
    it.  Probably the most natural way to do it would be either to add a
    "control argument" of -UNM to the syntax of STOR, now that there are
    enough UNIXtm's around so that this good old Multics trick isn't
    alien any more, or even to declare that STOR with no argument should
    cause a directory-unique name to be generated.  However, either of
    these would necessitate "reopening" the STOR command code, which is a
    distasteful sort of exercise.  Since most FTP's presumably do a
    dispatch sort of thing off a list of command names to begin with,
    then, an additional command would seem to be the way to go.

    Naming the command calls for a bit of thought.  STore Uniquely Named
    (-> STUN) is silly; UNIQue comes to close to free advertising or even
    trademark infringement (and confuses fingers if you're typing); Store
    Uniquely NaMed (-> SUNM) doesn't avoid free advertising either;
    Uniquely Named STore (-> UNST) might look like a synonym for DELEte,
    though it's not all that bad; SToRe Uniquely named (-> STRU) is
    taken; and so it goes.  The best bet seems to be STOU.

    Of somewhat more practical import, there's also the question of
    whether the sender needs to be apprised of what the unique name
    turned out to be.  Intuitively, sometimes this would be the case and
    sometimes it wouldn't.  Making it optional is almost certainly too

much like work, though--even if it does have the subtle virtue of
finally getting control arguments into FTP.  Therefore, why not just
include it in a suitable response-code's free text field (unless, of
course, an avalanche of comments comes in urging it not be done at
all)?

Note, by the way, that the intent here is emphatically not to
sidestep whatever access control, authentication, and accounting
mechanisms Hosts might have in play before the user can do an old
STOR or a new STOU, but with suitable publicized ID's and passwords
it could be almost as good as the proposal made in RFC 505.

RECOMMENDATION

Add a new command, STOU, to FTP, which behaves like STOR except that
the resultant file is to be created in the current directory under a
name unique to that directory.  The 250 Transfer Started response
should include the name generated (unless the copy of FTP I have is
so old that 250 isn't the right number any more).

Network Working Group                                              J. Postel
Request for Comments: 959                                      J. Reynolds
                                                                       ISI
Obsoletes RFC: 765 (IEN 149)                                 October 1985

FILE TRANSFER PROTOCOL (FTP)

Status of this Memo

   This memo is the official specification of the File Transfer
   Protocol (FTP).  Distribution of this memo is unlimited.

   The following new optional commands are included in this edition of
   the specification:

      CDUP (Change to Parent Directory), SMNT (Structure Mount), STOU
      (Store Unique), RMD (Remove Directory), MKD (Make Directory), PWD
      (Print Directory), and SYST (System).

   Note that this specification is compatible with the previous edition.

1.  INTRODUCTION

   The objectives of FTP are 1) to promote sharing of files (computer
   programs and/or data), 2) to encourage indirect or implicit (via
   programs) use of remote computers, 3) to shield a user from
   variations in file storage systems among hosts, and 4) to transfer
   data reliably and efficiently.  FTP, though usable directly by a user
   at a terminal, is designed mainly for use by programs.

   The attempt in this specification is to satisfy the diverse needs of
   users of maxi-hosts, mini-hosts, personal workstations, and TACs,
   with a simple, and easily implemented protocol design.

   This paper assumes knowledge of the Transmission Control Protocol
   (TCP) [2] and the Telnet Protocol [3].  These documents are contained
   in the ARPA-Internet protocol handbook [1].

2.  OVERVIEW

   In this section, the history, the terminology, and the FTP model are
   discussed.  The terms defined in this section are only those that
   have special significance in FTP.  Some of the terminology is very
   specific to the FTP model; some readers may wish to turn to the
   section on the FTP model while reviewing the terminology.

## 2.1.  HISTORY

FTP has had a long evolution over the years.  Appendix III is a
chronological compilation of Request for Comments documents
relating to FTP.  These include the first proposed file transfer
mechanisms in 1971 that were developed for implementation on hosts
at M.I.T. (RFC 114), plus comments and discussion in RFC 141.

RFC 172 provided a user-level oriented protocol for file transfer
between host computers (including terminal IMPs).  A revision of
this as RFC 265, restated FTP for additional review, while RFC 281
suggested further changes.  The use of a "Set Data Type"
transaction was proposed in RFC 294 in January 1982.

RFC 354 obsoleted RFCs 264 and 265.  The File Transfer Protocol
was now defined as a protocol for file transfer between HOSTs on
the ARPANET, with the primary function of FTP defined as
transfering files efficiently and reliably among hosts and
allowing the convenient use of remote file storage capabilities.
RFC 385 further commented on errors, emphasis points, and
additions to the protocol, while RFC 414 provided a status report
on the working server and user FTPs.  RFC 430, issued in 1973,
(among other RFCs too numerous to mention) presented further
comments on FTP.  Finally, an "official" FTP document was
published as RFC 454.

By July 1973, considerable changes from the last versions of FTP
were made, but the general structure remained the same.  RFC 542
was published as a new "official" specification to reflect these
changes.  However, many implementations based on the older
specification were not updated.

In 1974, RFCs 607 and 614 continued comments on FTP.  RFC 624
proposed further design changes and minor modifications.  In 1975,
RFC 686 entitled, "Leaving Well Enough Alone", discussed the
differences between all of the early and later versions of FTP.
RFC 691 presented a minor revision of RFC 686, regarding the
subject of print files.

Motivated by the transition from the NCP to the TCP as the
underlying protocol, a phoenix was born out of all of the above
efforts in RFC 765 as the specification of FTP for use on TCP.

This current edition of the FTP specification is intended to
correct some minor documentation errors, to improve the
explanation of some protocol features, and to add some new
optional commands.

In particular, the following new optional commands are included in this edition of the specification:

CDUP - Change to Parent Directory

SMNT - Structure Mount

STOU - Store Unique

RMD - Remove Directory

MKD - Make Directory

PWD - Print Directory

SYST - System

This specification is compatible with the previous edition.  A program implemented in conformance to the previous specification should automatically be in conformance to this specification.

2.2.  TERMINOLOGY

ASCII

The ASCII character set is as defined in the ARPA-Internet Protocol Handbook.  In FTP, ASCII characters are defined to be the lower half of an eight-bit code set (i.e., the most significant bit is zero).

access controls

Access controls define users' access privileges to the use of a system, and to the files in that system.  Access controls are necessary to prevent unauthorized or accidental use of files. It is the prerogative of a server-FTP process to invoke access controls.

byte size

There are two byte sizes of interest in FTP:  the logical byte size of the file, and the transfer byte size used for the transmission of the data.  The transfer byte size is always 8 bits.  The transfer byte size is not necessarily the byte size in which data is to be stored in a system, nor the logical byte size for interpretation of the structure of the data.

control connection

The communication path between the USER-PI and SERVER-PI for
the exchange of commands and replies.  This connection follows
the Telnet Protocol.

data connection

A full duplex connection over which data is transferred, in a
specified mode and type. The data transferred may be a part of
a file, an entire file or a number of files.  The path may be
between a server-DTP and a user-DTP, or between two
server-DTPs.

data port

The passive data transfer process "listens" on the data port
for a connection from the active transfer process in order to
open the data connection.

DTP

The data transfer process establishes and manages the data
connection.  The DTP can be passive or active.

End-of-Line

The end-of-line sequence defines the separation of printing
lines.  The sequence is Carriage Return, followed by Line Feed.

EOF

The end-of-file condition that defines the end of a file being
transferred.

EOR

The end-of-record condition that defines the end of a record
being transferred.

error recovery

A procedure that allows a user to recover from certain errors
such as failure of either host system or transfer process.  In
FTP, error recovery may involve restarting a file transfer at a
given checkpoint.

FTP commands

   A set of commands that comprise the control information flowing
   from the user-FTP to the server-FTP process.

file

   An ordered set of computer data (including programs), of
   arbitrary length, uniquely identified by a pathname.

mode

   The mode in which data is to be transferred via the data
   connection.  The mode defines the data format during transfer
   including EOR and EOF.  The transfer modes defined in FTP are
   described in the Section on Transmission Modes.

NVT

   The Network Virtual Terminal as defined in the Telnet Protocol.

NVFS

   The Network Virtual File System.  A concept which defines a
   standard network file system with standard commands and
   pathname conventions.

page

   A file may be structured as a set of independent parts called
   pages.  FTP supports the transmission of discontinuous files as
   independent indexed pages.

pathname

   Pathname is defined to be the character string which must be
   input to a file system by a user in order to identify a file.
   Pathname normally contains device and/or directory names, and
   file name specification.  FTP does not yet specify a standard
   pathname convention.  Each user must follow the file naming
   conventions of the file systems involved in the transfer.

PI

   The protocol interpreter.  The user and server sides of the
   protocol have distinct roles implemented in a user-PI and a
   server-PI.

record

    A sequential file may be structured as a number of contiguous
    parts called records. Record structures are supported by FTP
    but a file need not have record structure.

reply

    A reply is an acknowledgment (positive or negative) sent from
    server to user via the control connection in response to FTP
    commands. The general form of a reply is a completion code
    (including error codes) followed by a text string. The codes
    are for use by programs and the text is usually intended for
    human users.

server-DTP

    The data transfer process, in its normal "active" state,
    establishes the data connection with the "listening" data port.
    It sets up parameters for transfer and storage, and transfers
    data on command from its PI. The DTP can be placed in a
    "passive" state to listen for, rather than initiate a
    connection on the data port.

server-FTP process

    A process or set of processes which perform the function of
    file transfer in cooperation with a user-FTP process and,
    possibly, another server. The functions consist of a protocol
    interpreter (PI) and a data transfer process (DTP).

server-PI

    The server protocol interpreter "listens" on Port L for a
    connection from a user-PI and establishes a control
    communication connection. It receives standard FTP commands
    from the user-PI, sends replies, and governs the server-DTP.

type

    The data representation type used for data transfer and
    storage. Type implies certain transformations between the time
    of data storage and data transfer. The representation types
    defined in FTP are described in the Section on Establishing
    Data Connections.

user

   A person or a process on behalf of a person wishing to obtain
   file transfer service.  The human user may interact directly
   with a server-FTP process, but use of a user-FTP process is
   preferred since the protocol design is weighted towards
   automata.

user-DTP

   The data transfer process "listens" on the data port for a
   connection from a server-FTP process.  If two servers are
   transferring data between them, the user-DTP is inactive.

user-FTP process

   A set of functions including a protocol interpreter, a data
   transfer process and a user interface which together perform
   the function of file transfer in cooperation with one or more
   server-FTP processes.  The user interface allows a local
   language to be used in the command-reply dialogue with the
   user.

user-PI

   The user protocol interpreter initiates the control connection
   from its port U to the server-FTP process, initiates FTP
   commands, and governs the user-DTP if that process is part of
   the file transfer.

2.3.  THE FTP MODEL

    With the above definitions in mind, the following model (shown in
    Figure 1) may be diagrammed for an FTP service.

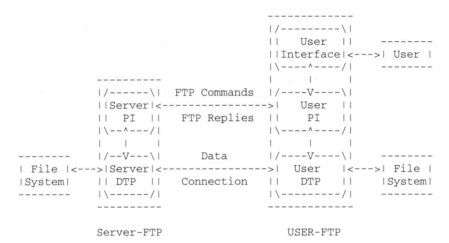

```
                                      -------------
                                      |/---------\|
                                      ||  User   ||     --------
                                      ||Interface|<--->| User |
                                      |\----^----/|     --------
                      ----------      |     |     |
                      |/------\|  FTP Commands  |/----V----\|
                      ||Server|<--------------->|  User   ||
                      || PI  ||  FTP Replies   ||  PI   ||
                      |\--^---/|                |\----^----/|
                      |   |    |                |     |     |
         --------     |/--V---\|     Data       |/----V----\|     --------
        | File |<--->|Server|<--------------->|  User   |<--->| File |
        |System|     || DTP  ||  Connection    ||  DTP   ||     |System|
         --------     |\------/|                |\---------/|     --------
                      ----------                -------------

                   Server-FTP                    USER-FTP
```

    NOTES: 1. The data connection may be used in either direction.
           2. The data connection need not exist all of the time.

                        Figure 1  Model for FTP Use

    In the model described in Figure 1, the user-protocol interpreter
    initiates the control connection.  The control connection follows
    the Telnet protocol.  At the initiation of the user, standard FTP
    commands are generated by the user-PI and transmitted to the
    server process via the control connection.  (The user may
    establish a direct control connection to the server-FTP, from a
    TAC terminal for example, and generate standard FTP commands
    independently, bypassing the user-FTP process.)  Standard replies
    are sent from the server-PI to the user-PI over the control
    connection in response to the commands.

    The FTP commands specify the parameters for the data connection
    (data port, transfer mode, representation type, and structure) and
    the nature of file system operation (store, retrieve, append,
    delete, etc.).  The user-DTP or its designate should "listen" on
    the specified data port, and the server initiate the data
    connection and data transfer in accordance with the specified
    parameters.  It should be noted that the data port need not be in

the same host that initiates the FTP commands via the control
connection, but the user or the user-FTP process must ensure a
"listen" on the specified data port.  It ought to also be noted
that the data connection may be used for simultaneous sending and
receiving.

In another situation a user might wish to transfer files between
two hosts, neither of which is a local host. The user sets up
control connections to the two servers and then arranges for a
data connection between them.  In this manner, control information
is passed to the user-PI but data is transferred between the
server data transfer processes.  Following is a model of this
server-server interaction.

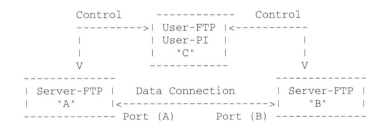

```
            Control        -----------   Control
            ---------->| User-FTP |<-----------
            |            | User-PI  |           |
            |            |   "C"    |           |
            V            -----------           V
    -------------                       -------------
    | Server-FTP |  Data Connection     | Server-FTP |
    |    "A"     |  |<------------------->|    "B"     |
    -------------  Port (A)    Port (B) -------------
```

Figure 2

The protocol requires that the control connections be open while
data transfer is in progress.  It is the responsibility of the
user to request the closing of the control connections when
finished using the FTP service, while it is the server who takes
the action.  The server may abort data transfer if the control
connections are closed without command.

The Relationship between FTP and Telnet:

   The FTP uses the Telnet protocol on the control connection.
   This can be achieved in two ways: first, the user-PI or the
   server-PI may implement the rules of the Telnet Protocol
   directly in their own procedures; or, second, the user-PI or
   the server-PI may make use of the existing Telnet module in the
   system.

   Ease of implementaion, sharing code, and modular programming
   argue for the second approach.  Efficiency and independence

argue for the first approach.  In practice, FTP relies on very
little of the Telnet Protocol, so the first approach does not
necessarily involve a large amount of code.

3.   DATA TRANSFER FUNCTIONS

Files are transferred only via the data connection.  The control
connection is used for the transfer of commands, which describe the
functions to be performed, and the replies to these commands (see the
Section on FTP Replies).  Several commands are concerned with the
transfer of data between hosts.  These data transfer commands include
the MODE command which specify how the bits of the data are to be
transmitted, and the STRUcture and TYPE commands, which are used to
define the way in which the data are to be represented.  The
transmission and representation are basically independent but the
"Stream" transmission mode is dependent on the file structure
attribute and if "Compressed" transmission mode is used, the nature
of the filler byte depends on the representation type.

3.1.   DATA REPRESENTATION AND STORAGE

Data is transferred from a storage device in the sending host to a
storage device in the receiving host.  Often it is necessary to
perform certain transformations on the data because data storage
representations in the two systems are different.  For example,
NVT-ASCII has different data storage representations in different
systems.  DEC TOPS-20s's generally store NVT-ASCII as five 7-bit
ASCII characters, left-justified in a 36-bit word. IBM Mainframe's
store NVT-ASCII as 8-bit EBCDIC codes.  Multics stores NVT-ASCII
as four 9-bit characters in a 36-bit word.  It is desirable to
convert characters into the standard NVT-ASCII representation when
transmitting text between dissimilar systems.  The sending and
receiving sites would have to perform the necessary
transformations between the standard representation and their
internal representations.

A different problem in representation arises when transmitting
binary data (not character codes) between host systems with
different word lengths.  It is not always clear how the sender
should send data, and the receiver store it.  For example, when
transmitting 32-bit bytes from a 32-bit word-length system to a
36-bit word-length system, it may be desirable (for reasons of
efficiency and usefulness) to store the 32-bit bytes
right-justified in a 36-bit word in the latter system.  In any
case, the user should have the option of specifying data
representation and transformation functions.  It should be noted

that FTP provides for very limited data type representations.
Transformations desired beyond this limited capability should be
performed by the user directly.

3.1.1.  DATA TYPES

Data representations are handled in FTP by a user specifying a
representation type.  This type may implicitly (as in ASCII or
EBCDIC) or explicitly (as in Local byte) define a byte size for
interpretation which is referred to as the "logical byte size."
Note that this has nothing to do with the byte size used for
transmission over the data connection, called the "transfer
byte size", and the two should not be confused.  For example,
NVT-ASCII has a logical byte size of 8 bits.  If the type is
Local byte, then the TYPE command has an obligatory second
parameter specifying the logical byte size.  The transfer byte
size is always 8 bits.

3.1.1.1.  ASCII TYPE

This is the default type and must be accepted by all FTP
implementations.  It is intended primarily for the transfer
of text files, except when both hosts would find the EBCDIC
type more convenient.

The sender converts the data from an internal character
representation to the standard 8-bit NVT-ASCII
representation (see the Telnet specification).  The receiver
will convert the data from the standard form to his own
internal form.

In accordance with the NVT standard, the <CRLF> sequence
should be used where necessary to denote the end of a line
of text.  (See the discussion of file structure at the end
of the Section on Data Representation and Storage.)

Using the standard NVT-ASCII representation means that data
must be interpreted as 8-bit bytes.

The Format parameter for ASCII and EBCDIC types is discussed
below.

3.1.1.2.  EBCDIC TYPE

This type is intended for efficient transfer between hosts
which use EBCDIC for their internal character
representation.

For transmission, the data are represented as 8-bit EBCDIC
characters.  The character code is the only difference
between the functional specifications of EBCDIC and ASCII
types.

End-of-line (as opposed to end-of-record--see the discussion
of structure) will probably be rarely used with EBCDIC type
for purposes of denoting structure, but where it is
necessary the <NL> character should be used.

3.1.1.3.  IMAGE TYPE

The data are sent as contiguous bits which, for transfer,
are packed into the 8-bit transfer bytes.  The receiving
site must store the data as contiguous bits.  The structure
of the storage system might necessitate the padding of the
file (or of each record, for a record-structured file) to
some convenient boundary (byte, word or block).  This
padding, which must be all zeros, may occur only at the end
of the file (or at the end of each record) and there must be
a way of identifying the padding bits so that they may be
stripped off if the file is retrieved.  The padding
transformation should be well publicized to enable a user to
process a file at the storage site.

Image type is intended for the efficient storage and
retrieval of files and for the transfer of binary data.  It
is recommended that this type be accepted by all FTP
implementations.

3.1.1.4.  LOCAL TYPE

The data is transferred in logical bytes of the size
specified by the obligatory second parameter, Byte size.
The value of Byte size must be a decimal integer; there is
no default value.  The logical byte size is not necessarily
the same as the transfer byte size.  If there is a
difference in byte sizes, then the logical bytes should be
packed contiguously, disregarding transfer byte boundaries
and with any necessary padding at the end.

When the data reaches the receiving host, it will be
transformed in a manner dependent on the logical byte size
and the particular host.  This transformation must be
invertible (i.e., an identical file can be retrieved if the
same parameters are used) and should be well publicized by
the FTP implementors.

For example, a user sending 36-bit floating-point numbers to
a host with a 32-bit word could send that data as Local byte
with a logical byte size of 36.  The receiving host would
then be expected to store the logical bytes so that they
could be easily manipulated; in this example putting the
36-bit logical bytes into 64-bit double words should
suffice.

In another example, a pair of hosts with a 36-bit word size
may send data to one another in words by using TYPE L 36.
The data would be sent in the 8-bit transmission bytes
packed so that 9 transmission bytes carried two host words.

3.1.1.5.  FORMAT CONTROL

The types ASCII and EBCDIC also take a second (optional)
parameter; this is to indicate what kind of vertical format
control, if any, is associated with a file.  The following
data representation types are defined in FTP:

A character file may be transferred to a host for one of
three purposes: for printing, for storage and later
retrieval, or for processing.  If a file is sent for
printing, the receiving host must know how the vertical
format control is represented.  In the second case, it must
be possible to store a file at a host and then retrieve it
later in exactly the same form.  Finally, it should be
possible to move a file from one host to another and process
the file at the second host without undue trouble.  A single
ASCII or EBCDIC format does not satisfy all these
conditions.  Therefore, these types have a second parameter
specifying one of the following three formats:

3.1.1.5.1.  NON PRINT

This is the default format to be used if the second
(format) parameter is omitted.  Non-print format must be
accepted by all FTP implementations.

The file need contain no vertical format information.  If
it is passed to a printer process, this process may
assume standard values for spacing and margins.

Normally, this format will be used with files destined
for processing or just storage.

3.1.1.5.2.  TELNET FORMAT CONTROLS

The file contains ASCII/EBCDIC vertical format controls
(i.e., <CR>, <LF>, <NL>, <VT>, <FF>) which the printer
process will interpret appropriately.  <CRLF>, in exactly
this sequence, also denotes end-of-line.

3.1.1.5.2.  CARRIAGE CONTROL (ASA)

The file contains ASA (FORTRAN) vertical format control
characters.  (See RFC 740 Appendix C; and Communications
of the ACM, Vol. 7, No. 10, p. 606, October 1964.)  In a
line or a record formatted according to the ASA Standard,
the first character is not to be printed.  Instead, it
should be used to determine the vertical movement of the
paper which should take place before the rest of the
record is printed.

The ASA Standard specifies the following control
characters:

    Character      Vertical Spacing

    blank          Move paper up one line
    0              Move paper up two lines
    1              Move paper to top of next page
    +              No movement, i.e., overprint

Clearly there must be some way for a printer process to
distinguish the end of the structural entity.  If a file
has record structure (see below) this is no problem;
records will be explicitly marked during transfer and
storage.  If the file has no record structure, the <CRLF>
end-of-line sequence is used to separate printing lines,
but these format effectors are overridden by the ASA
controls.

3.1.2.  DATA STRUCTURES

In addition to different representation types, FTP allows the
structure of a file to be specified.  Three file structures are
defined in FTP:

file-structure,      where there is no internal structure and
                     the file is considered to be a
                     continuous sequence of data bytes,

record-structure,    where the file is made up of sequential
                     records,

and page-structure,  where the file is made up of independent
                     indexed pages.

File-structure is the default to be assumed if the STRUcture
command has not been used but both file and record structures
must be accepted for "text" files (i.e., files with TYPE ASCII
or EBCDIC) by all FTP implementations.  The structure of a file
will affect both the transfer mode of a file (see the Section
on Transmission Modes) and the interpretation and storage of
the file.

The "natural" structure of a file will depend on which host
stores the file.  A source-code file will usually be stored on
an IBM Mainframe in fixed length records but on a DEC TOPS-20
as a stream of characters partitioned into lines, for example
by <CRLF>.  If the transfer of files between such disparate
sites is to be useful, there must be some way for one site to
recognize the other's assumptions about the file.

With some sites being naturally file-oriented and others
naturally record-oriented there may be problems if a file with
one structure is sent to a host oriented to the other.  If a
text file is sent with record-structure to a host which is file
oriented, then that host should apply an internal
transformation to the file based on the record structure.
Obviously, this transformation should be useful, but it must
also be invertible so that an identical file may be retrieved
using record structure.

In the case of a file being sent with file-structure to a
record-oriented host, there exists the question of what
criteria the host should use to divide the file into records
which can be processed locally.  If this division is necessary,
the FTP implementation should use the end-of-line sequence,

<CRLF> for ASCII, or <NL> for EBCDIC text files, as the
delimiter.  If an FTP implementation adopts this technique, it
must be prepared to reverse the transformation if the file is
retrieved with file-structure.

3.1.2.1.  FILE STRUCTURE

   File structure is the default to be assumed if the STRUcture
   command has not been used.

   In file-structure there is no internal structure and the
   file is considered to be a continuous sequence of data
   bytes.

3.1.2.2.  RECORD STRUCTURE

   Record structures must be accepted for "text" files (i.e.,
   files with TYPE ASCII or EBCDIC) by all FTP implementations.

   In record-structure the file is made up of sequential
   records.

3.1.2.3.  PAGE STRUCTURE

   To transmit files that are discontinuous, FTP defines a page
   structure.  Files of this type are sometimes known as
   "random access files" or even as "holey files".  In these
   files there is sometimes other information associated with
   the file as a whole (e.g., a file descriptor), or with a
   section of the file (e.g., page access controls), or both.
   In FTP, the sections of the file are called pages.

   To provide for various page sizes and associated
   information, each page is sent with a page header.  The page
   header has the following defined fields:

      Header Length

         The number of logical bytes in the page header
         including this byte.  The minimum header length is 4.

      Page Index

         The logical page number of this section of the file.
         This is not the transmission sequence number of this
         page, but the index used to identify this page of the
         file.

Data Length

The number of logical bytes in the page data.  The
minimum data length is 0.

Page Type

The type of page this is.  The following page types
are defined:

0 = Last Page

This is used to indicate the end of a paged
structured transmission.  The header length must
be 4, and the data length must be 0.

1 = Simple Page

This is the normal type for simple paged files
with no page level associated control
information.  The header length must be 4.

2 = Descriptor Page

This type is used to transmit the descriptive
information for the file as a whole.

3 = Access Controlled Page

This type includes an additional header field
for paged files with page level access control
information.  The header length must be 5.

Optional Fields

Further header fields may be used to supply per page
control information, for example, per page access
control.

All fields are one logical byte in length.  The logical byte
size is specified by the TYPE command.  See Appendix I for
further details and a specific case at the page structure.

A note of caution about parameters:  a file must be stored and
retrieved with the same parameters if the retrieved version is to

be identical to the version originally transmitted.  Conversely,
FTP implementations must return a file identical to the original
if the parameters used to store and retrieve a file are the same.

3.2.  ESTABLISHING DATA CONNECTIONS

The mechanics of transferring data consists of setting up the data
connection to the appropriate ports and choosing the parameters
for transfer.  Both the user and the server-DTPs have a default
data port.  The user-process default data port is the same as the
control connection port (i.e., U).  The server-process default
data port is the port adjacent to the control connection port
(i.e., L-1).

The transfer byte size is 8-bit bytes.  This byte size is relevant
only for the actual transfer of the data; it has no bearing on
representation of the data within a host's file system.

The passive data transfer process (this may be a user-DTP or a
second server-DTP) shall "listen" on the data port prior to
sending a transfer request command.  The FTP request command
determines the direction of the data transfer.  The server, upon
receiving the transfer request, will initiate the data connection
to the port.  When the connection is established, the data
transfer begins between DTP's, and the server-PI sends a
confirming reply to the user-PI.

Every FTP implementation must support the use of the default data
ports, and only the USER-PI can initiate a change to non-default
ports.

It is possible for the user to specify an alternate data port by
use of the PORT command.  The user may want a file dumped on a TAC
line printer or retrieved from a third party host.  In the latter
case, the user-PI sets up control connections with both
server-PI's.  One server is then told (by an FTP command) to
"listen" for a connection which the other will initiate.  The
user-PI sends one server-PI a PORT command indicating the data
port of the other.  Finally, both are sent the appropriate
transfer commands.  The exact sequence of commands and replies
sent between the user-controller and the servers is defined in the
Section on FTP Replies.

In general, it is the server's responsibility to maintain the data
connection--to initiate it and to close it.  The exception to this

is when the user-DTP is sending the data in a transfer mode that
requires the connection to be closed to indicate EOF.  The server
MUST close the data connection under the following conditions:

1. The server has completed sending data in a transfer mode
   that requires a close to indicate EOF.

2. The server receives an ABORT command from the user.

3. The port specification is changed by a command from the
   user.

4. The control connection is closed legally or otherwise.

5. An irrecoverable error condition occurs.

Otherwise the close is a server option, the exercise of which the
server must indicate to the user-process by either a 250 or 226
reply only.

3.3.  DATA CONNECTION MANAGEMENT

Default Data Connection Ports:  All FTP implementations must
support use of the default data connection ports, and only the
User-PI may initiate the use of non-default ports.

Negotiating Non-Default Data Ports:   The User-PI may specify a
non-default user side data port with the PORT command.  The
User-PI may request the server side to identify a non-default
server side data port with the PASV command.  Since a connection
is defined by the pair of addresses, either of these actions is
enough to get a different data connection, still it is permitted
to do both commands to use new ports on both ends of the data
connection.

Reuse of the Data Connection:  When using the stream mode of data
transfer the end of the file must be indicated by closing the
connection.  This causes a problem if multiple files are to be
transfered in the session, due to need for TCP to hold the
connection record for a time out period to guarantee the reliable
communication.  Thus the connection can not be reopened at once.

There are two solutions to this problem.  The first is to
negotiate a non-default port.  The second is to use another
transfer mode.

A comment on transfer modes.  The stream transfer mode is

inherently unreliable, since one can not determine if the
connection closed prematurely or not.  The other transfer modes
(Block, Compressed) do not close the connection to indicate the
end of file.  They have enough FTP encoding that the data
connection can be parsed to determine the end of the file.
Thus using these modes one can leave the data connection open
for multiple file transfers.

### 3.4.  TRANSMISSION MODES

The next consideration in transferring data is choosing the
appropriate transmission mode.  There are three modes: one which
formats the data and allows for restart procedures; one which also
compresses the data for efficient transfer; and one which passes
the data with little or no processing.  In this last case the mode
interacts with the structure attribute to determine the type of
processing.  In the compressed mode, the representation type
determines the filler byte.

All data transfers must be completed with an end-of-file (EOF)
which may be explicitly stated or implied by the closing of the
data connection.  For files with record structure, all the
end-of-record markers (EOR) are explicit, including the final one.
For files transmitted in page structure a "last-page" page type is
used.

NOTE:  In the rest of this section, byte means "transfer byte"
except where explicitly stated otherwise.

For the purpose of standardized transfer, the sending host will
translate its internal end of line or end of record denotation
into the representation prescribed by the transfer mode and file
structure, and the receiving host will perform the inverse
translation to its internal denotation.  An IBM Mainframe record
count field may not be recognized at another host, so the
end-of-record information may be transferred as a two byte control
code in Stream mode or as a flagged bit in a Block or Compressed
mode descriptor.  End-of-line in an ASCII or EBCDIC file with no
record structure should be indicated by <CRLF> or <NL>,
respectively.  Since these transformations imply extra work for
some systems, identical systems transferring non-record structured
text files might wish to use a binary representation and stream
mode for the transfer.

The following transmission modes are defined in FTP:

3.4.1.  STREAM MODE

   The data is transmitted as a stream of bytes.  There is no
   restriction on the representation type used; record structures
   are allowed.

   In a record structured file EOR and EOF will each be indicated
   by a two-byte control code.  The first byte of the control code
   will be all ones, the escape character.  The second byte will
   have the low order bit on and zeros elsewhere for EOR and the
   second low order bit on for EOF; that is, the byte will have
   value 1 for EOR and value 2 for EOF.  EOR and EOF may be
   indicated together on the last byte transmitted by turning both
   low order bits on (i.e., the value 3).  If a byte of all ones
   was intended to be sent as data, it should be repeated in the
   second byte of the control code.

   If the structure is a file structure, the EOF is indicated by
   the sending host closing the data connection and all bytes are
   data bytes.

3.4.2.  BLOCK MODE

   The file is transmitted as a series of data blocks preceded by
   one or more header bytes.  The header bytes contain a count
   field, and descriptor code.  The count field indicates the
   total length of the data block in bytes, thus marking the
   beginning of the next data block (there are no filler bits).
   The descriptor code defines:  last block in the file (EOF) last
   block in the record (EOR), restart marker (see the Section on
   Error Recovery and Restart) or suspect data (i.e., the data
   being transferred is suspected of errors and is not reliable).
   This last code is NOT intended for error control within FTP.
   It is motivated by the desire of sites exchanging certain types
   of data (e.g., seismic or weather data) to send and receive all
   the data despite local errors (such as "magnetic tape read
   errors"), but to indicate in the transmission that certain
   portions are suspect).  Record structures are allowed in this
   mode, and any representation type may be used.

   The header consists of the three bytes.  Of the 24 bits of
   header information, the 16 low order bits shall represent byte
   count, and the 8 high order bits shall represent descriptor
   codes as shown below.

Block Header

```
+----------------+----------------+----------------+
| Descriptor     |   Byte Count                    |
|          8 bits |                        16 bits |
+----------------+----------------+----------------+
```

The descriptor codes are indicated by bit flags in the
descriptor byte.  Four codes have been assigned, where each
code number is the decimal value of the corresponding bit in
the byte.

      Code      Meaning

      128       End of data block is EOR
       64       End of data block is EOF
       32       Suspected errors in data block
       16       Data block is a restart marker

With this encoding, more than one descriptor coded condition
may exist for a particular block.  As many bits as necessary
may be flagged.

The restart marker is embedded in the data stream as an
integral number of 8-bit bytes representing printable
characters in the language being used over the control
connection (e.g., default--NVT-ASCII).  <SP> (Space, in the
appropriate language) must not be used WITHIN a restart marker.

For example, to transmit a six-character marker, the following
would be sent:

```
+--------+--------+--------+
|Descrptr|  Byte count      |
|code= 16|            = 6   |
+--------+--------+--------+

+--------+--------+--------+
| Marker | Marker | Marker |
| 8 bits | 8 bits | 8 bits |
+--------+--------+--------+

+--------+--------+--------+
| Marker | Marker | Marker |
| 8 bits | 8 bits | 8 bits |
+--------+--------+--------+
```

3.4.3.  COMPRESSED MODE

    There are three kinds of information to be sent:  regular data,
sent in a byte string; compressed data, consisting of
replications or filler; and control information, sent in a
two-byte escape sequence.  If n>0 bytes (up to 127) of regular
data are sent, these n bytes are preceded by a byte with the
left-most bit set to 0 and the right-most 7 bits containing the
number n.

Byte string:

```
    1       7                8                       8
   +-+-+-+-+-+-+-+-+ +-+-+-+-+-+-+-+-+     +-+-+-+-+-+-+-+-+
   |0|     n       | |    d(1)       | ... |    d(n)       |
   +-+-+-+-+-+-+-+-+ +-+-+-+-+-+-+-+-+     +-+-+-+-+-+-+-+-+
                                    ^                   ^
                           |---n bytes---|
                                of data
```

    String of n data bytes d(1),..., d(n)
Count n must be positive.

    To compress a string of n replications of the data byte d, the
following 2 bytes are sent:

Replicated Byte:

```
     2      6                8
   +-+-+-+-+-+-+-+-+ +-+-+-+-+-+-+-+-+
   |1 0|   n       | |      d        |
   +-+-+-+-+-+-+-+-+ +-+-+-+-+-+-+-+-+
```

    A string of n filler bytes can be compressed into a single
byte, where the filler byte varies with the representation
type.  If the type is ASCII or EBCDIC the filler byte is <SP>
(Space, ASCII code 32, EBCDIC code 64).  If the type is Image
or Local byte the filler is a zero byte.

Filler String:

```
     2      6
   +-+-+-+-+-+-+-+-+
   |1 1|   n       |
   +-+-+-+-+-+-+-+-+
```

    The escape sequence is a double byte, the first of which is the

escape byte (all zeros) and the second of which contains
descriptor codes as defined in Block mode.  The descriptor
codes have the same meaning as in Block mode and apply to the
succeeding string of bytes.

Compressed mode is useful for obtaining increased bandwidth on
very large network transmissions at a little extra CPU cost.
It can be most effectively used to reduce the size of printer
files such as those generated by RJE hosts.

## 3.5.  ERROR RECOVERY AND RESTART

There is no provision for detecting bits lost or scrambled in data
transfer; this level of error control is handled by the TCP.
However, a restart procedure is provided to protect users from
gross system failures (including failures of a host, an
FTP-process, or the underlying network).

The restart procedure is defined only for the block and compressed
modes of data transfer.  It requires the sender of data to insert
a special marker code in the data stream with some marker
information.  The marker information has meaning only to the
sender, but must consist of printable characters in the default or
negotiated language of the control connection (ASCII or EBCDIC).
The marker could represent a bit-count, a record-count, or any
other information by which a system may identify a data
checkpoint.  The receiver of data, if it implements the restart
procedure, would then mark the corresponding position of this
marker in the receiving system, and return this information to the
user.

In the event of a system failure, the user can restart the data
transfer by identifying the marker point with the FTP restart
procedure.  The following example illustrates the use of the
restart procedure.

The sender of the data inserts an appropriate marker block in the
data stream at a convenient point.  The receiving host marks the
corresponding data point in its file system and conveys the last
known sender and receiver marker information to the user, either
directly or over the control connection in a 110 reply (depending
on who is the sender).  In the event of a system failure, the user
or controller process restarts the server at the last server
marker by sending a restart command with server's marker code as
its argument.  The restart command is transmitted over the control

connection and is immediately followed by the command (such as
RETR, STOR or LIST) which was being executed when the system
failure occurred.

4.  FILE TRANSFER FUNCTIONS

The communication channel from the user-PI to the server-PI is
established as a TCP connection from the user to the standard server
port.  The user protocol interpreter is responsible for sending FTP
commands and interpreting the replies received; the server-PI
interprets commands, sends replies and directs its DTP to set up the
data connection and transfer the data.  If the second party to the
data transfer (the passive transfer process) is the user-DTP, then it
is governed through the internal protocol of the user-FTP host; if it
is a second server-DTP, then it is governed by its PI on command from
the user-PI.  The FTP replies are discussed in the next section.  In
the description of a few of the commands in this section, it is
helpful to be explicit about the possible replies.

4.1.  FTP COMMANDS

4.1.1.  ACCESS CONTROL COMMANDS

The following commands specify access control identifiers
(command codes are shown in parentheses).

USER NAME (USER)

The argument field is a Telnet string identifying the user.
The user identification is that which is required by the
server for access to its file system.  This command will
normally be the first command transmitted by the user after
the control connections are made (some servers may require
this).  Additional identification information in the form of
a password and/or an account command may also be required by
some servers.  Servers may allow a new USER command to be
entered at any point in order to change the access control
and/or accounting information.  This has the effect of
flushing any user, password, and account information already
supplied and beginning the login sequence again.  All
transfer parameters are unchanged and any file transfer in
progress is completed under the old access control
parameters.

PASSWORD (PASS)

   The argument field is a Telnet string specifying the user's
   password.  This command must be immediately preceded by the
   user name command, and, for some sites, completes the user's
   identification for access control.  Since password
   information is quite sensitive, it is desirable in general
   to "mask" it or suppress typeout.  It appears that the
   server has no foolproof way to achieve this.  It is
   therefore the responsibility of the user-FTP process to hide
   the sensitive password information.

ACCOUNT (ACCT)

   The argument field is a Telnet string identifying the user's
   account.  The command is not necessarily related to the USER
   command, as some sites may require an account for login and
   others only for specific access, such as storing files.  In
   the latter case the command may arrive at any time.

   There are reply codes to differentiate these cases for the
   automation: when account information is required for login,
   the response to a successful PASSword command is reply code
   332.  On the other hand, if account information is NOT
   required for login, the reply to a successful PASSword
   command is 230; and if the account information is needed for
   a command issued later in the dialogue, the server should
   return a 332 or 532 reply depending on whether it stores
   (pending receipt of the ACCounT command) or discards the
   command, respectively.

CHANGE WORKING DIRECTORY (CWD)

   This command allows the user to work with a different
   directory or dataset for file storage or retrieval without
   altering his login or accounting information.  Transfer
   parameters are similarly unchanged.  The argument is a
   pathname specifying a directory or other system dependent
   file group designator.

CHANGE TO PARENT DIRECTORY (CDUP)

   This command is a special case of CWD, and is included to
   simplify the implementation of programs for transferring
   directory trees between operating systems having different

RFC 959

26

syntaxes for naming the parent directory.  The reply codes
shall be identical to the reply codes of CWD.  See
Appendix II for further details.

STRUCTURE MOUNT (SMNT)

This command allows the user to mount a different file
system data structure without altering his login or
accounting information.  Transfer parameters are similarly
unchanged.  The argument is a pathname specifying a
directory or other system dependent file group designator.

REINITIALIZE (REIN)

This command terminates a USER, flushing all I/O and account
information, except to allow any transfer in progress to be
completed.  All parameters are reset to the default settings
and the control connection is left open.  This is identical
to the state in which a user finds himself immediately after
the control connection is opened.  A USER command may be
expected to follow.

LOGOUT (QUIT)

This command terminates a USER and if file transfer is not
in progress, the server closes the control connection.  If
file transfer is in progress, the connection will remain
open for result response and the server will then close it.
If the user-process is transferring files for several USERs
but does not wish to close and then reopen connections for
each, then the REIN command should be used instead of QUIT.

An unexpected close on the control connection will cause the
server to take the effective action of an abort (ABOR) and a
logout (QUIT).

4.1.2.  TRANSFER PARAMETER COMMANDS

All data transfer parameters have default values, and the
commands specifying data transfer parameters are required only
if the default parameter values are to be changed.  The default
value is the last specified value, or if no value has been
specified, the standard default value is as stated here.  This
implies that the server must "remember" the applicable default
values.  The commands may be in any order except that they must
precede the FTP service request.  The following commands
specify data transfer parameters:

DATA PORT (PORT)

The argument is a HOST-PORT specification for the data port
to be used in data connection.  There are defaults for both
the user and server data ports, and under normal
circumstances this command and its reply are not needed.  If
this command is used, the argument is the concatenation of a
32-bit internet host address and a 16-bit TCP port address.
This address information is broken into 8-bit fields and the
value of each field is transmitted as a decimal number (in
character string representation).  The fields are separated
by commas.  A port command would be:

     PORT h1,h2,h3,h4,p1,p2

where h1 is the high order 8 bits of the internet host
address.

PASSIVE (PASV)

This command requests the server-DTP to "listen" on a data
port (which is not its default data port) and to wait for a
connection rather than initiate one upon receipt of a
transfer command.  The response to this command includes the
host and port address this server is listening on.

REPRESENTATION TYPE (TYPE)

The argument specifies the representation type as described
in the Section on Data Representation and Storage.  Several
types take a second parameter.  The first parameter is
denoted by a single Telnet character, as is the second
Format parameter for ASCII and EBCDIC; the second parameter
for local byte is a decimal integer to indicate Bytesize.
The parameters are separated by a <SP> (Space, ASCII code
32).

The following codes are assigned for type:

```
               \    /
    A - ASCII |    | N - Non-print
              |-><-| T - Telnet format effectors
    E - EBCDIC|    | C - Carriage Control (ASA)
               /    \
    I - Image

    L <byte size> - Local byte Byte size
```

The default representation type is ASCII Non-print.  If the
Format parameter is changed, and later just the first
argument is changed, Format then returns to the Non-print
default.

FILE STRUCTURE (STRU)

The argument is a single Telnet character code specifying
file structure described in the Section on Data
Representation and Storage.

The following codes are assigned for structure:

     F - File (no record structure)
     R - Record structure
     P - Page structure

The default structure is File.

TRANSFER MODE (MODE)

The argument is a single Telnet character code specifying
the data transfer modes described in the Section on
Transmission Modes.

The following codes are assigned for transfer modes:

     S - Stream
     B - Block
     C - Compressed

The default transfer mode is Stream.

4.1.3.  FTP SERVICE COMMANDS

The FTP service commands define the file transfer or the file
system function requested by the user.  The argument of an FTP
service command will normally be a pathname.  The syntax of
pathnames must conform to server site conventions (with
standard defaults applicable), and the language conventions of
the control connection.  The suggested default handling is to
use the last specified device, directory or file name, or the
standard default defined for local users.  The commands may be
in any order except that a "rename from" command must be
followed by a "rename to" command and the restart command must
be followed by the interrupted service command (e.g., STOR or
RETR).  The data, when transferred in response to FTP service

commands, shall always be sent over the data connection, except
for certain informative replies.  The following commands
specify FTP service requests:

RETRIEVE (RETR)

   This command causes the server-DTP to transfer a copy of the
   file, specified in the pathname, to the server- or user-DTP
   at the other end of the data connection.  The status and
   contents of the file at the server site shall be unaffected.

STORE (STOR)

   This command causes the server-DTP to accept the data
   transferred via the data connection and to store the data as
   a file at the server site.  If the file specified in the
   pathname exists at the server site, then its contents shall
   be replaced by the data being transferred.  A new file is
   created at the server site if the file specified in the
   pathname does not already exist.

STORE UNIQUE (STOU)

   This command behaves like STOR except that the resultant
   file is to be created in the current directory under a name
   unique to that directory.  The 250 Transfer Started response
   must include the name generated.

APPEND (with create) (APPE)

   This command causes the server-DTP to accept the data
   transferred via the data connection and to store the data in
   a file at the server site.  If the file specified in the
   pathname exists at the server site, then the data shall be
   appended to that file; otherwise the file specified in the
   pathname shall be created at the server site.

ALLOCATE (ALLO)

   This command may be required by some servers to reserve
   sufficient storage to accommodate the new file to be
   transferred.  The argument shall be a decimal integer
   representing the number of bytes (using the logical byte
   size) of storage to be reserved for the file.  For files
   sent with record or page structure a maximum record or page
   size (in logical bytes) might also be necessary; this is
   indicated by a decimal integer in a second argument field of

**RFC 959**

**30**

the command.  This second argument is optional, but when
present should be separated from the first by the three
Telnet characters <SP> R <SP>.  This command shall be
followed by a STORe or APPEnd command.  The ALLO command
should be treated as a NOOP (no operation) by those servers
which do not require that the maximum size of the file be
declared beforehand, and those servers interested in only
the maximum record or page size should acccpt a dummy value
in the first argument and ignore it.

RESTART (REST)

The argument field represents the server marker at which
file transfer is to be restarted.  This command does not
cause file transfer but skips over the file to the specified
data checkpoint.  This command shall be immediately followed
by the appropriate FTP service command which shall cause
file transfer to resume.

RENAME FROM (RNFR)

This command specifies the old pathname of the file which is
to be renamed.  This command must be immediately followed by
a "rename to" command specifying the new file pathname.

RENAME TO (RNTO)

This command specifies the new pathname of the file
specified in the immediately preceding "rename from"
command.  Together the two commands cause a file to be
renamed.

ABORT (ABOR)

This command tells the server to abort the previous FTP
service command and any associated transfer of data.  The
abort command may require "special action", as discussed in
the Section on FTP Commands, to force recognition by the
server.  No action is to be taken if the previous command
has been completed (including data transfer).  The control
connection is not to be closed by the server, but the data
connection must be closed.

There are two cases for the server upon receipt of this
command: (1) the FTP service command was already completed,
or (2) the FTP service command is still in progress.

In the first case, the server closes the data connection
(if it is open) and responds with a 226 reply, indicating
that the abort command was successfully processed.

In the second case, the server aborts the FTP service in
progress and closes the data connection, returning a 426
reply to indicate that the service request terminated
abnormally.  The server then sends a 226 reply,
indicating that the abort command was successfully
processed.

DELETE (DELE)

   This command causes the file specified in the pathname to be
   deleted at the server site.  If an extra level of protection
   is desired (such as the query, "Do you really wish to
   delete?"), it should be provided by the user-FTP process.

REMOVE DIRECTORY (RMD)

   This command causes the directory specified in the pathname
   to be removed as a directory (if the pathname is absolute)
   or as a subdirectory of the current working directory (if
   the pathname is relative).  See Appendix II.

MAKE DIRECTORY (MKD)

   This command causes the directory specified in the pathname
   to be created as a directory (if the pathname is absolute)
   or as a subdirectory of the current working directory (if
   the pathname is relative).  See Appendix II.

PRINT WORKING DIRECTORY (PWD)

   This command causes the name of the current working
   directory to be returned in the reply.  See Appendix II.

LIST (LIST)

   This command causes a list to be sent from the server to the
   passive DTP.  If the pathname specifies a directory or other
   group of files, the server should transfer a list of files
   in the specified directory.  If the pathname specifies a
   file then the server should send current information on the
   file.  A null argument implies the user's current working or
   default directory.  The data transfer is over the data
   connection in type ASCII or type EBCDIC.  (The user must

ensure that the TYPE is appropriately ASCII or EBCDIC).
Since the information on a file may vary widely from system
to system, this information may be hard to use automatically
in a program, but may be quite useful to a human user.

NAME LIST (NLST)

This command causes a directory listing to be sent from
server to user site.  The pathname should specify a
directory or other system-specific file group descriptor; a
null argument implies the current directory.  The server
will return a stream of names of files and no other
information.  The data will be transferred in ASCII or
EBCDIC type over the data connection as valid pathname
strings separated by <CRLF> or <NL>.  (Again the user must
ensure that the TYPE is correct.)  This command is intended
to return information that can be used by a program to
further process the files automatically.  For example, in
the implementation of a "multiple get" function.

SITE PARAMETERS (SITE)

This command is used by the server to provide services
specific to his system that are essential to file transfer
but not sufficiently universal to be included as commands in
the protocol.  The nature of these services and the
specification of their syntax can be stated in a reply to
the HELP SITE command.

SYSTEM (SYST)

This command is used to find out the type of operating
system at the server.  The reply shall have as its first
word one of the system names listed in the current version
of the Assigned Numbers document [4].

STATUS (STAT)

This command shall cause a status response to be sent over
the control connection in the form of a reply.  The command
may be sent during a file transfer (along with the Telnet IP
and Synch signals--see the Section on FTP Commands) in which
case the server will respond with the status of the
operation in progress, or it may be sent between file
transfers.  In the latter case, the command may have an
argument field.  If the argument is a pathname, the command
is analogous to the "list" command except that data shall be

transferred over the control connection.  If a partial
pathname is given, the server may respond with a list of
file names or attributes associated with that specification.
If no argument is given, the server should return general
status information about the server FTP process.  This
should include current values of all transfer parameters and
the status of connections.

HELP (HELP)

This command shall cause the server to send helpful
information regarding its implementation status over the
control connection to the user.  The command may take an
argument (e.g., any command name) and return more specific
information as a response.  The reply is type 211 or 214.
It is suggested that HELP be allowed before entering a USER
command. The server may use this reply to specify
site-dependent parameters, e.g., in response to HELP SITE.

NOOP (NOOP)

This command does not affect any parameters or previously
entered commands. It specifies no action other than that the
server send an OK reply.

The File Transfer Protocol follows the specifications of the Telnet
protocol for all communications over the control connection.  Since
the language used for Telnet communication may be a negotiated
option, all references in the next two sections will be to the
"Telnet language" and the corresponding "Telnet end-of-line code".
Currently, one may take these to mean NVT-ASCII and <CRLF>.  No other
specifications of the Telnet protocol will be cited.

FTP commands are "Telnet strings" terminated by the "Telnet end of
line code".  The command codes themselves are alphabetic characters
terminated by the character <SP> (Space) if parameters follow and
Telnet-EOL otherwise.  The command codes and the semantics of
commands are described in this section; the detailed syntax of
commands is specified in the Section on Commands, the reply sequences
are discussed in the Section on Sequencing of Commands and Replies,
and scenarios illustrating the use of commands are provided in the
Section on Typical FTP Scenarios.

FTP commands may be partitioned as those specifying access-control
identifiers, data transfer parameters, or FTP service requests.
Certain commands (such as ABOR, STAT, QUIT) may be sent over the
control connection while a data transfer is in progress.  Some

servers may not be able to monitor the control and data connections
simultaneously, in which case some special action will be necessary
to get the server's attention.  The following ordered format is
tentatively recommended:

    1. User system inserts the Telnet "Interrupt Process" (IP) signal
    in the Telnet stream.

    2. User system sends the Telnet "Synch" signal.

    3. User system inserts the command (e.g., ABOR) in the Telnet
    stream.

    4. Server PI, after receiving "IP", scans the Telnet stream for
    EXACTLY ONE FTP command.

(For other servers this may not be necessary but the actions listed
above should have no unusual effect.)

4.2.  FTP REPLIES

    Replies to File Transfer Protocol commands are devised to ensure
    the synchronization of requests and actions in the process of file
    transfer, and to guarantee that the user process always knows the
    state of the Server.  Every command must generate at least one
    reply, although there may be more than one; in the latter case,
    the multiple replies must be easily distinguished.  In addition,
    some commands occur in sequential groups, such as USER, PASS and
    ACCT, or RNFR and RNTO.  The replies show the existence of an
    intermediate state if all preceding commands have been successful.
    A failure at any point in the sequence necessitates the repetition
    of the entire sequence from the beginning.

        The details of the command-reply sequence are made explicit in
        a set of state diagrams below.

    An FTP reply consists of a three digit number (transmitted as
    three alphanumeric characters) followed by some text.  The number
    is intended for use by automata to determine what state to enter
    next; the text is intended for the human user.  It is intended
    that the three digits contain enough encoded information that the
    user-process (the User-PI) will not need to examine the text and
    may either discard it or pass it on to the user, as appropriate.
    In particular, the text may be server-dependent, so there are
    likely to be varying texts for each reply code.

    A reply is defined to contain the 3-digit code, followed by Space

<SP>, followed by one line of text (where some maximum line length
has been specified), and terminated by the Telnet end-of-line
code.  There will be cases however, where the text is longer than
a single line.  In these cases the complete text must be bracketed
so the User-process knows when it may stop reading the reply (i.e.
stop processing input on the control connection) and go do other
things.  This requires a special format on the first line to
indicate that more than one line is coming, and another on the
last line to designate it as the last.  At least one of these must
contain the appropriate reply code to indicate the state of the
transaction.  To satisfy all factions, it was decided that both
the first and last line codes should be the same.

   Thus the format for multi-line replies is that the first line
   will begin with the exact required reply code, followed
   immediately by a Hyphen, "-" (also known as Minus), followed by
   text.  The last line will begin with the same code, followed
   immediately by Space <SP>, optionally some text, and the Telnet
   end-of-line code.

      For example:
                        123-First line
                        Second line
                          234 A line beginning with numbers
                        123 The last line

   The user-process then simply needs to search for the second
   occurrence of the same reply code, followed by <SP> (Space), at
   the beginning of a line, and ignore all intermediary lines.  If
   an intermediary line begins with a 3-digit number, the Server
   must pad the front  to avoid confusion.

      This scheme allows standard system routines to be used for
      reply information (such as for the STAT reply), with
      "artificial" first and last lines tacked on.  In rare cases
      where these routines are able to generate three digits and a
      Space at the beginning of any line, the beginning of each
      text line should be offset by some neutral text, like Space.

   This scheme assumes that multi-line replies may not be nested.

The three digits of the reply each have a special significance.
This is intended to allow a range of very simple to very
sophisticated responses by the user-process.  The first digit
denotes whether the response is good, bad or incomplete.
(Referring to the state diagram), an unsophisticated user-process
will be able to determine its next action (proceed as planned,

redo, retrench, etc.) by simply examining this first digit. A
user-process that wants to know approximately what kind of error
occurred (e.g. file system error, command syntax error) may
examine the second digit, reserving the third digit for the finest
gradation of information (e.g., RNTO command without a preceding
RNFR).

There are five values for the first digit of the reply code:

   1yz   Positive Preliminary reply

      The requested action is being initiated; expect another
      reply before proceeding with a new command. (The
      user-process sending another command before the
      completion reply would be in violation of protocol; but
      server-FTP processes should queue any commands that
      arrive while a preceding command is in progress.) This
      type of reply can be used to indicate that the command
      was accepted and the user-process may now pay attention
      to the data connections, for implementations where
      simultaneous monitoring is difficult. The server-FTP
      process may send at most, one 1yz reply per command.

   2yz   Positive Completion reply

      The requested action has been successfully completed. A
      new request may be initiated.

   3yz   Positive Intermediate reply

      The command has been accepted, but the requested action
      is being held in abeyance, pending receipt of further
      information. The user should send another command
      specifying this information. This reply is used in
      command sequence groups.

   4yz   Transient Negative Completion reply

      The command was not accepted and the requested action did
      not take place, but the error condition is temporary and
      the action may be requested again. The user should
      return to the beginning of the command sequence, if any.
      It is difficult to assign a meaning to "transient",
      particularly when two distinct sites (Server- and
      User-processes) have to agree on the interpretation.
      Each reply in the 4yz category might have a slightly
      different time value, but the intent is that the

user-process is encouraged to try again.  A rule of thumb
in determining if a reply fits into the 4yz or the 5yz
(Permanent Negative) category is that replies are 4yz if
the commands can be repeated without any change in
command form or in properties of the User or Server
(e.g., the command is spelled the same with the same
arguments used; the user does not change his file access
or user name; the server does not put up a new
implementation.)

5yz    Permanent Negative Completion reply

The command was not accepted and the requested action did
not take place.  The User-process is discouraged from
repeating the exact request (in the same sequence).  Even
some "permanent" error conditions can be corrected, so
the human user may want to direct his User-process to
reinitiate the command sequence by direct action at some
point in the future (e.g., after the spelling has been
changed, or the user has altered his directory status.)

The following function groupings are encoded in the second
digit:

x0z    Syntax - These replies refer to syntax errors,
       syntactically correct commands that don't fit any
       functional category, unimplemented or superfluous
       commands.

x1z    Information -  These are replies to requests for
       information, such as status or help.

x2z    Connections - Replies referring to the control and
       data connections.

x3z    Authentication and accounting - Replies for the login
       process and accounting procedures.

x4z    Unspecified as yet.

x5z    File system - These replies indicate the status of the
       Server file system vis-a-vis the requested transfer or
       other file system action.

The third digit gives a finer gradation of meaning in each of
the function categories, specified by the second digit.  The
list of replies below will illustrate this.  Note that the text

associated with each reply is recommended, rather than
mandatory, and may even change according to the command with
which it is associated.  The reply codes, on the other hand,
must strictly follow the specifications in the last section;
that is, Server implementations should not invent new codes for
situations that are only slightly different from the ones
described here, but rather should adapt codes already defined.

A command such as TYPE or ALLO whose successful execution
does not offer the user-process any new information will
cause a 200 reply to be returned.  If the command is not
implemented by a particular Server-FTP process because it
has no relevance to that computer system, for example ALLO
at a TOPS20 site, a Positive Completion reply is still
desired so that the simple User-process knows it can proceed
with its course of action.  A 202 reply is used in this case
with, for example, the reply text:  "No storage allocation
necessary."  If, on the other hand, the command requests a
non-site-specific action and is unimplemented, the response
is 502.  A refinement of that is the 504 reply for a command
that is implemented, but that requests an unimplemented
parameter.

4.2.1  Reply Codes by Function Groups

    200 Command okay.
    500 Syntax error, command unrecognized.
        This may include errors such as command line too long.
    501 Syntax error in parameters or arguments.
    202 Command not implemented, superfluous at this site.
    502 Command not implemented.
    503 Bad sequence of commands.
    504 Command not implemented for that parameter.

110 Restart marker reply.
    In this case, the text is exact and not left to the
    particular implementation; it must read:
         MARK yyyy = mmmm
    Where yyyy is User-process data stream marker, and mmmm
    server's equivalent marker (note the spaces between markers
    and "=").
211 System status, or system help reply.
212 Directory status.
213 File status.
214 Help message.
    On how to use the server or the meaning of a particular
    non-standard command.  This reply is useful only to the
    human user.
215 NAME system type.
    Where NAME is an official system name from the list in the
    Assigned Numbers document.

120 Service ready in nnn minutes.
220 Service ready for new user.
221 Service closing control connection.
    Logged out if appropriate.
421 Service not available, closing control connection.
    This may be a reply to any command if the service knows it
    must shut down.
125 Data connection already open; transfer starting.
225 Data connection open; no transfer in progress.
425 Can't open data connection.
226 Closing data connection.
    Requested file action successful (for example, file
    transfer or file abort).
426 Connection closed; transfer aborted.
227 Entering Passive Mode (h1,h2,h3,h4,p1,p2).

230 User logged in, proceed.
530 Not logged in.
331 User name okay, need password.
332 Need account for login.
532 Need account for storing files.

      150 File status okay; about to open data connection.
      250 Requested file action okay, completed.
      257 "PATHNAME" created.
      350 Requested file action pending further information.
      450 Requested file action not taken.
          File unavailable (e.g., file busy).
      550 Requested action not taken.
          File unavailable (e.g., file not found, no access).
      451 Requested action aborted. Local error in processing.
      551 Requested action aborted. Page type unknown.
      452 Requested action not taken.
          Insufficient storage space in system.
      552 Requested file action aborted.
          Exceeded storage allocation (for current directory or
          dataset).
      553 Requested action not taken.
          File name not allowed.

4.2.2  Numeric  Order List of Reply Codes

      110 Restart marker reply.
          In this case, the text is exact and not left to the
          particular implementation; it must read:
              MARK yyyy = mmmm
          Where yyyy is User-process data stream marker, and mmmm
          server's equivalent marker (note the spaces between markers
          and "=").
      120 Service ready in nnn minutes.
      125 Data connection already open; transfer starting.
      150 File status okay; about to open data connection.

**41**

**RFC 959**

200 Command okay.
202 Command not implemented, superfluous at this site.
211 System status, or system help reply.
212 Directory status.
213 File status.
214 Help message.
    On how to use the server or the meaning of a particular
    non-standard command.  This reply is useful only to the
    human user.
215 NAME system type.
    Where NAME is an official system name from the list in the
    Assigned Numbers document.
220 Service ready for new user.
221 Service closing control connection.
    Logged out if appropriate.
225 Data connection open; no transfer in progress.
226 Closing data connection.
    Requested file action successful (for example, file
    transfer or file abort).
227 Entering Passive Mode (h1,h2,h3,h4,p1,p2).
230 User logged in, proceed.
250 Requested file action okay, completed.
257 "PATHNAME" created.

331 User name okay, need password.
332 Need account for login.
350 Requested file action pending further information.

421 Service not available, closing control connection.
    This may be a reply to any command if the service knows it
    must shut down.
425 Can't open data connection.
426 Connection closed; transfer aborted.
450 Requested file action not taken.
    File unavailable (e.g., file busy).
451 Requested action aborted: local error in processing.
452 Requested action not taken.
    Insufficient storage space in system.

                500 Syntax error, command unrecognized.
                    This may include errors such as command line too long.
                501 Syntax error in parameters or arguments.
                502 Command not implemented.
                503 Bad sequence of commands.
                504 Command not implemented for that parameter.
                530 Not logged in.
                532 Need account for storing files.
                550 Requested action not taken.
                    File unavailable (e.g., file not found, no access).
                551 Requested action aborted: page type unknown.
                552 Requested file action aborted.
                    Exceeded storage allocation (for current directory or
                    dataset).
                553 Requested action not taken.
                    File name not allowed.


5.  DECLARATIVE SPECIFICATIONS

    5.1.  MINIMUM IMPLEMENTATION

        In order to make FTP workable without needless error messages, the
        following minimum implementation is required for all servers:

            TYPE - ASCII Non-print
            MODE - Stream
            STRUCTURE - File, Record
            COMMANDS - USER, QUIT, PORT,
                       TYPE, MODE, STRU,
                         for the default values
                       RETR, STOR,
                       NOOP.

        The default values for transfer parameters are:

            TYPE - ASCII Non-print
            MODE - Stream
            STRU - File

        All hosts must accept the above as the standard defaults.

5.2.  CONNECTIONS

   The server protocol interpreter shall "listen" on Port L.  The
   user or user protocol interpreter shall initiate the full-duplex
   control connection.  Server- and user- processes should follow the
   conventions of the Telnet protocol as specified in the
   ARPA-Internet Protocol Handbook [1].  Servers are under no
   obligation to provide for editing of command lines and may require
   that it be done in the user host.  The control connection shall be
   closed by the server at the user's request after all transfers and
   replies are completed.

   The user-DTP must "listen" on the specified data port; this may be
   the default user port (U) or a port specified in the PORT command.
   The server shall initiate the data connection from his own default
   data port (L-1) using the specified user data port.  The direction
   of the transfer and the port used will be determined by the FTP
   service command.

   Note that all FTP implementation must support data transfer using
   the default port, and that only the USER-PI may initiate the use
   of non-default ports.

   When data is to be transferred between two servers, A and B (refer
   to Figure 2), the user-PI, C, sets up control connections with
   both server-PI's.  One of the servers, say A, is then sent a PASV
   command telling him to "listen" on his data port rather than
   initiate a connection when he receives a transfer service command.
   When the user-PI receives an acknowledgment to the PASV command,
   which includes the identity of the host and port being listened
   on, the user-PI then sends A's port, a, to B in a PORT command; a
   reply is returned.  The user-PI may then send the corresponding
   service commands to A and B.  Server B initiates the connection
   and the transfer proceeds.  The command-reply sequence is listed
   below where the messages are vertically synchronous but
   horizontally asynchronous:

```
        User-PI - Server A                  User-PI - Server B
        ------------------                  ------------------

        C->A : Connect                      C->B : Connect
        C->A : PASV
        A->C : 227 Entering Passive Mode. A1,A2,A3,A4,a1,a2
                                            C->B : PORT A1,A2,A3,A4,a1,a2
                                            B->C : 200 Okay
        C->A : STOR                         C->B : RETR
                  B->A : Connect to HOST-A, PORT-a
```

                                Figure 3

The data connection shall be closed by the server under the
conditions described in the Section on Establishing Data
Connections.  If the data connection is to be closed following a
data transfer where closing the connection is not required to
indicate the end-of-file, the server must do so immediately.
Waiting until after a new transfer command is not permitted
because the user-process will have already tested the data
connection to see if it needs to do a "listen"; (remember that the
user must "listen" on a closed data port BEFORE sending the
transfer request).  To prevent a race condition here, the server
sends a reply (226) after closing the data connection (or if the
connection is left open, a "file transfer completed" reply (250)
and the user-PI should wait for one of these replies before
issuing a new transfer command).

Any time either the user or server see that the connection is
being closed by the other side, it should promptly read any
remaining data queued on the connection and issue the close on its
own side.

5.3.  COMMANDS

The commands are Telnet character strings transmitted over the
control connections as described in the Section on FTP Commands.
The command functions and semantics are described in the Section
on Access Control Commands, Transfer Parameter Commands, FTP
Service Commands, and Miscellaneous Commands.  The command syntax
is specified here.

The commands begin with a command code followed by an argument
field.  The command codes are four or fewer alphabetic characters.
Upper and lower case alphabetic characters are to be treated
identically.  Thus, any of the following may represent the
retrieve command:

                    RETR     Retr     retr     ReTr     rETr

This also applies to any symbols representing parameter values,
such as A or a for ASCII TYPE.  The command codes and the argument
fields are separated by one or more spaces.

The argument field consists of a variable length character string
ending with the character sequence <CRLF> (Carriage Return, Line
Feed) for NVT-ASCII representation; for other negotiated languages
a different end of line character might be used.  It should be
noted that the server is to take no action until the end of line
code is received.

The syntax is specified below in NVT-ASCII.  All characters in the
argument field are ASCII characters including any ASCII
represented decimal integers.  Square brackets denote an optional
argument field.  If the option is not taken, the appropriate
default is implied.

5.3.1.  FTP COMMANDS

The following are the FTP commands:

```
USER <SP> <username> <CRLF>
PASS <SP> <password> <CRLF>
ACCT <SP> <account-information> <CRLF>
CWD  <SP> <pathname> <CRLF>
CDUP <CRLF>
SMNT <SP> <pathname> <CRLF>
QUIT <CRLF>
REIN <CRLF>
PORT <SP> <host-port> <CRLF>
PASV <CRLF>
TYPE <SP> <type-code> <CRLF>
STRU <SP> <structure-code> <CRLF>
MODE <SP> <mode-code> <CRLF>
RETR <SP> <pathname> <CRLF>
STOR <SP> <pathname> <CRLF>
STOU <CRLF>
APPE <SP> <pathname> <CRLF>
ALLO <SP> <decimal-integer>
     [<SP> R <SP> <decimal-integer>] <CRLF>
REST <SP> <marker> <CRLF>
RNFR <SP> <pathname> <CRLF>
RNTO <SP> <pathname> <CRLF>
ABOR <CRLF>
DELE <SP> <pathname> <CRLF>
RMD  <SP> <pathname> <CRLF>
MKD  <SP> <pathname> <CRLF>
PWD  <CRLF>
LIST [<SP> <pathname>] <CRLF>
NLST [<SP> <pathname>] <CRLF>
SITE <SP> <string> <CRLF>
SYST <CRLF>
STAT [<SP> <pathname>] <CRLF>
HELP [<SP> <string>] <CRLF>
NOOP <CRLF>
```

5.3.2.  FTP COMMAND ARGUMENTS

The syntax of the above argument fields (using BNF notation
where applicable) is:

```
<username> ::= <string>
<password> ::= <string>
<account-information> ::= <string>
<string> ::= <char> | <char><string>
<char> ::= any of the 128 ASCII characters except <CR> and
<LF>
<marker> ::= <pr-string>
<pr-string> ::= <pr-char> | <pr-char><pr-string>
<pr-char> ::= printable characters, any
              ASCII code 33 through 126
<byte-size> ::= <number>
<host-port> ::= <host-number>,<port-number>
<host-number> ::= <number>,<number>,<number>,<number>
<port-number> ::= <number>,<number>
<number> ::= any decimal integer 1 through 255
<form-code> ::= N | T | C
<type-code> ::= A [<sp> <form-code>]
              | E [<sp> <form-code>]
              | I
              | L <sp> <byte-size>
<structure-code> ::= F | R | P
<mode-code> ::= S | B | C
<pathname> ::= <string>
<decimal-integer> ::= any decimal integer
```

5.4.  SEQUENCING OF COMMANDS AND REPLIES

The communication between the user and server is intended to be an
alternating dialogue.  As such, the user issues an FTP command and
the server responds with a prompt primary reply.  The user should
wait for this initial primary success or failure response before
sending further commands.

Certain commands require a second reply for which the user should
also wait.  These replies may, for example, report on the progress
or completion of file transfer or the closing of the data
connection.  They are secondary replies to file transfer commands.

One important group of informational replies is the connection
greetings.  Under normal circumstances, a server will send a 220
reply, "awaiting input", when the connection is completed.  The
user should wait for this greeting message before sending any
commands.  If the server is unable to accept input right away, a
120 "expected delay" reply should be sent immediately and a 220
reply when ready.  The user will then know not to hang up if there
is a delay.

Spontaneous Replies

   Sometimes "the system" spontaneously has a message to be sent
   to a user (usually all users).  For example, "System going down
   in 15 minutes".  There is no provision in FTP for such
   spontaneous information to be sent from the server to the user.
   It is recommended that such information be queued in the
   server-PI and delivered to the user-PI in the next reply
   (possibly making it a multi-line reply).

The table below lists alternative success and failure replies for
each command.  These must be strictly adhered to; a server may
substitute text in the replies, but the meaning and action implied
by the code numbers and by the specific command reply sequence
cannot be altered.

Command-Reply Sequences

   In this section, the command-reply sequence is presented.  Each
   command is listed with its possible replies; command groups are
   listed together.  Preliminary replies are listed first (with
   their succeeding replies indented and under them), then
   positive and negative completion, and finally intermediary

replies with the remaining commands from the sequence
following.  This listing forms the basis for the state
diagrams, which will be presented separately.

```
    Connection Establishment
        120
            220
        220
        421
    Login
        USER
            230
            530
            500, 501, 421
            331, 332
        PASS
            230
            202
            530
            500, 501, 503, 421
            332
        ACCT
            230
            202
            530
            500, 501, 503, 421
        CWD
            250
            500, 501, 502, 421, 530, 550
        CDUP
            200
            500, 501, 502, 421, 530, 550
        SMNT
            202, 250
            500, 501, 502, 421, 530, 550
    Logout
        REIN
            120
                220
            220
            421
            500, 502
        QUIT
            221
            500
```

```
         Transfer parameters
            PORT
               200
               500, 501, 421, 530
            PASV
               227
               500, 501, 502, 421, 530
            MODE
               200
               500, 501, 504, 421, 530
            TYPE
               200
               500, 501, 504, 421, 530
            STRU
               200
               500, 501, 504, 421, 530
         File action commands
            ALLO
               200
               202
               500, 501, 504, 421, 530
            REST
               500, 501, 502, 421, 530
               350
            STOR
            125, 150
               (110)
               226, 250
               425, 426, 451, 551, 552
            532, 450, 452, 553
            500, 501, 421, 530
            STOU
            125, 150
               (110)
               226, 250
               425, 426, 451, 551, 552
            532, 450, 452, 553
            500, 501, 421, 530
            RETR
            125, 150
               (110)
               226, 250
               425, 426, 451
            450, 550
            500, 501, 421, 530
```

```
                LIST
                   125, 150
                      226, 250
                      425, 426, 451
                   450
                   500, 501, 502, 421, 530
                NLST
                   125, 150
                      226, 250
                      425, 426, 451
                   450
                   500, 501, 502, 421, 530
                APPE
                   125, 150
                      (110)
                      226, 250
                      425, 426, 451, 551, 552
                   532, 450, 550, 452, 553
                   500, 501, 502, 421, 530
                RNFR
                   450, 550
                   500, 501, 502, 421, 530
                   350
                RNTO
                   250
                   532, 553
                   500, 501, 502, 503, 421, 530
                DELE
                   250
                   450, 550
                   500, 501, 502, 421, 530
                RMD
                   250
                   500, 501, 502, 421, 530, 550
                MKD
                   257
                   500, 501, 502, 421, 530, 550
                PWD
                   257
                   500, 501, 502, 421, 550
                ABOR
                   225, 226
                   500, 501, 502, 421
```

```
        Informational commands
           SYST
              215
              500, 501, 502, 421
           STAT
              211, 212, 213
              450
              500, 501, 502, 421, 530
           HELP
              211, 214
              500, 501, 502, 421
        Miscellaneous commands
           SITE
              200
              202
              500, 501, 530
           NOOP
              200
              500 421
```

6.   STATE DIAGRAMS

   Here we present state diagrams for a very simple minded FTP
   implementation.  Only the first digit of the reply codes is used.
   There is one state diagram for each group of FTP commands or command
   sequences.

   The command groupings were determined by constructing a model for
   each command then collecting together the commands with structurally
   identical models.

   For each command or command sequence there are three possible
   outcomes: success (S), failure (F), and error (E).  In the state
   diagrams below we use the symbol B for "begin", and the symbol W for
   "wait for reply".

   We first present the diagram that represents the largest group of FTP
   commands:

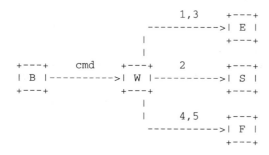

   This diagram models the commands:

       ABOR, ALLO, DELE, CWD, CDUP, SMNT, HELP, MODE, NOOP, PASV,
       QUIT, SITE, PORT, SYST, STAT, RMD, MKD, PWD, STRU, and TYPE.

The other large group of commands is represented by a very similar
diagram:

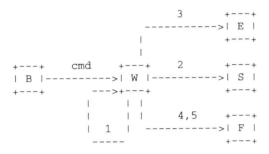

```
                              3       +---+
                          --------->| E |
                              |       +---+
                              |
    +---+     cmd    +---+     2      +---+
    | B |--------->| W |--------->| S |
    +---+          --->+---+         +---+
                     | | |
                     | | |   4,5    +---+
                     | 1 |  --------->| F |
                     -----           +---+
```

This diagram models the commands:

    APPE, LIST, NLST, REIN, RETR, STOR, and STOU.

Note that this second model could also be used to represent the first
group of commands, the only difference being that in the first group
the 100 series replies are unexpected and therefore treated as error,
while the second group expects (some may require) 100 series replies.
Remember that at most, one 100 series reply is allowed per command.

The remaining diagrams model command sequences, perhaps the simplest
of these is the rename sequence:

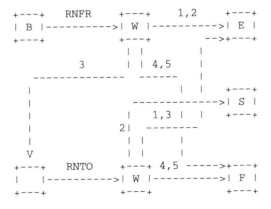

```
    +---+    RNFR    +---+    1,2    +---+
    | B |--------->| W |--------->| E |
    +---+          +---+          -->+---+
                    | |            |
            3       | | 4,5        |
        -------------  ------      |
        |                 | |   +---+
        |                 ------------->| S |
        |               | 1,3 | |   +---+
        |              2|  --------
        |               | |      |
        |               | |      |
        V               | |      |
    +---+    RNTO    +---+ 4,5 ----->+---+
    |   |--------->| W |--------->| F |
    +---+          +---+          +---+
```

The next diagram is a simple model of the Restart command:

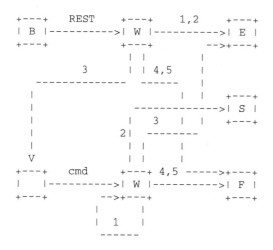

         Where "cmd" is APPE, STOR, or RETR.

We note that the above three models are similar.  The Restart differs
from the Rename two only in the treatment of 100 series replies at
the second stage, while the second group expects (some may require)
100 series replies.  Remember that at most, one 100 series reply is
allowed per command.

The most complicated diagram is for the Login sequence:

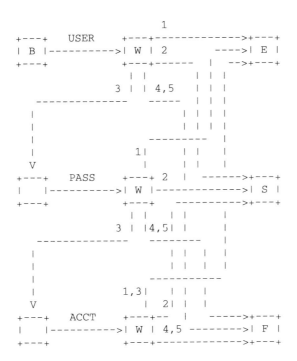

Finally, we present a generalized diagram that could be used to model
the command and reply interchange:

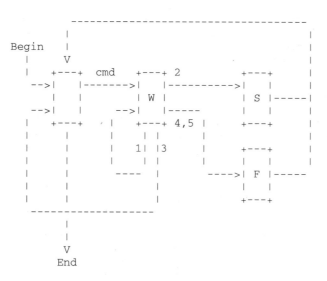

7.  TYPICAL FTP SCENARIO

    User at host U wanting to transfer files to/from host S:

    In general, the user will communicate to the server via a mediating
    user-FTP process.  The following may be a typical scenario.  The
    user-FTP prompts are shown in parentheses, '---->' represents
    commands from host U to host S, and '<----' represents replies from
    host S to host U.

```
        LOCAL COMMANDS BY USER                  ACTION INVOLVED

        ftp (host) multics<CR>            Connect to host S, port L,
                                          establishing control connections.
                                          <---- 220 Service ready <CRLF>.
        username Doe <CR>                 USER Doe<CRLF>---->
                                          <---- 331 User name ok,
                                                    need password<CRLF>.
        password mumble <CR>              PASS mumble<CRLF>---->
                                          <---- 230 User logged in<CRLF>.
        retrieve (local type) ASCII<CR>
        (local pathname) test 1 <CR>      User-FTP opens local file in ASCII.
        (for. pathname) test.pl1<CR>      RETR test.pl1<CRLF> ---->
                                          <---- 150 File status okay;
                                                    about to open data
                                                    connection<CRLF>.
                                          Server makes data connection
                                          to port U.

                                          <---- 226 Closing data connection,
                                                    file transfer successful<CRLF>.
        type Image<CR>                    TYPE I<CRLF> ---->
                                          <---- 200 Command OK<CRLF>
        store (local type) image<CR>
        (local pathname) file dump<CR>    User-FTP opens local file in Image.
        (for.pathname) >udd>cn>fd<CR>     STOR >udd>cn>fd<CRLF> ---->
                                          <---- 550 Access denied<CRLF>
        terminate                         QUIT <CRLF> ---->
                                          Server closes all
                                          connections.
```

8.  CONNECTION ESTABLISHMENT

    The FTP control connection is established via TCP between the user
    process port U and the server process port L.  This protocol is
    assigned the service port 21 (25 octal), that is L=21.

APPENDIX I -  PAGE STRUCTURE

   The need for FTP to support page structure derives principally from
   the  need to support efficient transmission of files between TOPS-20
   systems, particularly the files used by NLS.

   The file system of TOPS-20 is based on the concept of pages.  The
   operating system is most efficient at manipulating files as pages.
   The operating system provides an interface to the file system so that
   many applications view files as sequential streams of characters.
   However, a few applications use the underlying page structures
   directly, and some of these create holey files.

   A TOPS-20 disk file consists of four things: a pathname, a page
   table, a (possibly empty) set of pages, and a set of attributes.

   The pathname is specified in the RETR or STOR command.  It includes
   the directory name, file name, file name extension, and generation
   number.

   The page table contains up to 2**18 entries.  Each entry may be
   EMPTY, or may point to a page.  If it is not empty, there are also
   some page-specific access bits; not all pages of a file need have the
   same access protection.

      A page is a contiguous set of 512 words of 36 bits each.

   The attributes of the file, in the File Descriptor Block (FDB),
   contain such things as creation time, write time, read time, writer's
   byte-size, end-of-file pointer, count of reads and writes, backup
   system tape numbers, etc.

   Note that there is NO requirement that entries in the page table be
   contiguous.  There may be empty page table slots between occupied
   ones.  Also, the end of file pointer is simply a number.  There is no
   requirement that it in fact point at the "last" datum in the file.
   Ordinary sequential I/O calls in TOPS-20 will cause the end of file
   pointer to be left after the last datum written, but other operations
   may cause it not to be so, if a particular programming system so
   requires.

   In fact, in both of these special cases, "holey" files and
   end-of-file pointers NOT at the end of the file, occur with NLS data
   files.

The TOPS-20 paged files can be sent with the FTP transfer parameters:
TYPE L 36, STRU P, and MODE S (in fact, any mode could be used).

Each page of information has a header.  Each header field, which is a
logical byte, is a TOPS-20 word, since the TYPE is L 36.

The header fields are:

   Word 0: Header Length.

      The header length is 5.

   Word 1: Page Index.

      If the data is a disk file page, this is the number of that
      page in the file's page map.  Empty pages (holes) in the file
      are simply not sent.  Note that a hole is NOT the same as a
      page of zeros.

   Word 2: Data Length.

      The number of data words in this page, following the header.
      Thus, the total length of the transmission unit is the Header
      Length plus the Data Length.

   Word 3: Page Type.

      A code for what type of chunk this is.  A data page is type 3,
      the FDB page is type 2.

   Word 4: Page Access Control.

      The access bits associated with the page in the file's page
      map.  (This full word quantity is put into AC2 of an SPACS by
      the program reading from net to disk.)

After the header are Data Length data words.  Data Length is
currently either 512 for a data page or 31 for an FDB.  Trailing
zeros in a disk file page may be discarded, making Data Length less
than 512 in that case.

APPENDIX II -  DIRECTORY COMMANDS

   Since UNIX has a tree-like directory structure in which directories
   are as easy to manipulate as ordinary files, it is useful to expand
   the FTP servers on these machines to include commands which deal with
   the creation of directories.  Since there are other hosts on the
   ARPA-Internet which have tree-like directories (including TOPS-20 and
   Multics), these commands are as general as possible.

   Four directory commands have been added to FTP:

      MKD pathname

         Make a directory with the name "pathname".

      RMD pathname

         Remove the directory with the name "pathname".

      PWD

         Print the current working directory name.

      CDUP

         Change to the parent of the current working directory.

   The  "pathname"  argument should be created (removed) as a
   subdirectory of the current working directory, unless the "pathname"
   string contains sufficient information to specify otherwise to the
   server, e.g., "pathname" is an absolute pathname (in UNIX and
   Multics), or pathname is something like "<abso.lute.path>" to
   TOPS-20.

REPLY CODES

   The CDUP command is a special case of CWD, and is included to
   simplify the implementation of programs for transferring directory
   trees between operating systems having different syntaxes for
   naming the parent directory.  The reply codes for CDUP be
   identical to the reply codes of CWD.

   The reply codes for RMD be identical to the reply codes for its
   file analogue, DELE.

   The reply codes for MKD, however, are a bit more complicated.  A
   freshly created directory will probably be the object of a future

CWD command.  Unfortunately, the argument to MKD may not always be
a suitable argument for CWD.  This is the case, for example, when
a TOPS-20 subdirectory is created by giving just the subdirectory
name.  That is, with a TOPS-20 server FTP, the command sequence

      MKD MYDIR
      CWD MYDIR

will fail.  The new directory may only be referred to by its
"absolute" name; e.g., if the MKD command above were issued while
connected to the directory <DFRANKLIN>, the new subdirectory
could only be referred to by the name <DFRANKLIN.MYDIR>.

Even on UNIX and Multics, however, the argument given to MKD may
not be suitable.  If it is a "relative" pathname (i.e., a pathname
which is interpreted relative to the current directory), the user
would need to be in the same current directory in order to reach
the subdirectory.  Depending on the application, this may be
inconvenient.  It is not very robust in any case.

To solve these problems, upon successful completion of an MKD
command, the server should return a line of the form:

      257<space>"<directory-name>"<space><commentary>

That is, the server will tell the user what string to use when
referring to the created  directory.  The directory name can
contain any character; embedded double-quotes should be escaped by
double-quotes (the "quote-doubling" convention).

For example, a user connects to the directory /usr/dm, and creates
a subdirectory, named pathname:

      CWD /usr/dm
      200 directory changed to /usr/dm
      MKD pathname
      257 "/usr/dm/pathname" directory created

An example with an embedded double quote:

      MKD foo"bar
      257 "/usr/dm/foo""bar" directory created
      CWD /usr/dm/foo"bar
      200 directory changed to /usr/dm/foo"bar

The prior existence of a subdirectory with the same name is an
error, and the server must return an "access denied" error reply
in that case.

```
CWD /usr/dm
200 directory changed to /usr/dm
MKD pathname
521-"/usr/dm/pathname" directory already exists;
521 taking no action.
```

The failure replies for MKD are analogous to its file  creating
cousin, STOR.  Also, an "access denied" return is given if a file
name with the same name as the subdirectory will conflict with the
creation of the subdirectory (this is a problem on UNIX, but
shouldn't be one on TOPS-20).

Essentially because the PWD command returns the same type of
information as the successful MKD command, the successful PWD
command uses the 257 reply code as well.

SUBTLETIES

Because these commands will be most useful in transferring
subtrees from one machine to another, carefully observe that the
argument to MKD is to be interpreted as a sub-directory of  the
current working directory, unless it contains enough information
for the destination host to tell otherwise.  A hypothetical
example of its use in the TOPS-20 world:

```
CWD <some.where>
200 Working directory changed
MKD overrainbow
257 "<some.where.overrainbow>" directory created
CWD overrainbow
431 No such directory
CWD <some.where.overrainbow>
200 Working directory changed

CWD <some.where>
200 Working directory changed to <some.where>
MKD <unambiguous>
257 "<unambiguous>" directory created
CWD <unambiguous>
```

Note that the first example results in a subdirectory of the
connected directory.  In contrast, the argument in the second
example contains enough information for TOPS-20 to tell that  the

        <unambiguous> directory is a top-level directory.  Note also that
in the first example the user "violated" the protocol by
attempting to access the freshly created directory with a name
other than the one returned by TOPS-20.  Problems could have
resulted in this case had there been an <overrainbow> directory;
this is an ambiguity inherent in some TOPS-20 implementations.
Similar considerations apply to the RMD command.  The point is
this: except where to do so would violate a host's conventions for
denoting relative versus absolute pathnames, the host should treat
the operands of the MKD and RMD commands as subdirectories.  The
257 reply to the MKD command must always contain the absolute
pathname of the created directory.

APPENDIX III - RFCs on FTP

Bhushan, Abhay, "A File Transfer Protocol", RFC 114 (NIC 5823),
MIT-Project MAC, 16 April 1971.

Harslem, Eric, and John Heafner, "Comments on RFC 114 (A File
Transfer Protocol)", RFC 141 (NIC 6726), RAND, 29 April 1971.

Bhushan, Abhay, et al, "The File Transfer Protocol", RFC 172
(NIC 6794), MIT-Project MAC, 23 June 1971.

Braden, Bob, "Comments on DTP and FTP Proposals", RFC 238 (NIC 7663),
UCLA/CCN, 29 September 1971.

Bhushan, Abhay, et al, "The File Transfer Protocol", RFC 265
(NIC 7813), MIT-Project MAC, 17 November 1971.

McKenzie, Alex, "A Suggested Addition to File Transfer Protocol",
RFC 281 (NIC 8163), BBN, 8 December 1971.

Bhushan, Abhay, "The Use of "Set Data Type" Transaction in File
Transfer Protocol", RFC 294 (NIC 8304), MIT-Project MAC,
25 January 1972.

Bhushan, Abhay, "The File Transfer Protocol", RFC 354 (NIC 10596),
MIT-Project MAC, 8 July 1972.

Bhushan, Abhay, "Comments on the File Transfer Protocol (RFC 354)",
RFC 385 (NIC 11357), MIT-Project MAC, 18 August 1972.

Hicks, Greg, "User FTP Documentation", RFC 412 (NIC 12404), Utah,
27 November 1972.

Bhushan, Abhay, "File Transfer Protocol (FTP) Status and Further
Comments", RFC 414 (NIC 12406), MIT-Project MAC, 20 November 1972.

Braden, Bob, "Comments on File Transfer Protocol", RFC 430
(NIC 13299), UCLA/CCN, 7 February 1973.

Thomas, Bob, and Bob Clements, "FTP Server-Server Interaction",
RFC 438 (NIC 13770), BBN, 15 January 1973.

Braden, Bob, "Print Files in FTP", RFC 448 (NIC 13299), UCLA/CCN,
27 February 1973.

McKenzie, Alex, "File Transfer Protocol", RFC 454 (NIC 14333), BBN,
16 February 1973.

Bressler, Bob, and Bob Thomas, "Mail Retrieval via FTP", RFC 458
(NIC 14378), BBN-NET and BBN-TENEX, 20 February 1973.

Neigus, Nancy, "File Transfer Protocol", RFC 542 (NIC 17759), BBN,
12 July 1973.

Krilanovich, Mark, and George Gregg, "Comments on the File Transfer
Protocol", RFC 607 (NIC 21255), UCSB, 7 January 1974.

Pogran, Ken, and Nancy Neigus, "Response to RFC 607 - Comments on the
File Transfer Protocol", RFC 614 (NIC 21530), BBN, 28 January 1974.

Krilanovich, Mark, George Gregg, Wayne Hathaway, and Jim White,
"Comments on the File Transfer Protocol", RFC 624 (NIC 22054), UCSB,
Ames Research Center, SRI-ARC, 28 February 1974.

Bhushan, Abhay, "FTP Comments and Response to RFC 430", RFC 463
(NIC 14573), MIT-DMCG, 21 February 1973.

Braden, Bob, "FTP Data Compression", RFC 468 (NIC 14742), UCLA/CCN,
8 March 1973.

Bhushan, Abhay, "FTP and Network Mail System", RFC 475 (NIC 14919),
MIT-DMCG, 6 March 1973.

Bressler, Bob, and Bob Thomas "FTP Server-Server Interaction - II",
RFC 478 (NIC 14947), BBN-NET and BBN-TENEX, 26 March 1973.

White, Jim, "Use of FTP by the NIC Journal", RFC 479 (NIC 14948),
SRI-ARC, 8 March 1973.

White, Jim, "Host-Dependent FTP Parameters", RFC 480 (NIC 14949),
SRI-ARC, 8 March 1973.

Padlipsky, Mike, "An FTP Command-Naming Problem", RFC 506
(NIC 16157), MIT-Multics, 26 June 1973.

Day, John, "Memo to FTP Group (Proposal for File Access Protocol)",
RFC 520 (NIC 16819), Illinois, 25 June 1973.

Merryman, Robert, "The UCSD-CC Server-FTP Facility", RFC 532
(NIC 17451), UCSD-CC, 22 June 1973.

Braden, Bob, "TENEX FTP Problem", RFC 571 (NIC 18974), UCLA/CCN,
15 November 1973.

67

RFC 959

    McKenzie, Alex, and Jon Postel, "Telnet and FTP Implementation -
    Schedule Change", RFC 593 (NIC 20615), BBN and MITRE,
    29 November 1973.

    Sussman, Julie, "FTP Error Code Usage for More Reliable Mail
    Service", RFC 630 (NIC 30237), BBN, 10 April 1974.

    Postel, Jon, "Revised FTP Reply Codes", RFC 640 (NIC 30843),
    UCLA/NMC, 5 June 1974.

    Harvey, Brian, "Leaving Well Enough Alone", RFC 686 (NIC 32481),
    SU-AI, 10 May 1975.

    Harvey, Brian, "One More Try on the FTP", RFC 691 (NIC 32700), SU-AI,
    28 May 1975.

    Lieb, J., "CWD Command of FTP", RFC 697 (NIC 32963), 14 July 1975.

    Harrenstien, Ken, "FTP Extension: XSEN", RFC 737 (NIC 42217), SRI-KL,
    31 October 1977.

    Harrenstien, Ken, "FTP Extension: XRSQ/XRCP", RFC 743 (NIC 42758),
    SRI-KL, 30 December 1977.

    Lebling, P. David, "Survey of FTP Mail and MLFL", RFC 751, MIT,
    10 December 1978.

    Postel, Jon, "File Transfer Protocol Specification", RFC 765, ISI,
    June 1980.

    Mankins, David, Dan Franklin, and Buzz Owen, "Directory Oriented FTP
    Commands", RFC 776, BBN, December 1980.

    Padlipsky, Michael, "FTP Unique-Named Store Command", RFC 949, MITRE,
    July 1985.

**RFC 959**

**68**

REFERENCES

   [1]  Feinler, Elizabeth, "Internet Protocol Transition Workbook",
        Network Information Center, SRI International, March 1982.

   [2]  Postel, Jon, "Transmission Control Protocol - DARPA Internet
        Program Protocol Specification", RFC 793, DARPA, September 1981.

   [3]  Postel, Jon, and Joyce Reynolds, "Telnet Protocol
        Specification", RFC 854, ISI, May 1983.

   [4]  Reynolds, Joyce, and Jon Postel, "Assigned Numbers", RFC 943,
        ISI, April 1985.

Network Working Group                                    A. DeSchon
Request for Comments: 1068                                R. Braden
                                                                ISI
                                                        August 1988

Background File Transfer Program (BFTP)

Status of This Memo

   This memo describes an Internet background file transfer service that
   is built upon the third-party transfer model of FTP.  No new
   protocols are involved.  The purpose of this memo is to stimulate
   discussion on new Internet service modes.  Distribution of this memo
   is unlimited.

1. Introduction

   For a variety of reasons, file transfer in the Internet has generally
   been implemented as an interactive or "foreground" service.  That is,
   a user runs the appropriate local FTP user interface program as an
   interactive command and requests a file transfer to occur in real
   time.  If the transfer should fail to complete for any reason, the
   user must reissue the transfer request.  Foreground file transfer is
   relatively simple to implement -- no subtleties of queuing or stable
   storage -- and in the early days of networking it provided excellent
   service, because the Internet/ARPANET was lightly loaded and
   reasonably reliable.

   More recently, the Internet has become increasingly subject to
   congestion and long delays, particularly during times of peak usage.
   In addition, as more of the world becomes interconnected, planned and
   unplanned outages of hosts, gateways, and networks sometimes make it
   difficult for users to successfully transfer files in foreground.

   Performing file transfer asynchronously (i.e., in "background"),
   provides a solution to some of these problems, by eliminating the
   requirement for a human user to be directly involved at the time that
   a file transfer takes place.  A background file transfer service
   requires two components: a user interface program to collect the
   parameters describing the required transfer(s), and a file transfer
   control (FTC) daemon to carry them out.

Background file transfer has a number of potential advantages for a
user:

o    No Waiting

     The user can request a large transfer and ignore it until a
     notification message arrives through some common channel (e.g.,
     electronic mail).

o    End-to-end Reliability

     The FTC daemon can try a transfer repeatedly until it either
     succeeds or fails permanently.  This provides reliable end-to-
     end delivery of a file, in spite of the source or destination
     host being down or poor Internet connectivity during some time
     period.

o    Multiple File Delivery

     In order for background file transfer to be accepted in the
     Internet, it may have to include some "value-added" services.
     One such service would be an implementation of a multiple file
     transfer capability for all hosts.  Such a facility is suggested
     in RFC-959 (see the description of "NLST") and implemented in
     some User-FTP programs.

o    Deferred Delivery

     The user may wish to defer a large transfer until an off-peak
     period.  This may become important when parts of the Internet
     adopt accounting and traffic-based cost-recovery mechanisms.


There is a serious human-engineering problem with background file
transfer: if the user makes a mistake in entering parameters, this
mistake may not become apparent until much later.  This can be the
cause of severe user frustration.  To avoid this problem, the user
interface program ought to verify the correctness of as many of the
parameters as possible when they are entered.  Of course, such
foreground verification of parameters is not possible if the remote
host to which the parameters apply is currently unreachable.

To explore the usefulness of background file transfer in the present
Internet, we have implemented a file-mover service which we call the
Background File Transfer Program or BFTP.

Section 2 describes BFTP and Section 3 presents our experience and
conclusions.  The appendices contain detailed information about the

user interface language for BFTP, a description of the program
organization, and sample execution scripts.

2. Background File Transfer Program

   2.1 General Model

      In the present BFTP design, its user interface program and its FTC
      daemon program must execute on the same host, which we call the
      BFTP control host.

      Through the user interface program, a BFTP user will supply all of
      the parameters needed to transfer a file from source host S to
      destination host D, where S and D may be different from the BFTP
      control host.  These parameters include:

      o     S and D host names,

      o     login names and passwords on S and D hosts, and

      o     S and D file names (and optionally, directories).


      The user may also specify a number of optional control parameters:

      *     Source file disposition -- Copy, move (i.e., copy and
            delete), or simply delete the source file.  The default is
            copy.

      *     Destination file operation -- Create/Replace, append to, or
            create a unique destination file.  The default is
            create/replace ("STOR").

      *     FTP Parameters -- Explicitly set any of the FTP type, mode,
            or structure parameters at S and D hosts.

      *     Multiple Transfers -- Enable "wildcard" matching to perform
            multiple transfers.

      *     Start Time -- Set the time of day for the first attempt of
            the transfer. The default is "now" (i.e., make the first
            attempt as soon as the request has been queued for the FTC
            daemon).


      Finally, the user specifies a mailbox to which a completion
      notification message will be sent, and "submits" the request to
      the FTC daemon queue.  The user can then exit the BFTP user

interface program.

If the transfer should fail permanently, the FTC daemon will send
a notification message to the user's mailbox.  In the event of a
temporary failure (e.g., a broken TCP connection), the FTC daemon
will log the failure and retry the transfer after some timeout
period.  The retry cycles will be repeated until the transfer
succeeds or until some maximum number of tries specified has been
reached.  In either case, a notification message will then be sent
to the user's mailbox.

The user can check on the progress of the transfer by reentering
the BFTP user interface program, supplying a key that was defined
with the request, and displaying the current status of the
request.  The user may then cancel the request or leave it in the
queue.

The BFTP program includes a server-Telnet module, so it can be
executed as a remotely-accessible service that can be reached via
a Telnet connection to the BFTP well-known port (152).  This
allows a user on any Internet host to perform background file
transfers without running BFTP locally, but instead opening a
Telnet connection to port 152 on a BFTP service host.  Of course,
a user can also run the local BFTP user interface program directly
on any host that supports it and for which the user has login
privileges.

The next section discusses how BFTP uses standard FTP servers to
perform the transfers, while the following section covers the user
interface of BFTP.

2.2 File Transfer Mechanics for BFTP

The BFTP makes use of the "third party" or "Server-Server" model
incorporated in the Internet File Transfer Protocol [RFC-959].
Thus, the FTC daemon opens FTP control connections to the existing
FTP servers on source host S and destination host D and instructs
them to transfer the desired file(s) from S to D.  The S and D
hosts may be any two Internet hosts supporting FTP servers (but at
least one of them must support the FTP "PASV" command).  This
approach allows the implementation of a background file transfer
capability for the entire Internet at a very low cost.

Figure 1 illustrates the BFTP model of operation.  Note that the
BFTP control host is not necessarily the same as S or D.  Figure 2
illustrates the FTP command interchange used in a typical Server-
Server file transfer operation; this may be compared with the
User-Server FTP scenario illustrated in Section 7 of RFC-959.

Since BFTP may be asked to transfer files between any two hosts in
the Internet, it must support all the file types and transfer
modes that are defined in RFC-959, not just a subset implemented
by particular hosts.

BFTP supports the transfer of a set of files in a single request,
using the standard technique:

(1)  Send an NLST command to the source host S, specifying a
     pathname containing "wildcard" characters.  The reply will
     contain a list of matching source file names.

(2)  Execute a separate transfer operation for each file in this
     list.  The destination file name in each case is assumed to
     be the same as the source file name; this requires that these
     names be compatible with the naming conventions of D.

It will typically be necessary to specify working directories for
the transfers at S and D, so the file names will be simple,
unstructured names on each system.

This approach depends upon the wildcard matching capability of the
source host S.  A more general implementation would acquire a
complete list of the file names from the source host and do the
matching in the FTC daemon, for example using a regular-expression
matcher.  Another useful extension would be a general pattern-
matching file name transformation capability (e.g., like the one
included in the 4.3BSD version of FTP) to generate appropriate
destination pathnames for multiple requests.

Figure 1 -- BFTP Model of Operation

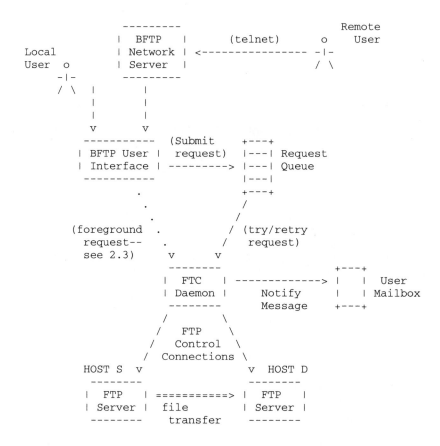

Figure 2 -- Server-Server File Transfer


```
        Server FTP              BFTP Daemon              Server FTP
          HOST S                   HOST C                  HOST D
        ----------               ----------              ----------

                        <-------- Open TCP Ctrl conn
                              Open TCP Ctrl conn -------->

                        <-------- (log in)
              (login confirm.) -------->
                                        (log in) -------->
                                             <-------- (login confirm.)

                        <-------- TYPE, STRU, MODE, CWD
             (confirmations) -------->
                            TYPE, STRU, MODE, CWD -------->
                                             <-------- (confirmations)

                        <-------- PASV command
              PASV confirm -------->
                                  PORT command -------->
                                             <-------- PORT confirm

                                    RETR file   -------->
                        <--------   STOR file
                        <---------------------------- Open TCP Data conn
                        <---------------------------- Send file
                        <---------------------------- Close Data conn
                                             <-------- RETR confirm
              STOR confirm -------->

                        <-------- QUIT command
                                  QUIT command -------->
              Close Ctrl conn -------->

                                             <-------- Close Ctrl conn
```

BFTP currently utilizes the following Server-FTP commands [RFC-959]: USER, PASS, ACCT, PASV, PORT, RETR, STOR, STOU, CWD, NLST, MODE, STRU, TYPE, and QUIT.

The FTC daemon attempts to work around FTP servers that fail to support certain commands. For example, if a server does not support the optional command "CWD", the FTC daemon will attempt to construct a complete path name using the source directory name and the source file name. However, it is necessary that at least one of the two hosts support the FTP passive (PASV) command. While many FTP server implementations support do this command, some (in particular, the 4.2BSD FTP) do not. The PASV command was officially listed as being optional in RFC-959.

## 2.3 Reliable Delivery

The reliable delivery function of BFTP is analogous to reliable delivery in a transport protocol like TCP. Both depend upon repeated delivery attempts until success is achieved, and in both cases the choice of the retry interval requires some care to balance overhead against unresponsiveness.

Humans are impatient, but even their impatience has a limit. If the file cannot be transferred "soon", a human will turn to another project; typically, there is a tendency for the transfer to become less urgent the longer the wait. The FTC daemon of BFTP therefore starts each transfer request with a very short retry interval -- e.g., 10 minutes -- and then doubles this interval for successive retries, until a maximum interval -- e.g., 4 hours -- is reached. This is essentially the exponential backoff algorithm of the Ethernet, which is also used by transport protocols such as TCP, although BFTP and TCP have quite different rationales for the algorithm.

We must also define the meaning of reliable transmission for a multiple-transfer request. For example, the set of files selected by wildcard characters in a pathname is not well defined; the set may change while the request is pending, as files are created and deleted. Furthermore, it is unreasonable to regard the entire multiple transfer as a single atomic operation. Suppose that transferring a set of files fails part way through; for an atomic operation, the files which had been successfully transferred would have to be deleted pending the next retry of the entire set. This would be ridiculously inefficient and may be impossible (since the communication path may be broken when it is time to issue the deletion requests).

BFTP addresses these issues in the following manner:

*   For a multiple file operation, the FTC daemon saves the file
    name list returned by the first successful NLST command in
    the request queue entry.  This name list determines the set
    of source files for the transfer; there can be no later
    additions to the set.

*   The FTC daemon maintains a transfer status pointer.  On each
    retry cycle, it tries to transfer only those files that have
    not already been successfully transferred.

*   The request is complete when all the individual file
    transfers have been successful, a permanent failure has
    occured, or when the retry limit is reached.

*   The notification message to the user lists the status of each
    of the multiple files.


2.4 BFTP User Interface

The purpose of BFTP is to simplify the file transfer process and
to place the burden of reliability on the BFTP control host.  We
have attempted to provide a "user friendly" command interface to
BFTP, similar in flavor to the user interface of the TOPS-20
operating system.  This interface provides extensive prompting,
defaulting, and help facilities for every command.

For a list of all BFTP commands, the user may enter "?<Return>" at
the main BFTP prompt ("BFTP>").  Entering "help<Return>" and
"explain<Return>" will provide increasing levels of explanatory
material.  To obtain information on a particular command, "help
<command name><Return>" may be entered.  The 'quit' or 'exit'
command will exit from BFTP.  Command and subcommand names may be
abbreviated to the shortest unique sequence for that context;
alternatively, a partial name can be automatically completed by
typing <Return>.

The normal procedure for a BFTP user is to set up a set of
parameters defining the desired transfer and then submit the
request to the FTC daemon.  To give the user the maximum
flexibility, BFTP supports three modes of submission:

o   Background Operation

    To request a reliable background file transfer, the user will
    issue the BFTP 'submit' command to the FTC daemon.

o      Foreground Verification, Background Operation

The BFTP 'verify' command may be used to ascertain that file
transfer parameters are valid.  It causes BFTP to connect to
the FTP servers on both the source and the destination hosts
(if possible), log into both, verify the FTP parameters, and
verify that the specified source file is present.

Once the 'verify' command has successfully completed, the
user can issue the 'submit' command to schedule the actual
file transfer.


o      Foreground Operation

The BFTP 'transfer' command will perform the specified
third-party transfer in foreground mode.  This is illustrated
by the dotted path bypassing the queue in Figure 1.


The easiest way to set up the parameters is to issue the 'prompt'
command, which will prompt the user for all of the basic
parameters required for most transfers.  Certain unusual
parameters must be set with the 'set' command (see Appendix B for
details).

When entering any parameter, the following control characters may
be used:

?      will display help text for the parameter, indicating its
       meaning, the choices, and the default, and then reprompt for
       the parameter.

<ESC> will display the default value (or the last value set) for
       this parameter.  The user can accept this default by entering
       <Return>, or else erase it with Control-W and enter a
       different value for the parameter, followed by <Return> to
       accept the entered value.

<Control-W>
       will erase the value typed or displayed for current
       parameter.

<Return>
       will accept the value displayed for this parameter, and
       continue to the next parameter, if any.  If the user has not
       typed a value or used <ESC> to display the default, <Return>
       will display the default and then accept it.

It is important to provide a means for a user to obtain status
information about an earlier request or even to cancel an earlier
request.  However, these functions, especially cancellation, must
be controlled by some user authentication.  We did not want to
build a user authentication database with each BFTP instance or
require login to BFTP itself, and there is no Internet-wide user
authentication mechanism.  We adopted the following weak
authentication mechanism as a compromise:

*    When the 'submit' command is issued, it prompts the user for
     a character string called a "keyword", which recorded with
     the request.

*    This keyword can be entered later as the argument to a 'find'
     command, which will display the status of all requests with
     matching keywords.

*    Similarly, the keyword may be used to cancel the
     corresponding request.

If two different users happen to choose the same keywords, of
course, this scheme will not protect each other's requests from
accidental or malicious cancellation.  However, a notification
message will be sent at the time that a cancellation occurs.

To make a series of similar requests, the user needs only to
change the individual parameters that differ from the preceding
request and then issue a new 'submit' command, for each request.
There are commands for individually setting each of the parameters
that 'prompt' sets -- and 'time' -- to provide a shortcut for BFTP
experts.  A simpler but lengthier procedure is to use the 'prompt'
command to run through the current set of parameters, reentering
the parameters that must change and using the sequence
<ESC><return> to retain the previous value for each of the others.
The same procedures may be used to correct a mistake made in
entering a particular parameter.

The current settings of all the BFTP parameters can be displayed
at any time with the 'status' command, while the 'clear' command
will return all parameters to their initial values.  Finally, the
'request' command allows the user to save the current set of
parameters in a file or to restore the parameters from a
previously-saved file.

There is also a window-based BFTP user interface for use on a Sun
Workstation, described in Appendix A.  The complete list of BFTP
commands is presented in Appendix B.

3. Experience and Conclusions

BFTP has been available to users at ISI for some months.  Users have
reported a number of advantages of using BFTP:

(a)   Some users prefer the prompting style of BFTP to the user
      interface of the foreground FTP they normally use.

(b)   The BFTP "verify" command allows the user to verify that host
      names, passwords, and filenames are correct without having to
      wait for the entire transfer to take place.

(c)   Since results are returned through the mail system, a transfer
      can occur without tying up a terminal line, a phone line, or
      even a window.

BFTP must be able to communicate with a variety of Server-FTP
implementations, and we have observed much variation in the commands
supported, error handling, and the timing in these servers.  Some of
the problems we have encountered are:

(1)   Some systems (e.g., 4.2BSD) do not support the PASV command.

(2)   4.2/3BSD systems return a non-standard response to the NLST
      command.  Instead of returning a list of complete path-names,
      they use an ad hoc format consisting of a directory name
      followed by a list of files.

(3)   4.2/3BSD systems may return a "permanent negative completion
      reply" (a 5xx FTP reply code) as a result of a communications
      failure such as a broken TCP connection.  According to RFC-959,
      the appropriate response is a "transient negative completion
      reply" (a 4xx FTP reply code), which would inform the BFTP that
      the transfer should be retried.

(4)   A number of servers return badly formatted responses.  An
      example of this is the 4.2/3BSD response to an NLST command for
      a non-existent file name: an error string which is not preceded
      by a numerical response code.

To diagnose problems that do occur, we have found it very useful to
have a complete record of the interchange between the FTC daemon and
the two FTP servers.  This record is saved and is currently always
included in the notification message mailed to the user (see Appendix
D for an example).  As we get more experience with this program, some
of the details of the transfer may be omitted from this log.

The use of library routines shared between modules makes it relatively easy to implement additional user interface programs. We are currently experimenting with a window version of BFTP, the "bftptool", which runs in the SunView environment, and is described in Appendix A. Some additional interfaces that might be useful are:

o    A command line interface for use in shell scripts and "Makefiles".

o    A more general library interface which would make it easy to invoke BFTP from a variety of programs.

o    Additional full-screen form based interfaces, for example a tool running in X-Window system environment.

Lastly, BFTP would benefit from the resolution of the following open protocol issues:

o    There currently exist no provisions for Internet-wide user authentication. In the BFTP context, this means that passwords required for a file transfer must be present in BFTP request files. The security of these passwords is subject to the limitations of the file system security on the BFTP control host. Anonymous file transfer provides a partial solution, but a more general, long term solution is needed.

o    Better mechanisms are needed to cope with the diversity of real file systems in the Internet.

     For example, an extension could be made to the FTP protocol to allow the daemon to learn the delimiter conventions of each host file system. This could allow a more flexible and powerful multiple-file facility in BFTP. This could include the automatic transfer of directory subtrees, for example.

4. References

    [RFC-959] Postel, J., and J. Reynolds, "File Transfer Protocol (FTP)", RFC-959, USC/Information Sciences Institute, October 1985.

Appendix A -- BFTP Implementation Structure

BFTP has been implemented on both a Sun workstation running Sun OS
3.4 (based on 4.2BSD) and a VAX running 4.3BSD.  The program modules
are: the local user interface programs "bftp", the Internet server
program "bftpd", and the FTC daemon "fts".  BFTP makes use of the
"at" command, a UNIX batch job facility, to submit requests and
execute the daemon.  An additional user interface program, the
"bftptool", is available for Sun OS 3.4, and runs in the SunView
environment.

BFTP keeps its state in a set of control files: request files,
command files, and message files.  These files are stored in the home
directory specified for the environment of the process running
"bftp".  If a user is running "bftp" directly, this will typically be
the user's home directory.  In the case where a user has made a
Telnet connection to the well-known port 152 on a BFTP service host,
"bftp" is started by "bftpd" (or "inetd", indirectly).  As a result,
the control files will be owned by the user-id under which "inetd"
was started, normally "root", and stored in the top level directory
"/".  Note, however, that under BFTP all user files are written by
the FTP servers, which are presumed to enforce the operating systems'
access control conventions.  Hence, BFTP does not constitute a system
integrity exposure.

A.1  User Interface Program

   The BFTP user interface program "bftp" may be run directly via a
   UNIX shell.  Once the program has been started, the prompt "BFTP>"
   will appear and commands may be entered.  These commands are
   described in detail in Appendix B.

A.2  Tool-Style User Interface Program

   The BFTP user interface program "bftptool" may be started from a
   shell window in the SunView environment on a Sun workstation.  The
   BFTP commands may be selected via the left mouse button.  The
   various file transfer parameters appear in a form-style interface;
   defaults and multiple-choice style parameter values can be filled
   in via menus.  An advantage of this form-style interface program
   is that it is possible to view all of the file transfer parameters
   simultaneously, providing the user with a sense for which
   parameter values might be mutually exclusive.

   Help information can be displayed in a text subwindow by
   positioning the on-screen mouse pointer over a command or a
   parameter, and clicking the center mouse button.  (No standard
   mechanism for displaying help information is currently included in

the SunView package.)

The commands used in the "bftptool" are for the most part very
similar to the commands described in Appendix B.  Request
submittal and the execution of the FTC daemon are identical for
the "bftp" and the "bftptool" interface programs.

A.3  Internet Server

The Internet server program "bftpd" can be invoked by opening a
Telnet connection to a well-known port, and does not require
login.  The "bftpd" program runs under "inetd", the standard
BSD4.x well-known port dispatcher.  When a SYN arrives for the
BFTP well-known port, "bftpd" opens the TCP connection and
performs Telnet negotiations.  It then passes control to the user
interface "bftp" which allows the user to enter file transfer
requests.

A.4  BFTP Server Daemon

The BFTP file transfer control daemon program is named "fts" (for
"File Transfer Service").  This module contains code to actually
cause a single file transfer operation using the FTP server-server
model as shown in Figures 1 and 2.  It is invoked with the command
"fts <request-file>".  The <request-file> contains the necessary
parameters for the file transfer, in ASCII format, separated by
linefeeds.  Such a request file may be created by the user
interface program, "bftp".

As a byproduct of the development of BFTP, "fts" represents a
server-server FTP driver that can be run independent of the "bftp"
program.  Parameters used in the file transfer are read from a
request file, which is created and accessed via library routines
which can be shared between modules.  This could be used to
perform FTP's under program control.

Appendix B: BFTP Command Summary

   B.1 Special Editing Characters

      In the "bftp" program, the special editing characters for command
      words, subcommands, and parameter fields are as follows:

         <return>     Accept current command/field.
         <escape>     Complete current command/field, or display default.
         <space>      Complete and delimit current command.
         <delete>     Erase last character.
         control-L    Refresh screen.
         control-R    Refresh line.
         control-U    Erase line.
         control-W    Erase current token.
         ?            List legal options.

   B.2 BFTP Commands

      The remainder of Appendix B consists of a list of the BFTP
      commands.  Each command should be followed by a carriage-return.
      In the description of the syntax for each command, square brackets
      "[]" are used to indicate a ssubcommand, or a list of possible
      subcommands, which are separated by the "|" character.  Angle
      brackets "<>" are used to indicate a description of a parameter
      where the choices would be too numerous to list, for example
      "<host name/number>".

   B.2.1 Clear Command


      Return all parameters to their default values.

            clear

   B.2.2 Destination Commands

      Set the destination directory.

            ddir <directory name>

      Set the destination file name.

            dfile <file name>

      Set the destination host, user, and password.

            dhost <host name/number> <login> <password>

B.2.3 Explain Command

Display a short explanation of how to use BFTP.

        explain

B.2.4 Find Command

Find and display a previous request.

        find

BFTP will prompt for the request id, which is printed when the
request is first submitted.  An example of a request id is
"bftp583101774".  BFTP also prompts for the request keyword, which
was determined by the user when the request was first submitted.
If no keyword was specified, a <CR> should be typed.  If no
request id is entered, BFTP will display all requests which
contain a matching keyword.

        RequestID (optional): <bftp-request-id>
        RequestKeyword: <keyword>

After BFTP has displayed a summary of a matching request, it asks
whether the request is to be changed, or canceled.

        Do you wish to change this request? [yes | no]
        Do you wish to cancel this request? [yes | no]

If the user indicates that the request is to be changed, BFTP will
read in the parameters and cancel the existing request.  At this
point the user may make any desired changes and use the "submit"
command to requeue the request.  At this point a new request id
will be assigned and displayed.

Although this may happen extremely rarely, if at all, it is
possible that a system crash (or the interruption of the BFTP
program) at a particularly inopportune moment may leave a request
which is not queued.  When the "find" command locates such a
request, it displays the warning:

        Your request is NOT currently queued.

If this happens, the request may be read in and resubmitted using
the following procedure:

        Your request is NOT currently queued.
        Do you wish to change this request? yes

          (BFTP displays the parameters that have been read in.)

        Previous request canceled.
        Use the 'submit' command to submit a new request.

B.2.5 Help Command

    Print local help information.

        help
        help <command>

B.2.6 Quit Command

    Clear parameters and exit the BFTP program.

        quit

B.2.7 Prompt Command

    Prompt for commonly-used parameters.

        prompt

The following are the parameters that BFTP prompts for:

```
copy/move/delete: [copy | move | delete]
ascii/ebcdic/image/local:
        [ascii|ebcdic] [nonprint|telnet|carriage-control]
or
        [image]
or
        [local] <byte size>
(see "set type" for additional information)

Source --
    Host: <host name/number>
    User: <login>
    Password: <password>
    Dir: <directory including a delimiter, e.g., "/" or ">">
         (either an absolute path, or relative to the login)
    File: <file name>

Destination --
    Host: <host name/number>
    User: <login>
    Password: <password>
    Dir: <directory>
    File: <file name>
```

Once the prompting has been completed, the current values of all
parameters will be displayed.  Parameters not mentioned in the
prompting will be initialized with default values, and may be
changed via the "set" commands.

B.2.8 Request Commands

The request commands enable the user to save a set of BFTP parameters in a "request-file" for future use. Subcommands are provided to to list all available request-files, or to read, write, or delete a request-file. All request-files are stored in the user's home directory. Therefore, this facility is not available when the user is accessing BFTP by telneting to port 152.

Delete request file "bftp-save.name".

        request delete <name>

List all bftp-save files.

        request list

Read a request file in as the current request.

        request load <name>

Save the current request in a file named "bftp-save.name".

        request store <name>

B.2.9 Set Commands

The "set" commands have complex subcommand structures and are used to set many of the less commonly used FTP parameters. The subcommands of "set" are as follows:

Set the account for the source/destination login.

        set account [source | destination] <account string>

Set to true to append to destination file.

        set append [true | false]

The source file will be copied to the destination file name.

        set copy

The source file will be deleted after the file has been moved or copied.

        set delete

Set the mailbox to which the results will be returned.  The
mailbox should be in standard internet format, for example:
"deschon@isi.edu".

        set mailbox <mailbox string>

Set the FTP transfer mode.

        set mode [stream | block | compress]

The source file will be deleted after it has been copied.

        set move

Set to true to transfer multiple files.

        set multiple [true | false]

Set the port for the source/destination FTP connection.

        set port [source | destination] <port number>

Set the FTP structure.

        set structure [file | record | page]

Set the FTP type and format / byte size parameters.  Note that a
normal text file is usually "ascii", and a "binary" file is often
the same as an "image" file.

        set type [ascii|ebcdic] [nonprint|telnet|carriage-control]
or
        set type [image]
or
        set type [local] <byte size>

Set to true if the STOU command is to be used.  If the STOU
command is supported by the destination host, the file will be
stored into a file having a unique file name.

        set unique [true | false]

Set to true to display full FTP conversations for "verify" and
"transfer" commands.

        set verbose [true | false]

**21**

**RFC 1068**

B.2.10 Source Commands

    Set the source directory.

        sdir <directory name>

    Set the source file name.

        sfile <file name>

    Set the source host, user, and password.

        shost <host name/number> <login> <password>

B.2.11 Status Command

    Display the current parameter values.

        status

B.2.12 Submit Command

    Submit the current request for background FTP.

        submit

    BFTP prompts for the following information:

        StartTime: <date and/or time>
        ReturnMailbox: <internet mailbox>
        RequestKeyword: <made-up keyword>

B.2.13 Time Command

    Set the start time, the starting retry interval, and the maximum
    number of tries.

        time <date and/or time> <minutes between tries>
            <maximum number of tries>

B.2.14 Transfer Command

    Perform the current request in the foreground.

        transfer

B.2.15 Verify Command

Make the connections now to check parameters.

        verify

Appendix C: Example BFTP User Script

```
    deschon.isi.edu 1% telnet hobgoblin.isi.edu 152
    Trying 128.9.0.42 ...
    Connected to hobgoblin.isi.edu.
    Escape character is '^]'.

    BFTP Server (hobgoblin.isi.edu)

    Background File Transfer: For help, type '?', 'help', or 'explain'.

    BFTP> prompt

    Copy/Move/Delete: copy

    Source --
        Host: deschon.isi.edu
        User: deschon
        Password:
        Dir: ./
        File: foo*

    Destination --
        Host: venera.isi.edu
        User: deschon
        Password:
        Dir: ./temp/
        File: foo*

    StartTime: Tue Oct  6 10:14:43 1987 (interval) 60 (tries) 5
    ReturnMailbox: deschon@isi.edu
    RequestPassword:

    BFTP> set multiple true
    BFTP> status
        Request type: COPY

        Source --
            Host: 'deschon.isi.edu'
            User: 'deschon'
            Pass: SET
            Acct: ''
            Dir: './'
            File: 'foo*'
            Port: 21

        Destination --
            Host: 'venera.isi.edu'
```

```
             User: 'deschon'
             Pass: SET
             Acct: ''
             Dir: './temp/'
             File:'foo*'
             Port: 21

        Structure: file, Mode: stream, Type: ascii, Format: nonprint
        Multiple matching: TRUE
        Return mailbox: 'deschon@isi.edu', Password: SET
        Remaining tries: 5, Retry interval: 60 minutes

        Start after Tue Oct  6 10:14:43 1987.

    BFTP> submit
    Checking parameters...

    Request bftp560538880 submitted to run at 10:14 Oct 6.

    BFTP> quit
    bye
    Connection closed by foreign host.
    deschon.isi.edu 2%
```

Appendix D: Sample BFTP Notification Message

```
   Received-Date: Tue, 6 Oct 87 10:15:52 PDT
   Date: Tue, 6 Oct 87 10:15:47 PDT
   From: root (Operator)
   Posted-Date: Tue, 6 Oct 87 10:15:47 PDT
   To: deschon
   Subject: BFTP Results: bftp560538880

   Request bftp560538880 submitted to run at 10:14 Oct 6.

     Tue Oct  5 10:15:22 1987: starting...

       Request type: COPY
       Source: deschon.isi.edu-deschon-XXX--21-./-foo*
       Destination: venera.isi.edu-deschon-XXX--21-./temp/-
       Stru: F, Mode: S, Type: A N, Creation: STOR
       Multiple matching: TRUE
       Return mailbox: 'deschon@isi.edu', Password: SET
       Remaining tries: 5, Retry interval: 60 minutes

   Connect to: deschon.isi.edu, 21
   deschon.isi.edu ==> 220 deschon.isi.edu FTP server (Version 4.7
                          Sun Sep 14 12:44:57 PDT 1986) ready.
   Connect to: venera.isi.edu, 21
   venera.isi.edu ==> 220 venera.isi.edu FTP server (Version 4.107
                          Thu Mar 19 20:54:37 PST 1987) ready.
   deschon.isi.edu <== USER deschon
   deschon.isi.edu ==> 331 Password required for deschon.
   deschon.isi.edu <== PASS XXX
   deschon.isi.edu ==> 230 User deschon logged in.
   venera.isi.edu <== USER deschon
   venera.isi.edu ==> 331 Password required for deschon.
   venera.isi.edu <== PASS XXX
   venera.isi.edu ==> 230 User deschon logged in.
   deschon.isi.edu <== CWD ./
   deschon.isi.edu ==> 200 CWD command okay.
   venera.isi.edu <== CWD ./temp/
   venera.isi.edu ==> 250 CWD command successful.
   deschon.isi.edu <== PORT 128,9,1,56,4,106
   deschon.isi.edu ==> 200 PORT command okay.
   deschon.isi.edu <== NLST foo*
   deschon.isi.edu ==> 150 Opening data connection for /bin/ls
                          (128.9.1.56,1130) (0 bytes).
   deschon.isi.edu ==> 226 Transfer complete.
   deschon.isi.edu <== PASV
   deschon.isi.edu ==> 502 PASV command not implemented.
   venera.isi.edu <== PASV
```

```
venera.isi.edu ==> 227 Entering Passive Mode (128,9,0,32,6,200)
deschon.isi.edu <== PORT 128,9,0,32,6,200
deschon.isi.edu ==> 200 PORT command okay.
deschon.isi.edu <== RETR foo
venera.isi.edu <== STOR foo
deschon.isi.edu ==> 150 Opening data connection for foo
                        (128.9.0.32,1736) (0 bytes).
deschon.isi.edu ==> 226 Transfer complete.
venera.isi.edu ==> 150 Openning data connection for foo
                        (128.9.1.56,20).
venera.isi.edu ==> 226 Transfer complete.
venera.isi.edu <== PASV
venera.isi.edu ==> 227 Entering Passive Mode (128,9,0,32,6,201)
deschon.isi.edu <== PORT 128,9,0,32,6,201
deschon.isi.edu ==> 200 PORT command okay.
deschon.isi.edu <== RETR foo1
venera.isi.edu <== STOR foo1
deschon.isi.edu ==> 150 Opening data connection for foo1
                        (128.9.0.32,1737) (4 bytes).
deschon.isi.edu ==> 226 Transfer complete.
venera.isi.edu ==> 150 Openning data connection for foo1
                        (128.9.1.56,20).
venera.isi.edu ==> 226 Transfer complete.
deschon.isi.edu <== QUIT
venera.isi.edu <== QUIT

   Tue Oct  6 10:15:39 1987: completed successfully.
```

Network Working Group                                          K. Sollins
Request For Comments: 1350                                            MIT
STD: 33                                                         July 1992
Obsoletes: RFC 783

THE TFTP PROTOCOL (REVISION 2)

Status of this Memo

Summary

   TFTP is a very simple protocol used to transfer files.  It is from
   this that its name comes, Trivial File Transfer Protocol or TFTP.
   Each nonterminal packet is acknowledged separately.  This document
   describes the protocol and its types of packets.  The document also
   explains the reasons behind some of the design decisions.

Acknowlegements

   The protocol was originally designed by Noel Chiappa, and was
   redesigned by him, Bob Baldwin and Dave Clark, with comments from
   Steve Szymanski.  The current revision of the document includes
   modifications stemming from discussions with and suggestions from
   Larry Allen, Noel Chiappa, Dave Clark, Geoff Cooper, Mike Greenwald,
   Liza Martin, David Reed, Craig Milo Rogers (of USC-ISI), Kathy
   Yellick, and the author.  The acknowledgement and retransmission
   scheme was inspired by TCP, and the error mechanism was suggested by
   PARC's EFTP abort message.

   The May, 1992 revision to fix the "Sorcerer's Apprentice" protocol
   bug [4] and other minor document problems was done by Noel Chiappa.

   This research was supported by the Advanced Research Projects Agency
   of the Department of Defense and was monitored by the Office of Naval
   Research under contract number N00014-75-C-0661.

1. Purpose

   TFTP is a simple protocol to transfer files, and therefore was named
   the Trivial File Transfer Protocol or TFTP.  It has been implemented
   on top of the Internet User Datagram protocol (UDP or Datagram) [2]

so it may be used to move files between machines on different
networks implementing UDP.  (This should not exclude the possibility
of implementing TFTP on top of other datagram protocols.)  It is
designed to be small and easy to implement.  Therefore, it lacks most
of the features of a regular FTP.  The only thing it can do is read
and write files (or mail) from/to a remote server.  It cannot list
directories, and currently has no provisions for user authentication.
In common with other Internet protocols, it passes 8 bit bytes of
data.

Three modes of transfer are currently supported: netascii (This is
ascii as defined in "USA Standard Code for Information Interchange"
[1] with the modifications specified in "Telnet Protocol
Specification" [3].)  Note that it is 8 bit ascii.  The term
"netascii" will be used throughout this document to mean this
particular version of ascii.); octet (This replaces the "binary" mode
of previous versions of this document.) raw 8 bit bytes; mail,
netascii characters sent to a user rather than a file.  (The mail
mode is obsolete and should not be implemented or used.)  Additional
modes can be defined by pairs of cooperating hosts.

Reference [4] (section 4.2) should be consulted for further valuable
directives and suggestions on TFTP.

2. Overview of the Protocol

Any transfer begins with a request to read or write a file, which
also serves to request a connection.  If the server grants the
request, the connection is opened and the file is sent in fixed
length blocks of 512 bytes.  Each data packet contains one block of
data, and must be acknowledged by an acknowledgment packet before the
next packet can be sent.  A data packet of less than 512 bytes
signals termination of a transfer.  If a packet gets lost in the
network, the intended recipient will timeout and may retransmit his
last packet (which may be data or an acknowledgment), thus causing
the sender of the lost packet to retransmit that lost packet.  The
sender has to keep just one packet on hand for retransmission, since
the lock step acknowledgment guarantees that all older packets have
been received.  Notice that both machines involved in a transfer are
considered senders and receivers.  One sends data and receives
acknowledgments, the other sends acknowledgments and receives data.

Most errors cause termination of the connection.  An error is
signalled by sending an error packet.  This packet is not
acknowledged, and not retransmitted (i.e., a TFTP server or user may
terminate after sending an error message), so the other end of the
connection may not get it.  Therefore timeouts are used to detect
such a termination when the error packet has been lost.  Errors are

caused by three types of events: not being able to satisfy the
request (e.g., file not found, access violation, or no such user),
receiving a packet which cannot be explained by a delay or
duplication in the network (e.g., an incorrectly formed packet), and
losing access to a necessary resource (e.g., disk full or access
denied during a transfer).

TFTP recognizes only one error condition that does not cause
termination, the source port of a received packet being incorrect.
In this case, an error packet is sent to the originating host.

This protocol is very restrictive, in order to simplify
implementation.  For example, the fixed length blocks make allocation
straight forward, and the lock step acknowledgement provides flow
control and eliminates the need to reorder incoming data packets.

3. Relation to other Protocols

As mentioned TFTP is designed to be implemented on top of the
Datagram protocol (UDP).  Since Datagram is implemented on the
Internet protocol, packets will have an Internet header, a Datagram
header, and a TFTP header.  Additionally, the packets may have a
header (LNI, ARPA header, etc.)  to allow them through the local
transport medium.  As shown in Figure 3-1, the order of the contents
of a packet will be: local medium header, if used, Internet header,
Datagram header, TFTP header, followed by the remainder of the TFTP
packet.  (This may or may not be data depending on the type of packet
as specified in the TFTP header.)  TFTP does not specify any of the
values in the Internet header.  On the other hand, the source and
destination port fields of the Datagram header (its format is given
in the appendix) are used by TFTP and the length field reflects the
size of the TFTP packet.  The transfer identifiers (TID's) used by
TFTP are passed to the Datagram layer to be used as ports; therefore
they must be between 0 and 65,535.  The initialization of TID's is
discussed in the section on initial connection protocol.

The  TFTP header consists of a 2 byte opcode field which indicates
the packet's type (e.g., DATA, ERROR, etc.)  These opcodes and  the
formats of  the various types of packets are discussed further in the
section on TFTP packets.

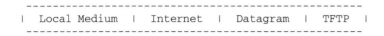

```
-----------------------------------------------------
|  Local Medium  |  Internet  |  Datagram  |  TFTP  |
-----------------------------------------------------
```

Figure 3-1: Order of Headers

4. Initial Connection Protocol

   A transfer is established by sending a request (WRQ to write onto a
   foreign file system, or RRQ to read from it), and receiving a
   positive reply, an acknowledgment packet for write, or the first data
   packet for read.  In general an acknowledgment packet will contain
   the block number of the data packet being acknowledged.  Each data
   packet has associated with it a block number; block numbers are
   consecutive and begin with one.  Since the positive response to a
   write request is an acknowledgment packet, in this special case the
   block number will be zero.  (Normally, since an acknowledgment packet
   is acknowledging a data packet, the acknowledgment packet will
   contain the block number of the data packet being acknowledged.)  If
   the reply is an error packet, then the request has been denied.

   In order to create a connection, each end of the connection chooses a
   TID for itself, to be used for the duration of that connection.  The
   TID's chosen for a connection should be randomly chosen, so that the
   probability that the same number is chosen twice in immediate
   succession is very low.  Every packet has associated with it the two
   TID's of the ends of the connection, the source TID and the
   destination TID.  These TID's are handed to the supporting UDP (or
   other datagram protocol) as the source and destination ports.  A
   requesting host chooses its source TID as described above, and sends
   its initial request to the known TID 69 decimal (105 octal) on the
   serving host.  The response to the request, under normal operation,
   uses a TID chosen by the server as its source TID and the TID chosen
   for the previous message by the requestor as its destination TID.
   The two chosen TID's are then used for the remainder of the transfer.

   As an example, the following shows the steps used to establish a
   connection to write a file.  Note that WRQ, ACK, and DATA are the
   names of the write request, acknowledgment, and data types of packets
   respectively.  The appendix contains a similar example for reading a
   file.

1. Host A sends a "WRQ" to host B with source= A's TID, destination= 69.

2. Host B sends a "ACK" (with block number= 0) to host A with source= B's TID, destination= A's TID.

At this point the connection has been established and the first data packet can be sent by Host A with a sequence number of 1.  In the next step, and in all succeeding steps, the hosts should make sure that the source TID matches the value that was agreed on in steps 1 and 2.  If a source TID does not match, the packet should be discarded as erroneously sent from somewhere else.  An error packet should be sent to the source of the incorrect packet, while not disturbing the transfer.  This can be done only if the TFTP in fact receives a packet with an incorrect TID.  If the supporting protocols do not allow it, this particular error condition will not arise.

The following example demonstrates a correct operation of the protocol in which the above situation can occur.  Host A sends a request to host B. Somewhere in the network, the request packet is duplicated, and as a result two acknowledgments are returned to host A, with different TID's chosen on host B in response to the two requests.  When the first response arrives, host A continues the connection.  When the second response to the request arrives, it should be rejected, but there is no reason to terminate the first connection.  Therefore, if different TID's are chosen for the two connections on host B and host A checks the source TID's of the messages it receives, the first connection can be maintained while the second is rejected by returning an error packet.

5. TFTP Packets

TFTP supports five types of packets, all of which have been mentioned above:

```
opcode   operation
  1      Read request (RRQ)
  2      Write request (WRQ)
  3      Data (DATA)
  4      Acknowledgment (ACK)
  5      Error (ERROR)
```

The TFTP header of a packet contains the  opcode  associated  with that packet.

```
           2 bytes      string    1 byte     string   1 byte
           -------------------------------------------------
          | Opcode |  Filename  |   0  |    Mode    |  0  |
           -------------------------------------------------
```

Figure 5-1: RRQ/WRQ packet

RRQ and WRQ packets (opcodes 1 and 2 respectively) have the format
shown in Figure 5-1.  The file name is a sequence of bytes in
netascii terminated by a zero byte.  The mode field contains the
string "netascii", "octet", or "mail" (or any combination of upper
and lower case, such as "NETASCII", NetAscii", etc.) in netascii
indicating the three modes defined in the protocol.  A host which
receives netascii mode data must translate the data to its own
format.  Octet mode is used to transfer a file that is in the 8-bit
format of the machine from which the file is being transferred.  It
is assumed that each type of machine has a single 8-bit format that
is more common, and that that format is chosen.  For example, on a
DEC-20, a 36 bit machine, this is four 8-bit bytes to a word with
four bits of breakage.  If a host receives a octet file and then
returns it, the returned file must be identical to the original.
Mail mode uses the name of a mail recipient in place of a file and
must begin with a WRQ.  Otherwise it is identical to netascii mode.
The mail recipient string should be of the form "username" or
"username@hostname".  If the second form is used, it allows the
option of mail forwarding by a relay computer.

The discussion above assumes that both the sender and recipient are
operating in the same mode, but there is no reason that this has to
be the case.  For example, one might build a storage server.  There
is no reason that such a machine needs to translate netascii into its
own form of text.  Rather, the sender might send files in netascii,
but the storage server might simply store them without translation in
8-bit format.  Another such situation is a problem that currently
exists on DEC-20 systems.  Neither netascii nor octet accesses all
the bits in a word.  One might create a special mode for such a
machine which read all the bits in a word, but in which the receiver
stored the information in 8-bit format.  When such a file is
retrieved from the storage site, it must be restored to its original
form to be useful, so the reverse mode must also be implemented.  The
user site will have to remember some information to achieve this.  In
both of these examples, the request packets would specify octet mode
to the foreign host, but the local host would be in some other mode.
No such machine or application specific modes have been specified in
TFTP, but one would be compatible with this specification.

It is also possible to define other modes for cooperating pairs of

hosts, although this must be done with care.   There is no requirement
that any other hosts implement these.   There is no central authority
that will define these modes or assign them names.

```
         2 bytes      2 bytes       n bytes
       ----------------------------------
       | Opcode  |  Block #  |   Data     |
       ----------------------------------
```

Figure 5-2: DATA packet


Data is actually transferred in DATA packets depicted in Figure 5-2.
DATA packets (opcode = 3) have a block number and data field.   The
block numbers on data packets begin with one and increase by one for
each new block of data.   This restriction allows the program to use a
single number to discriminate between new packets and duplicates.
The data field is from zero to 512 bytes long.   If it is 512 bytes
long, the block is not the last block of data; if it is from zero to
511 bytes long, it signals the end of the transfer.   (See the section
on Normal Termination for details.)

All  packets other than duplicate ACK's and those used for
termination are acknowledged unless a timeout occurs [4].   Sending a
DATA packet is an acknowledgment for the first ACK packet of the
previous DATA packet. The WRQ and DATA packets are acknowledged by
ACK or ERROR packets, while RRQ

```
         2 bytes      2 bytes
       --------------------
       | Opcode  |  Block #  |
       --------------------
```

Figure 5-3: ACK packet


and ACK packets are acknowledged by  DATA  or ERROR packets.  Figure
5-3 depicts an ACK packet; the opcode is 4.   The  block  number   in
an  ACK echoes the block number of the DATA packet being
acknowledged.   A WRQ is acknowledged with an ACK packet having a
block number of zero.

```
     2 bytes      2 bytes       string      1 byte
    ------------------------------------------------
   | Opcode |   ErrorCode |   ErrMsg    |   0  |
    ------------------------------------------------
```

Figure 5-4: ERROR packet

An ERROR packet (opcode 5) takes the form depicted in Figure 5-4.  An
ERROR packet can be the acknowledgment of any other type of packet.
The error code is an integer indicating the nature of the error.  A
table of values and meanings is given in the appendix.  (Note that
several error codes have been added to this version of this
document.) The error message is intended for human consumption, and
should be in netascii.  Like all other strings, it is terminated with
a zero byte.

6. Normal Termination

   The end of a transfer is marked by a DATA packet that contains
   between 0 and 511 bytes of data (i.e., Datagram length < 516).  This
   packet is acknowledged by an ACK packet like all other DATA packets.
   The host acknowledging the final DATA packet may terminate its side
   of the connection on sending the final ACK.  On the other hand,
   dallying is encouraged.  This means that the host sending the final
   ACK will wait for a while before terminating in order to retransmit
   the final ACK if it has been lost.  The acknowledger will know that
   the ACK has been lost if it receives the final DATA packet again.
   The host sending the last DATA must retransmit it until the packet is
   acknowledged or the sending host times out.  If the response is an
   ACK, the transmission was completed successfully.  If the sender of
   the data times out and is not prepared to retransmit any more, the
   transfer may still have been completed successfully, after which the
   acknowledger or network may have experienced a problem.  It is also
   possible in this case that the transfer was unsuccessful.  In any
   case, the connection has been closed.

7. Premature Termination

   If a request can not be granted, or some error occurs during the
   transfer, then an ERROR packet (opcode 5) is sent.  This is only a
   courtesy since it will not be retransmitted or acknowledged, so it
   may never be received.  Timeouts must also be used to detect errors.

I. Appendix

Order of Headers

```
                                                2 bytes
      ----------------------------------------------------------
      |  Local Medium  |  Internet  |  Datagram  |  TFTP Opcode  |
      ----------------------------------------------------------
```

TFTP Formats

```
   Type    Op #      Format without header

           2 bytes      string    1 byte      string    1 byte
           ------------------------------------------------
   RRQ/    | 01/02 |  Filename  |  0  |    Mode    |  0  |
   WRQ     ------------------------------------------------
           2 bytes     2 bytes          n bytes
           ----------------------------------------
   DATA    | 03     |  Block #  |    Data     |
           ----------------------------------------
           2 bytes     2 bytes
           ------------------
   ACK     | 04     |  Block #  |
           ------------------
           2 bytes   2 bytes         string    1 byte
           ----------------------------------------
   ERROR  | 05     |  ErrorCode  |  ErrMsg  |  0  |
           ----------------------------------------
```

Initial Connection Protocol for reading a file

   1. Host  A  sends  a  "RRQ"  to  host  B  with  source= A's TID,
      destination= 69.

   2. Host B sends a "DATA" (with block number= 1) to host  A  with
      source= B's TID, destination= A's TID.

Error Codes

    Value     Meaning

    0         Not defined, see error message (if any).
    1         File not found.
    2         Access violation.
    3         Disk full or allocation exceeded.
    4         Illegal TFTP operation.
    5         Unknown transfer ID.
    6         File already exists.
    7         No such user.

Internet User Datagram Header [2]

    (This has been included only for convenience.  TFTP need not be
    implemented on top of the Internet User Datagram Protocol.)

        Format

    0                   1                   2                   3
     0 1 2 3 4 5 6 7 8 9 0 1 2 3 4 5 6 7 8 9 0 1 2 3 4 5 6 7 8 9 0 1
    +-+-+-+-+-+-+-+-+-+-+-+-+-+-+-+-+-+-+-+-+-+-+-+-+-+-+-+-+-+-+-+-+
    |          Source Port          |       Destination Port        |
    +-+-+-+-+-+-+-+-+-+-+-+-+-+-+-+-+-+-+-+-+-+-+-+-+-+-+-+-+-+-+-+-+
    |            Length             |           Checksum            |
    +-+-+-+-+-+-+-+-+-+-+-+-+-+-+-+-+-+-+-+-+-+-+-+-+-+-+-+-+-+-+-+-+


    Values of Fields


    Source Port    Picked by originator of packet.

    Dest. Port     Picked by destination machine (69 for RRQ or WRQ).

    Length         Number of bytes in UDP packet, including UDP header.

    Checksum       Reference 2 describes rules for computing checksum.
                   (The implementor of this should be sure that the
                   correct algorithm is used here.)
                   Field contains zero if unused.

    Note: TFTP passes transfer identifiers (TID's) to the Internet User
    Datagram protocol to be used as the source and destination ports.

References

[1]  USA Standard Code for Information Interchange, USASI X3.4-1968.

[2]  Postel, J., "User Datagram  Protocol," RFC 768, USC/Information
     Sciences Institute, 28 August 1980.

[3]  Postel, J., "Telnet Protocol Specification," RFC 764,
     USC/Information Sciences Institute, June, 1980.

[4]  Braden, R., Editor, "Requirements for Internet Hosts --
     Application and Support", RFC 1123, USC/Information Sciences
     Institute, October 1989.

Security Considerations

   Since TFTP includes no login or access control mechanisms, care must
   be taken in the rights granted to a TFTP server process so as not to
   violate the security of the server hosts file system.  TFTP is often
   installed with controls such that only files that have public read
   access are available via TFTP and writing files via TFTP is
   disallowed.

Author's Address

   Karen R. Sollins
   Massachusetts Institute of Technology
   Laboratory for Computer Science
   545 Technology Square
   Cambridge, MA 02139-1986

   Phone: (617) 253-6006

   EMail: SOLLINS@LCS.MIT.EDU

Network Working Group                                          J. Mindel
Request for Comments: 1415                                     R. Slaski
                                                      Open Networks, Inc.
                                                           January 1993

FTP-FTAM Gateway Specification

Status of the Memo

Abstract

   This memo describes a dual protocol stack application layer gateway
   that performs protocol translation, in an interactive environment,
   between the FTP and FTAM file transfer protocols.

   Two key assumptions are made:  1) POSIX file naming conventions and
   hierarchical organization, rather than proprietary conventions are in
   use; and 2) X.500 Directory Services are available.

Acknowledgments

   The authors of this RFC would like to express their appreciation to
   the individuals and organizations that participated in the
   implementation of the FTP-FTAM Application Layer Gateway and its
   fielding on the MILNET.  Implementation credits go to Mr. John Scott,
   formerly of the MITRE Corporation, while fielding credits are
   extended to James Graham and R. Greg Lavender of Open Networks, Inc.
   (formerly NetWorks One) and Robert Cooney of the Naval Computer and
   Telecommunications Station (NCTS) Washington.  Dr. Marshall Rose is
   to be commended for recognizing the importance of the FTP-FTAM
   gateway and promulgating it as a part of the ISO Development
   Environment (ISODE).   The following individuals have provided
   valuable editorial comments:  Larry Friedman, Donna Vincent and
   Michael Resnick of Digital Equipment Corporation; Robert Cooney of
   NCTS; and S.E. Hardcastle-Kille of University College London. Funding
   of the FTP-FTAM Gateway Request for Comments effort was provided by
   Open Networks Inc. and the Defense Information Systems Agency (DISA),
   formerly the Defense Communications Agency.  DISA sponsors include
   Len Tabacchi, George Bradshaw, Tom Clarke, and Betsy Turner.

Table of Contents

1.  Introduction.....................................................2
1.1.    Relationship to Other Work ................................3
1.2.    Overview of Gateway Operation .............................4
2.  Gateway Architecture............................................6
3.  Network Naming and Addressing...................................8
4.  Use of the Gateway Services.....................................9
4.1.    FTP-Initiated Gateway Service .............................9
4.2.    FTAM-Initiated Gateway Service ...........................11
4.3.    Summary of Usage .........................................12
5.  Gateway State Variables and Transitions........................13
5.1.    FTP-Initiated Gateway Service ............................14
5.2.    FTAM-Initiated Gateway Service ...........................16
6.  Document Type Support..........................................18
6.1.    Notes on NBS-9 ...........................................18
7.  Functional Comparison of FTP and FTAM..........................19
7.1.    Loss of Functionality ....................................20
8. Mapping of Protocol Functions and Representations..............20
8.1.    FTP-Initiated Gateway Service ............................22
8.2.    FTAM-Initiated Gateway Service ...........................38
9. Mapping between FTP Reply Codes and FTAM Parameters............47
9.1.    FTP Reply Codes to FTAM Parameters .......................48
9.2.    FTAM Parameters to FTP Reply Codes .......................50
9.3.    Future Mapping Problem ...................................54
9.4.    Error Handling ...........................................54
10. Implementation and Configuration Guidelines...................54
10.1.   Robustness ...............................................54
10.2.   Well-Known TCP/IP Port ...................................55
10.3.   Gateway Listener Processes ...............................55
10.4.   Implementation Testing ...................................55
10.5.   POSIX File Naming and Organization .......................55
11. Security Considerations........................................55
12. References....................................................56
13. Authors' Addresses............................................58

1. Introduction

   The TCP/IP and OSI protocol suites will coexist in the Internet
   community for several years to come.  As more and more OSI hosts are
   fielded on the Internet, the requirement for gateways between the two
   protocol suites becomes more pressing.

   This specification describes an application layer gateway providing
   interoperability between the TCP/IP File Transfer Protocol (FTP) and
   the OSI File Transfer, Access, and Management (FTAM) protocol.  The
   proposed application layer gateway is based on a bi-directional set
   of mappings between the FTP and FTAM protocols.  Since the protocols

have quite different command structures, the mappings between them
are not one-to-one.  This paper assumes knowledge of the File
Transfer Protocol (FTP) [RFC959] and the File Transfer, Access, and
Management Protocol (FTAM) [ISO8571-1,2,3,4,5].

Two important goals of the mappings are to:

   Provide FTP users with as much emulated FTP capability on an
   FTAM Responder as possible, and

   Provide FTAM users with as much emulated FTAM capability on an
   FTP Server as possible.

Though it is anticipated that the application layer gateway will be
implemented on full protocol suites of both TCP/IP and OSI, at least
one implementation of such a gateway (included in the ISO Development
Environment) can be configured to operate FTAM over either OSI or
TCP/IP lower-layer services.

1.1. Relationship to Other Work

   Ideas presented in this specification are based on lessons learned in
   fielding the gateway on the MILNET, operational at NCTS Washington
   D.C. since 1989, and on the efforts of M. A. Wallace et al. of the
   National Institute of Standards and Technology (NIST) [NIST86].  In
   1986, NIST published a design document for an FTP-FTAM gateway.
   Since that time, at least one implementation (for a subset of the FTP
   and FTAM protocols) of the gateway has been developed [MITRE87] and
   is included with the ISODE.  This implementation is based on the NIST
   protocol translator gateway design [NIST86].

   This document's contribution to the advancement of the FTP-FTAM
   gateway concept is to:

      * Enhance the user interaction capability provided by the ISODE
        implementation of the FTP-FTAM application layer gateway.

      * Clarify and enhance the mappings (FTP to FTAM, FTAM to FTP)
        documented by NIST.

      * Provide guidelines for fielding the FTP-FTAM application layer
        gateway on the Internet so that it is useful as an Internet
        resource.

      * Produce a formal specification for the FTP-FTAM gateway suitable
        for implementors to use in building additional FTP-FTAM
        gateways.

    * Provide a formal specification for organizations wishing to
      procure FTP-FTAM gateways.

1.2. Overview of Gateway Operation

    The gateway provides a virtual end-to-end application file transfer
    service.  As data is sent via FTP, the gateway immediately maps the
    requested function to FTAM and passes it to the FTAM host.  In a
    similar fashion, but using a different set of mappings, an FTAM
    request is sent to the gateway, immediately mapped to an FTP
    function, and passed along to the FTP host.

    In FTP, the two parties involved in a file transfer are the Client
    and Server.  The Client is responsible for initiating a connection to
    the Server.  Once the connection is established, all service requests
    originate from the Client.  The FTP-FTAM gateway does not support the
    FTP three node model.

    In FTAM, the two parties involved in a file transfer are the
    Initiator and Responder.  The Initiator is responsible for initiating
    a connection to the Responder.  Once the connection is established,
    either the Initiator or Responder may issue service requests to the
    other.

    The FTP-FTAM gateway provides two sets of services:

        1. FTP-Initiated Gateway Services

           Utilized when an FTP Client contacts the FTP-FTAM gateway to
           instigate a file transfer with an FTAM Responder.

        2. FTAM-Initiated Gateway Services

           Utilized when an FTAM Initiator contacts the FTP-FTAM
           gateway to instigate a file transfer with an FTP Server.

    The gateway services' names were selected to identify the roles that
    the FTP-FTAM gateway plays when performing file transfers.  For
    example, when a file transfer is instigated by an FTP Client, it
    contacts the FTP Server portion of the gateway, which maps protocol
    information to the FTAM Initiator portion of the gateway, which in
    turn contacts the remote FTAM Responder.  This example scenario uses
    the FTP-Initiated Gateway Services.

    Figure 1 illustrates the perspective of the application process in
    the FTP-Initiated service.  Figure 2 illustrates that of the FTAM-
    Initiated service.

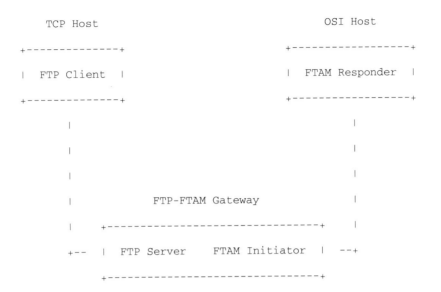

Figure 1  -  FTP-Initiated Gateway Service

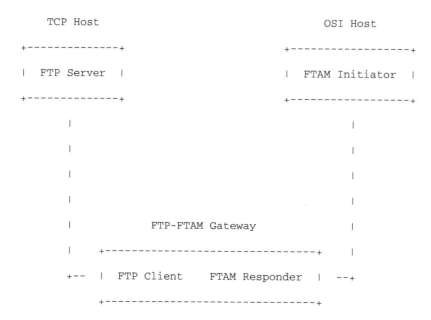

Figure 2  -  FTAM-Initiated Gateway Service

2. Gateway Architecture

The gateway architecture, termed a protocol translator [NIST86], is
depicted in Figure 3.  It implements TCP/IP and OSI protocol stacks
with an application level process providing the link between the two.
The link between FTP and FTAM is defined by two sets of protocol
mappings, one each for the FTP-Initiated and FTAM-Initiated service
sets.

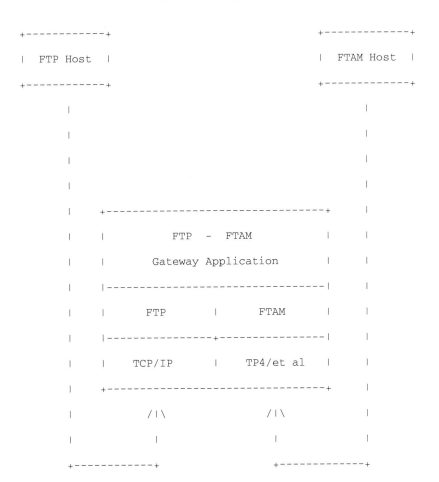

Figure 3  -  Gateway Protocol Stack

A fundamental aspect of this gateway architecture is that data is
mapped and transmitted immediately; i.e., no transferred file need
ever reside on the gateway file system.  In the context of this
document, the term "filesystem" refers to the file access and
maintenance mechanisms provided by the operating system.  This lack
of gateway filesystem interaction helps speed up the end-to-end data
transfer.  Another speed-enhancing feature of this architecture is
that both the FTP and FTAM network connections can operate

simultaneously.  Additional advantages include:

   1. FTP and FTAM hosts require no modification to utilize gateway
      services.

   2. Users require no knowledge of the other protocol.

   3. Gateway access control is not impaired (since users cannot
      directly access the gateway filesystem).

   4. No additional filesystem space is required on the gateway.

   5. Interactive nature of protocols is preserved.

   6. Users become aware of fatal errors immediately.

Disadvantages of this design include the initial coding effort
required to develop the gateway and the subsequent re-coding efforts
required to keep it current.

3. Network Naming and Addressing

   The network naming and addressing schemes used by FTP (Domain Names
   (DN), IP Addresses) and FTAM (Distinguished Names, Presentation
   Addresses) are quite different.  This issue is quite apparent when a
   user of one protocol needs to identify a destination host of the
   other protocol.

   In the TCP/IP naming and addressing scheme, the identity of the FTP
   Server is its DN and its IP address [RFC1101].  To initiate a
   connection to an FTP Server, the FTP Client looks up a DN in either
   the Domain Name System (DNS) or static host table and obtains an IP
   address.

   In the OSI naming and addressing scheme, the identity of the FTAM
   Responder service is its Distinguished Name in the OSI Directory
   (X.500 or static table) and its Presentation address.  The
   Distinguished Name is an authoritative description of the service.  A
   Presentation address consists of a Presentation selector, a session
   selector, a transport selector, and a network address.  To initiate a
   connection to an FTAM Responder, the FTAM Initiator contacts the OSI
   Directory, presents the Distinguished Name of the desired FTAM
   Responder and asks for the Presentation address attribute associated
   with that name.

   An alternative to the direct use of Distinguished Names is to use
   "User Friendly Naming", as defined in [Kille92].  Gateway support for
   "User Friendly Naming" is recommended, but not required.

4. Use of the Gateway Services

4.1. FTP-Initiated Gateway Service

   The FTP Client uses the FTP-Initiated gateway service to utilize the
   resources of an FTAM Responder.

   To initiate a file transfer from an FTP Client, the Client connects
   to the FTP-Initiated gateway service via TCP/IP.  The gateway then
   establishes a connection, via OSI, to the FTAM Responder.  At this
   point, the user can initiate file transfer operations.

   The FTP Client is responsible for providing the gateway with an
   authoritative Distinguished Name, or a User Friendly Name, of the
   desired OSI filestore.  It is the responsibility of the gateway to
   resolve this Distinguished Name, or User Friendly Name, to its
   corresponding Presentation address.

   The logon sequence taken by an FTP Client when initiating a file
   transfer with an FTAM Responder is given below:

                    % ftp gateway
                    ftp> site Distinguished-Name-of-FTAM Responder
                    ftp> user username
                    ftp> pass password

   The "ftp gateway" command initiates the connection between the FTP
   Client and the gateway.  Once connected to the gateway, the FTP
   Client should identify the desired FTAM Responder service via the
   Responder's Distinguished Name, or User Friendly Name, which is
   resolved by an algorithm running on the Directory Services provider.
   This information is sent via a "site Distinguished-Name-of-FTAM
   Responder" or "site UFN-of-FTAM Responder" command.

   Upon receipt of a Distinguished Name or a User Friendly Name, it is
   the gateway's responsibility to resolve it to the Presentation
   Address associated with that name.  This resolution is done by
   contacting the OSI Directory (X.500 or local static table) and
   presenting the Distinguished Name or User Friendly Name.  Once the
   Presentation address is obtained, the gateway can attempt a
   connection with the ultimate destination file transfer service
   represented by this Presentation address.

   The userid is passed via the "user username" command, and the
   password is passed via the "pass password".  If the FTAM Responder
   requires a password, a password prompt should appear after issuing
   the "user username" command.  It is anticipated that stronger
   authentication mechanisms will be required for DoD gateways in the

future.

Using a specific example, suppose an FTAM Responder has the following
Distinguished Name:

```
CountryName            =        "US"
Organization           =        "Open Networks"
OrganizationalUnit     =        "Network Services"
CommonName             =        "netwrx1"
CommonName             =        "FTAM service"
```

and the FTP-FTAM gateway is available at "washdc1-osigw.navy.mil".

The FTP user action will appear as:

```
% ftp washdc1-osigw.navy.mil
ftp> site "c=US@o=Open Networks@ou=Network Services@cn=netwrx1
     @cn=FTAM service"
ftp> user mindel
ftp> pass ***********
```

The "ftp washdc1-osigw.navy.mil" command initiates the connection
between the FTP Client and the FTP-FTAM gateway at the Washington
Navy Yard, Washington D.C.  Once connected, the OSI filestore at Open
Networks is identified via its Distinguished Name, "@c=US@o=Open
Networks@ou=Network Services@cn=netwrx1@cn=FTAM service".
Alternatively, a User Friendly Name, such as:

```
"netwrx1, Open Networks, us"
```

can be specified, enabling the following FTP user action:

```
% ftp washdc1-osigw.navy.mil
ftp> site "netwrx1, Open Networks, us"
ftp> user mindel
ftp> pass ***********
```

As this example indicates, use of an intermediate gateway is not
transparent.  To partially alleviate this awkwardness, the gateway
can be made more transparent through the registration of the FTAM
host in the DNS using the address of the gateway [RFC1279].

An example will clarify this point.  Suppose that the "netwrx1, Open
Networks, us" FTAM host is registered in the TCP/IP DNS with the DN
of "ftam-service.netwrx1.com" and the IP address of the "washdc1-
osigw.navy.mil" gateway.  In this example, the following set of user
actions is required:

```
                    % ftp ftam-service.netwrx1.com
                    ftp> user mindel
                    ftp> pass ***********
```

Since the "ftam-service.netwrx1.com" really points to the gateway
address, the first command will connect the FTP Client to the
gateway.  The gateway will then use the name (using [RFC1279]) to
determine where the actual FTAM host is resident.  Gateway support
for RFC1279 is recommended, but not required.

## 4.2. FTAM-Initiated Gateway Service

The FTAM Initiator uses the FTAM-Initiated gateway service to utilize
the resources of an FTP Server.

To initiate a file transfer from an FTAM Initiator, the Initiator
connects to the FTAM-Initiated gateway service via OSI.  The gateway
then establishes a connection, via TCP/IP, to the FTP Server.  At
this point, the user can initiate file transfer operations.

The FTAM Initiator is responsible for providing the gateway with an
authoritative DN of the desired TCP/IP filestore.  It is the
responsibility of the gateway to resolve this DN to its corresponding
IP address.

The logon sequence taken by an FTAM Initiator when initiating a file
transfer with an FTP Server is given below:

```
                    % ftam gateway
                    ftam> user username@DNS-string
                    ftam> pass password
```

The "ftam gateway" command initiates the connection between the FTAM
Initiator and the gateway.  Once connected, userid and TCP/IP
filestore are identified in the "username@DNS-string" argument to the
user command.  If the FTP Server requires a password, a password
prompt should appear after issuing the user command.

The gateway should incorporate the BIND Resolver functionality so
that upon receipt of a Domain Name, the Gateway FTP Client can
resolve it via the distributed Domain Name System.

Using a specific example, suppose that a FTP Server has the following
Domain Name:  "ftp-service.netwrx1.com" and an FTP-FTAM gateway is
available at:

```
                CountryName           =         "US"
                Organization          =         "GOV"
                OrganizationalUnit    =         "DOD"
                OrganizationalUnit    =         "DISA"
                Locality              =         "Washington Navy Yard"
                CommonName            =         "wnyosi7"
```

   The FTAM user action will appear as:

```
        % ftam @c=US@o=GOV@ou=DOD@ou=DISA@l=Washington Navy Yard
            @cn=wnyosi7
        ftam> user mindel@ftp-service.netwrx1.com
        ftam> pass ***********
```

   Alternatively, a User Friendly Name could be used rather than the
   Distinguished Name.

   As mentioned in the previous section, "Use of the FTP-Initiated
   Gateway Service", use of an intermediate gateway is not transparent.
   The gateway can be made more transparent through the registration of
   the FTP host in the X.500 OSI Directory.  By querying the X.500 OSI
   Directory, the gateway can identify where the actual host is
   resident.

   For example, suppose that the FTP Server in the previous example
   ("ftp-service.netwrx1.com") is registered in the X.500 Directory with
   the following Distinguished Name:

```
                CountryName           =         "US"
                Organization          =         "Open Networks"
                OrganizationalUnit    =         "Network Services"
                CommonName            =         "netwrx1"
                CommonName            =         "FTP service"
```

   and the Presentation Address of the FTP-FTAM gateway.  This approach,
   described in [RFC1279], would permit the following user interactions:

```
        % ftam @c=US@o=Open Networks@ou=Network Services
            @cn=netwrx1@cn=FTP Service"
        ftam> user mindel
        ftam> pass ***********
```

4.3. Summary of Usage

   As shown in the discussions of the FTP-Initiated and FTAM-Initiated
   Gateway Services, the gateway user does not have access to the
   gateway filesystem; he merely makes use of the gateway logon
   procedure to specify the ultimate destination userid and password.

Two methods of interaction with the gateway were described.  In the
former, the user must:

1. Be aware that a gateway is required to reach the
   destination FTP or FTAM host.

2. Determine which gateway is most appropriate for their
   respective source-destination pair.

3. Explicitly connect to the gateway host prior to connecting
   to the destination host.

Needless to say, the exchange of files between FTP and FTAM hosts
requires more effort than that required for the exchange of files
between a pair of hosts utilizing the same file transfer protocol.

The latter, more transparent method does not necessarily require that
the user determine which gateway is most appropriate for their
respective source-destination pair.  In fact, filestore service
providers are registered using the address of a predetermined
gateway.  With this approach, the user:

1. Must be aware that a gateway is required to reach the
   destination FTP or FTAM host.

2. Need not determine which gateway is most appropriate to
   access their ultimate destination host.

3. Need not explicitly connect to the gateway prior to
   connecting to the destination FTP or FTAM host.

5. Gateway State Variables and Transitions

As described, the FTP-FTAM gateway provides two sets of services:
FTP-Initiated and FTAM-Initiated.  Each service has its own mutually
exclusive set of state variables and transitions that
deterministically define the actions of the gateway.  Gateway support
for these state variables and transitions is required.

For conciseness in this discussion, FTP-Initiated will be abbreviated
with "FTP-I", and FTAM-Initiated will be abbreviated with "FTAM-I".

Concerning error conditions, if a connection is dropped when the
gateway is in any state other than FTP-I:Initial-State or FTAM-
I:Initial-State, then the gateway will issue a fatal error message to
the host with the remaining connection, and then drop that
connection.  If the remaining host is an FTP Client, then the gateway
will send an ABOR, QUIT, and 426 reply code (Connection closed,

transfer aborted).  If it is an FTAM Initiator, then the gateway will
send an F-P-ABORT with a <Diagnostic> value with identifier 1011
(Lower layer failure), as well as any known <Further Details>.

Other error conditions are not addressed in this discussion.

## 5.1. FTP-Initiated Gateway Service

The set of state variables for the FTP-Initiated Gateway service
follow:

| State Variable | State Definition |
| --- | --- |
| FTP-I:Initial-State | Initial state of FTP-Initiated Gateway service. |
| | Gateway is waiting for an FTP Client to issue a USER command in order to proceed with connection establishment with remote FTAM Responder.  If SITE or ACCT commands are sent while waiting for USER command, save arguments for subsequent use. |
| FTP-I:Wait-for-PASS | Gateway has already received USER command from FTP Client, as well as userid and destination host DN. Gateway is waiting for the FTAM Responder logon password. |
| FTP-I:Wait-for-PAddress | Gateway has already received PASS command from FTP Client.  Gateway is resolving the provided FTAM Responder's address to a Presentation Address.  The provided address may be a Distinguished Name, User Friendly Name, or Domain Name.  Resolution will typically be done using X.500 directory services. |
| FTP-I:Wait-for-Connection | Gateway has initiated a connection to the FTAM Responder and is waiting for notification as to whether or not the logon is successful. |
| FTP-I:Wait-for-ClientCmd | Connection exists between FTP Client and FTAM Responder.  Gateway is waiting for next command or response from FTP |

                                    Client.  Commands and responses are
                                    mapped as they are received.

    FTP-I:Wait-for-RespondrCmd      Connection exists between FTP Client
                                    and FTAM Responder.  Gateway is waiting
                                    for next command or response from FTAM
                                    Responder.  Commands and responses are
                                    mapped as they are received.

    Each of the possible state transitions is provided in the remainder
    of Section 5.1.  For each state transition, the actions causing the
    transition are listed.

5.1.1. FTP-I:Initial-State   -->    FTP-I:Initial-State

        1. Gateway receives SITE or ACCT command from FTP Client.
           SITE argument includes Distinguish Name of FTAM Responder.

5.1.2. FTP-I:Initial-State   -->    FTP-I:Wait-for-PASS

        1. Gateway receives USER command from FTP Client.  Arguments
           include Distinguished Name of FTAM Responder and userid on
           FTAM responder.

5.1.3. FTP-I:Wait-for-PASS   -->    FTP-I:Wait-for-PAddress

        1. Gateway receives PASS command from FTP Client.

5.1.4. FTP-I:Wait-for-PAddress   -->    FTP-I:Wait-for-Connection

        1. Gateway resolves received Distinguished Name, User Friendly
           Name, or Domain Name of FTAM Responder to OSI Presentation
           address.
        2. Gateway sends F-INITIALIZE to FTAM Responder with
           Presentation Address in <Called Presentation Address>,
           userid in <Initiator Identity>, and password in <Filestore
           Password>.

5.1.5. FTP-I:Wait-for-Connection   -->    FTP-I:Wait-for-NextMapping

        1. Gateway receives <State Result> of "Success" .
        2. Gateway sends 230 reply code (User Logged In) to FTP
           Client.

5.1.6. FTP-I:Wait-for-ClientCmd   -->    FTP-I:Wait-for-RespondrCmd

        1. Gateway receives command or response from FTP Client and
           maps it to FTAM protocol, as defined in section 8.1.

5.1.7. FTP-I:Wait-for-RespondrCmd   -->    FTP-I:Wait-for-ClientCmd

    1. Gateway receives command or response from FTAM Responder
      and maps it to FTP protocol, as defined in section 8.1.

5.1.8. FTP-I:Wait-for-ClientCmd   -->    FTP-I:Wait-for-USER

    1. Gateway receives QUIT command from FTP Client; maps QUIT as
      per Section 8.1.

5.2. FTAM-Initiated Gateway Service

    The set of state variables for the FTAM-Initiated Gateway service
    follow:

| State Variable | State Definition |
| --- | --- |
| FTAM-I:Initial-State | Initial state of FTAM-Initiated Gateway Service. |
| | Gateway is waiting for an FTAM Initiator to issue an F-INITIALIZE command in order to proceed with connection establishment with remote FTP Server. |
| FTAM-I:Wait-for-IPAddress | Gateway has already received F-INITIALIZE from FTAM Initiator. Gateway is resolving the provided FTP Server's address to an IP address.  The provided address may be a Domain Name, Distinguished Name, or User Friendly Name. |
| FTAM-I:Wait-for-Connection | Gateway has initiated a connection to the FTP Server and is waiting for notification as to whether or not the logon is successful. |
| FTAM-I:Wait-for-InitiatrCmd | Connection exists between FTAM Initiator and FTP Server.  Gateway is waiting for next command or response from FTAM Initiator.  Commands and responses are mapped as they are received. |

   FTP-I:Wait-for-ServerCmd          Connection exists between FTAM
                                     Initiator and FTP Server.  Gateway is
                                     waiting for next command or response
                                     from FTP Server.  Commands and
                                     responses are mapped as they are
                                     received.

   Each of the possible state transitions is provided in the remainder
   of Section 5.2.  For each state transition, the actions causing the
   transition are listed.

5.2.1. FTAM-I:Initial-State   -->   FTAM-I:Wait-for-IPAddress

       1. Gateway receives F-INITIALIZE from FTAM Initiator.  Domain
          Name of FTP Server is either in <Responding Presentation
          Address> or in the "@host" portion of the <Initiator
          Identity> parameter.  The userid is in <Initiator
          Identity>, and password is in <Filestore Password>
          parameter.

5.2.2. FTAM-I:Wait-for-IPAddress   -->   FTAM-I:Wait-for-Connection

       1. Gateway resolves received Domain Name, Distinguished Name,
          or User Friendly Name of FTP Server to IP address.
       2. Gateway sends USER to FTP Server.
       3. Gateway sends PASS to FTP Server.

5.2.3. FTAM-I:Wait-for-Connection   -->   FTAM-I:Wait-for-NextMapping

       1. Gateway receives 230 reply code (User Logged In) from FTP
          Server.
       2. Gateway sends <State Result> of "Success" to FTAM
          Initiator.

5.2.4  FTAM-I:Wait-for-InitiatrCmd   -->   FTAM-I:Wait-for-ServerCmd

       1. Gateway receives command or response from FTAM Initiator
          and maps it to FTP protocol, as defined in section 8.2.

5.2.5. FTAM-I:Wait-for-ServerCmd   -->   FTAM-I:Wait-for-InitiatrCmd

       1. Gateway receives command or response from FTP Server and
          maps it to FTAM protocol, as defined in section 8.2.

5.2.6. FTAM-I:Wait-for-InitiatrCmd   -->   FTAM-I:Wait-for-INITIALIZE

       1. Gateway receives F-CLOSE primitive from FTAM Initiator;
          maps F-CLOSE as per Section 8.2.

6. Document Type Support

The set of FTAM document types supported by the FTP-FTAM gateway is a
subset of the document types identified in the Stable Implementation
Agreements for Open Systems Interconnection Protocols:  Part 9 - FTAM
Phase 2, produced by the March 1992 Open Systems Environment
Implementors' Workshop [NIST92].  This subset was chosen for its
equivalence to those document types supported by FTP.  The set
includes:

              FTAM-1      "ISO FTAM Unstructured text file

              FTAM-3      "ISO FTAM Unstructured binary file

              NBS-9       "NBS-9 FTAM File directory file"

    FTAM document types map to FTP document types as follows:

              FTAM      <->        FTP
              ---------------------------------

              FTAM-1    <->        ASCII

              FTAM-3    <->        8 bit binary

              NBS-9     <->        Directory

Gateway support for FTAM-1 and FTAM-2 is required, whereas support
for NBS-9 is recommended.

6.1. Notes on NBS-9

NBS-9 is optional in GOSIP versions 1 and 2 [NIST91].  NBS-9 will be
superseded by its replacement when ISO/IEC ISP 10607-2 and ISO/IEC
ISP 10607-2/Amendment 1 are published [NIST92].

For conformance to NBS-9, an FTAM Responder is only required to
return the <Filename> file attribute, subject to local security and
access control.  All other requested attributes need not be returned.

Systems supporting the NBS-9 document type shall make available an
NBS-9 document called 'DIRLIS'.  This document can be used to obtain
a listing of files and their associated attributes from a remote
Filestore.

7. Functional Comparison of FTP and FTAM

A comprehensive comparison of the services offered by FTP and FTAM is beyond the scope of this specification. What follows is an analysis of several key points. Refer to [NIST 86a] and [ROSE90] for a more complete discourse on this topic.

FTAM is not a superset of FTP; each protocol has functions that only it performs. The set of FTAM functions is, however, larger than the set of FTP functions.

FTP combines file management and file transfer into one protocol engine, whereas FTAM separates management and transfer as they relate to files.

The file transfer services of both FTP and FTAM expect a reliable underlying end-to-end service. At a minimum, this service includes the capability to transfer entire files between remote hosts and to display remote filenames.

In addition to this basic file transfer service, FTAM supports the capability to: access a few records from a file server, create a network file system (similar to Sun's Network File System), handle printing and spooling, and access remote database records. FTP does not support these additional capabilities.

FTP uses TELNET services to set up a connection between the FTP Client and FTP Server. A three-digit reply code followed by explanatory text indicates the status of the preceding request and provides diagnostic information explaining each transaction.

FTAM relies on the Association Control Service Element (ACSE) to start and stop the network for network file interaction. Generally, the ASCE establishes the application association and related application context needed to support the FTAM protocol.

The FTAM protocol is modularized so as to keep the allowable number of actions in any particular state relatively small. There are many more possible sequences of FTP operations than possible sequences of FTAM operations [NIST86].

Because FTAM is more robust than FTP, FTAM allows greater flexibility for conveying information about files. FTAM deals only with aspects of application processes, and leaves data representation and data management facilities to other OSI service elements.

In contrast to the Client/Server model present in the FTP scheme, FTAM is based on the Initiator/Responder model. The key distinction

is that once the FTAM Initiator has established a connection with a
remote host, either the Initiator or Responder can request services
of the other.  In the FTP realm, the Client both initiates a
connection and requests all services.

The FTP Client knows the real properties of the remote host
filesystem.  FTAM, in contrast, embraces a conceptual model of a
filesystem, labeled a virtual filestore model.  The virtual filestore
is a collection of files, each of which has a name that uniquely
identifies it.  Each file has a set of attributes, such as ownership
information and contents, which is the data associated with the file.
One file attribute is the <Contents Type> of the file, typically of
value "FTAM-1", "FTAM-3", or "NBS-9".  The FTAM Initiator only knows
the properties of the corresponding Responder and virtual filestore,
not the real properties of the filesystem on the remote host.

7.1. Loss of Functionality

As happens whenever two dissimilar protocols, or languages for that
matter, are translated, some loss of functionality is inevitable.
With reference to the FTP-FTAM gateway, several of the most blatant
losses of functionality are:

    1. Diagnostics passed between protocols may not be precisely
       translated.

    2. The FTAM partial file (record) transfer may not be
       supported.

    3. Some FTAM attributes are not supported by FTP.

The primary goal of the gateway protocol mappings are to minimize
this loss of functionality. As this gateway specification and
subsequent implementations evolve, means to partially overcome loss
of functionality may become more obvious.  For example, the gateway
may be able to emulate file record transfers between FTAM Initiators
and FTP Servers.

8. Mapping of Protocol Functions and Representations

The mappings presented are based upon the FTAM protocol
implementation as defined in Stable Implementation Agreements for
Open Systems Interconnection Protocols:  Part 9 - FTAM Phase 2,
produced by the March 1992 Open Systems Environment Implementors'
Workshop [NIST92], and in [ISO8571-1], [ISO8571-2],[ISO8571-
3],[ISO8571-4], and [ISO8571-5].  The FTP protocol as defined in
Request for Comments [RFC959].  The mappings are strongly influenced
by the work of M. A. Wallace et. al. at NIST [NIST86] and John Scott

at MITRE [MITRE87].

A key goal of the mappings presented in this document is to minimize
the loss of functionality between the two protocols.  The specific
approach taken to implement the mappings is left to the discretion of
the gateway implementor.  The focus of the protocol function and
representation mappings is on non-error encumbered processing.  The
mapping of diagnostic and error messages is treated separately in
section 9.

At a minimum, the FTAM implementation in the FTP-FTAM gateway support
for Implementation Profiles T1 (Simple File Transfer) and M1
(Management), as defined in [NIST92], is required.  These
Implementation Profiles correspond to the A/111 and A/13 Profiles of
Standards Promotion and Application Group in Europe, respectively
[NIST92].

At a minimum, the gateway support for the following is required:

    ASCII and 8 bit binary file types.  It should also support FTP
    File Stream Mode.

    The following FTAM document types: FTAM-1 (unstructured text
    file), FTAM-3 (unstructured binary file), and NBS-9 (set of
    directory entries).

POSIX file naming and organization conventions are assumed in these
mappings; i.e., files in the systems are assumed to be organized in a
hierarchical structure in which all of the non-terminal nodes are
directories and all of the terminal nodes are any other type of file.

The following terminology is used in the mapping specifications:

    argument .......FTP Service Command argument, as used in [RFC959].

    parameter ......FTAM Service Primitive parameters and attributes,
                    as enumerated in Tables 6, 50, and 51 of [ISO8571-
                    3].

The following notation is used in the mapping specifications:

    Arguments and parameters are enclosed in angle brackets; e.g.,
    <Action Result>

    Values of arguments and parameters are enclosed in quotation
    marks; e.g., "Success"

FTP Service Commands and FTAM Primitives are in uppercase; e.g., F-INITIALIZE

8.1.  FTP-Initiated Gateway Service

The protocol mapping between FTP and FTAM may be one-to-zero (i.e., not mappable), one-to-one, or one-to-many.

The general steps taken by the FTP-FTAM gateway to provide the FTP-Initiated service are:

1. Accept an FTP Client request at the FTP Server side of the gateway service.

2. Map the request to the (set of) corresponding FTAM Initiator function(s).

3. Acting as an FTAM Initiator, send the FTAM Initiator function(s) to the FTAM Responder.

4. Accept information returned to the FTAM Initiator side of the gateway.  This information originated at the FTAM Responder.

5. Map this returned information to the protocol form understood by the FTP Server side of the gateway.

6. Send this returned information from the FTP Server side of the gateway to the FTP Client.

For each FTP protocol function, the FTAM protocol functions required to map it are identified:

```
FTP       FTAM

----------------------------------------------------------------

ABOR      F-BEGIN-GROUP, F-CANCEL, F-CLOSE, F-DESELECT, F-END-GROUP

ACCT      F-INITIALIZE,

ALLO      none

APPE      F-BEGIN-GROUP, F-CLOSE, F-CREATE, F-DATA, F-DATA-END, F-
          DESELECT, F-END-GROUP, F-OPEN, F-READ-ATTRIBUTES, F-SELECT,
          F-TRANSFER-END, F-WRITE

CDUP      F-BEGIN-GROUP, F-DESELECT, F-END-GROUP, F-SELECT
```

CWD      F-BEGIN-GROUP, F-END-GROUP, F-DESELECT, F-SELECT

DELE     F-BEGIN-GROUP, F-DELETE, F-END-GROUP, F-SELECT

HELP     none

LIST     F-BEGIN-GROUP, F-CLOSE, F-DATA, F-DATA-END, F-DESELECT, F-
         END-GROUP, F-OPEN, F-READ, F-READ-ATTRIBUTES, F-SELECT, F-
         TRANSFER-END

MKD      none

MODE     none

NLST     F-BEGIN-GROUP, F-CLOSE, F-DATA, F-DATA-END, F-DESELECT, F-
         END-GROUP, F-OPEN, F-READ, F-SELECT, F-TRANSFER-END

NOOP     none

PASS     F-INITIALIZE

PASV     none

PORT     none

PWD      F-BEGIN-GROUP, F-DESELECT, F-END-GROUP, F-READ-ATTRIBUTES,
         F-SELECT

QUIT     F-P-ABORT or F-U-ABORT, F-TERMINATE

REIN     F-BEGIN-GROUP, F-CANCEL, F-CLOSE, F-DESELECT, F-END-GROUP

REST     F-CHECK, F-RESTART

RETR     F-BEGIN-GROUP, F-CLOSE, F-DATA, F-DATA-END, F-DESELECT, F-
         END-GROUP, F-OPEN, F-READ, F-SELECT, F-TRANSFER-END

RMD      none

RNFR     F-BEGIN-GROUP, F-DESELECT, F-END-GROUP, F-SELECT

RNTO     F-BEGIN-GROUP, F-CHANGE-ATTRIBUTES, F-DESELECT, F-END-
         GROUP, F-SELECT

SITE     F-INITIALIZE

SMNT     none

STAT          none

STOR          F-BEGIN-GROUP,F-CLOSE, F-CREATE, F-DATA, F-DATA-END, F-
              DESELECT, F-END-GROUP, F-OPEN, F-READ-ATTRIBUTES, F-SELECT,
              F-TRANSFER-END, F-WRITE

STOU          F-BEGIN-GROUP, F-CLOSE, F-CREATE, F-DATA, F-DATA-END, F-
              DESELECT, F-END-GROUP, F-OPEN, F-READ-ATTRIBUTES, F-SELECT,
              F-TRANSFER-END, F-WRITE

STRU          none

TYPE          none

USER          F-INITIALIZE

The remainder of this section presents detailed mapping procedures
for each of the FTP protocol functions.  Gateway support for these
mappings is required.

8.1.1. ABOR

        1. Send F-CANCEL to FTAM Responder.
        2. Send the following grouped request to the FTAM Responder.
           F-BEGIN-GROUP
           F-CLOSE
           F-DESELECT
           F-END-GROUP
        3. Translate FTAM Responder <Action Result> and <Diagnostic>
           parameters to equivalent FTP reply code(s) and send reply
           codes to FTP Client.
        4. Translate FTP Client reply codes to equivalent FTAM <Action
           Result> and <Diagnostic> parameters and send parameters to
           FTAM Responder.

8.1.2. ACCT

        1. Set <Account> parameter value for issuing F-INITIALIZE to
           FTAM Responder.
        2. If <Called Presentation Address>, <Initiator Identity>, and
           <Filestore Password> parameters are available, attempt
           connection with FTAM Responder;
           Otherwise wait for additional ACCT commands.
        3. Translate FTAM Responder <Action Result> and <Diagnostic>
           parameters to equivalent FTP reply code(s) and send reply
           codes to FTP Client.
        4. Translate FTP Client reply codes to equivalent FTAM <Action
           Result> and <Diagnostic> parameters and send parameters to

FTAM Responder.

Note:
a. The ACCT command will be effective with the next PASS
   command.

8.1.3. ALLO

1. Return a 200 reply code to FTP Client.

8.1.4. APPE

1. Save current pathname by appending saved CWD string with
   <pathname> argument.  If no saved CWD string, proceed to
   step 12.
2. Send the following grouped request to FTAM Responder.
   F-BEGIN-GROUP
   F-SELECT
   F-READ-ATTRIBUTES
       Save <Contents Type> parameter value
   F-DESELECT
   F-END-GROUP
3. If the <Contents Type> parameter value returned with the
   F-READ-ATTRIBUTES has a value of "NBS-9", proceed to step
   12.
4. Send the following grouped request to the FTAM responder.
   F-BEGIN-GROUP
   F-CREATE
       Set the <Override> parameter in the F-CREATE to
       "Select Old File".
   F-OPEN
   F-END-GROUP
5. If the file existed, set the <Contents Type> parameter in
   the F-CREATE to match that returned by the
   F-READ-ATTRIBUTES.
6. If the file did not exist and no previous FTP TYPE "Image"
   command was issued, then set the <Contents Type> parameter
   to "FTAM-1";
   Otherwise, set the <Contents Type> parameter to "FTAM-3".
7. Send F-WRITE, with <Bulk Data Transfer Specification, FADU
   Operation> parameter set to "File Extend", to FTAM
   Responder.
8. Loop reading data from FTP data connection, sending the
   data in F-DATA PDUs until end-of-file on the FTP
   connection.
9. Send F-DATA-END to FTAM Responder.
10. Send F-TRANSFER-END to FTAM Responder.
11. Send the following grouped request to the FTAM Responder.

                    F-BEGIN-GROUP
                    F-CLOSE
                    F-DESELECT
                    F-END-GROUP
            12. Translate FTAM Responder <Action Result> and <Diagnostic>
                parameters to equivalent FTP reply code(s) and send reply
                code(s) to FTP Client.
            13. Translate FTP Client reply codes to equivalent FTAM
                <Action Result> and <Diagnostic> parameters and send
                parameters to FTAM Responder.

        Note:
        a. <pathname> argument is assumed to be a filename, relative
           to the currently saved CWD.
        b. CWD of the FTAM system must be defined prior to issuance of
           APPE.

8.1.5. CDUP

        1. Determine parent directory from saved CWD string.  If no
           saved CWD string, proceed to step 4.
        2. Set <Contents Type> parameter to "NBS-9".
        3. Send the following grouped request to FTAM Responder.
           F-BEGIN-GROUP
           F-SELECT
           F-DESELECT
           F-END-GROUP
        4. Translate FTAM Responder <Action Result> and <Diagnostic>
           parameters to equivalent FTP reply code(s) and send reply
           code(s) to FTP Client.
        5. Translate FTP Client reply codes to equivalent FTAM <Action
           Result> and <Diagnostic> parameters and send parameters to
           FTAM Responder.

        Note:
        a. A POSIX file organization is assumed; i.e., files in the
           systems are organized in a hierarchical structure in which
           all of the non-terminal nodes are directories and all of
           the terminal nodes are any other type of file.
        b. If the parent directory does not exist, the current working
           directory remains unchanged.
        c. CWD of the FTAM system must be defined prior to issuance of
           CDUP.

8.1.6. CWD

        1. Save <pathname> argument as CWD string.
        2. Set <Contents Type> parameter to "NBS-9".

3. Send the following grouped request to FTAM Responder.
   F-BEGIN-GROUP
   F-SELECT
   F-DESELECT
   F-END-GROUP
4. Translate FTAM Responder <Action Result> and <Diagnostic>
   parameters to equivalent FTP reply code(s) and send reply
   code(s) to FTP Client.
5. Translate FTP Client reply codes to equivalent FTAM <Action
   Result> and <Diagnostic> parameters and send parameters to
   FTAM Responder.

Note:
a. The <pathname> argument is assumed to be an absolute
   directory specification.
b. If the specified directory does not exist, the current
   working directory remains unchanged.
c. Saved CWD string is used in other FTP-to-FTAM mappings,
   such as APPE.

## 8.1.7. DELE

1. Save current pathname by appending saved CWD string with
   <pathname> argument.  If no saved CWD string, proceed to
   step 3.
2. Send the following grouped request to FTAM Responder.
   F-BEGIN-GROUP
   F-SELECT
   F-DELETE
   F-END-GROUP
3. Translate FTAM Responder <Action Result> and <Diagnostic>
   parameters to equivalent FTP reply code(s) and send reply
   code(s) to FTP Client.
4. Translate FTP Client reply codes to equivalent FTAM
   parameters and send parameters to FTAM Responder.

Note:
a. <pathname> argument is assumed to be a filename, relative
   to the currently saved CWD.
b. CWD of the FTAM system must be defined prior to issuance of
   DELE.

## 8.1.8. HELP

1. If no <string> argument is provided, send helpful
   information about the implementation of the gateway to the
   FTP Client.  If an argument is provided, send more specific
   information.

   2. Return the FTP reply code 214 to the FTP Client.

8.1.9. LIST

   1. If <pathname> argument is provided, proceed to step 3.
   2. Save current pathname by appending saved CWD string with
      <pathname> argument; If no saved CWD string, proceed to
      step 11.
   3. Send the following grouped request to the FTAM Responder.
        F-BEGIN-GROUP
        F-SELECT
        F-READ-ATTRIBUTES
           Save <Filename>, <Contents Type>, <Data/Time of Last
      Modification>, and <Filesize> parameters
        F-DESELECT
        F-END-GROUP
   4. If the <Contents Type> parameter of the F-READ-ATTRIBUTES
      is not "NBS-9", then return the <Filename>, <Contents
      Type>, <Date/Time of Last Modification>, and <Filesize>
      parameter values, obtained with the previous
      F-READ-ATTRIBUTES, to the FTP data connection;
      and proceed to step 8.
   5. Send the following grouped request to the FTAM Responder.
        F-BEGIN-GROUP
        F-SELECT
        F-OPEN
        F-END-GROUP
   6. Send F-READ to FTAM Responder.
   7. Loop reading F-DATA until F-DATA-END.  As data is received,
      write the <Filename>, <Permitted Actions>, <Contents Type>,
      and <Date/Time of Last Modification> parameter values from
      the PDU to the FTP data connection.
   8. Send F-TRANSFER-END to FTAM Responder.
   9. Send the following grouped request to the FTAM responder.
        F-BEGIN-GROUP
        F-CLOSE
        F-DESELECT
        F-END-GROUP
   10. Translate FTAM Responder <Action Result> and <Diagnostic>
       parameters to equivalent FTP reply code(s) and send reply
       code(s) to FTP Client.
   11. Translate FTP Client reply codes to equivalent FTAM <Action
       Result> and <Diagnostic> parameters and send parameters to
       FTAM Responder.

   Note:
   a. Assume the <pathname> argument is relative to the saved
      CWD, whether filename or directory specification.

b. CWD of the FTAM system must be defined prior to issuance of
   LIST.
c. Transfers over data connection should be in ASCII.
e. If list of files with full directory/file specification is
   received from FTAM Responder, then gateway should parse
   list to strip off directory portion.

8.1.10. MKD

1. Return a 502 reply code (Command not implemented) to the
   FTP Client.

Note:
a. As indicated in the NIST Stable Implementation Agreements
   for FTAM [NIST92], creation or deletion of NBS-9 files is
   outside the scope of the agreements.

8.1.11. MODE

1. If <argument> is "Stream", return 200 reply code to FTP
   Client; Otherwise return a 504 reply code (Command not
   implemented for that parameter).

8.1.12. NLST

1. If <pathname> argument is provided, use <pathname> argument
   as <Filename> parameter value in F-SELECT issued in step 3.
2. If no argument is provided, use saved CWD value as
   <Filename> parameter value in F-SELECT issued in step 3; If
   no CWD string is saved and no argument is provided, proceed
   to step 9.
3. Set <Contents Type> parameter to "NBS-9".
4. Send the following grouped request to the FTAM Responder.
   F-BEGIN-GROUP
   F-SELECT
   F-OPEN
   F-END-GROUP
5. Send F-READ to FTAM Responder.
6. Loop reading F-DATA until F-DATA-END.  As data is received,
   write the filenames and other useful information from the
   PDU to the FTP data connection.
7. Send F-TRANSFER-END to FTAM Responder.
8. Send the following grouped request to the FTAM responder.
   F-BEGIN-GROUP
   F-CLOSE
   F-DESELECT
   F-END-GROUP
9. Translate FTAM Responder <Action Result> and <Diagnostic>

parameters to equivalent FTP reply code(s) and send reply
code(s) to FTP Client.
10. Translate FTP Client reply codes to equivalent FTAM <Action
Result> and <Diagnostic> parameters and send parameters to
FTAM Responder.

Note:
a. As per RFC 959 (FTP), the NLST <pathname> argument is a
directory.
b. Assume the argument is relative to the saved CWD, whether
filename or directory specification.
c. CWD of the FTAM system must be defined prior to issuance of
NLST.
d. Transfers over data connection should be in ASCII.
e. Gateway should parse full directory/file specifications
received from FTAM Responder to strip off directory
portion.  This is required to support the "FTP multiple
get" function that pipes NLST output to the STOR command.

## 8.1.13. NOOP

1. Return a 200 reply code to FTP Client.

## 8.1.14. PASS

1. Set <Filestore Password> parameter for F-INITIALIZE.
2. If <Called Presentation Address>, <User Identity>, and
<Filestore Password> are available, issue F- INITIALIZE to
FTAM Responder.
3. Translate FTAM Responder <Action Result> and <Diagnostic>
parameters to equivalent FTP reply code(s) and send reply
code(s) to FTP Client.
4. Translate FTP Client reply codes to equivalent FTAM <Action
Result> and <Diagnostic> parameters and send parameters to
FTAM Responder.

## 8.1.15. PASV

1. Wait for data transfer on default data port or data port
specified by PORT command.
2. Return a 200 reply code to FTP Client.

## 8.1.16. PORT

1. Return a 200 reply code to FTP Client.

8.1.17. PWD

   1. If there is a saved CWD string, return it to the FTP client
      and proceed to step 4.
   2. Set <Contents Type> attribute to "NBS-9".
   3. Send the following grouped request to FTAM Responder.
      F-BEGIN-GROUP
      F-SELECT
      F-READ-ATTRIBUTES
      F-DESELECT
      F-END-GROUP
   4. Return the current directory name to the FTP client.
   5. Translate FTAM Responder <Action Result> and <Diagnostic>
      parameters to equivalent FTP reply code(s) and send reply
      code(s) to FTP Client.
   6. Translate FTP Client reply codes to equivalent FTAM <Action
      Result> and <Diagnostic> parameters and send parameters to
      FTAM Responder.

8.1.18. QUIT

   1. If user is not logged in, proceed to step 5.
   2. If file transfer is in progress, send F-P-ABORT or
      F-U-ABORT to FTAM Responder.
   3. If file transfer is not in progress, send and F-TERMINATE
      to FTAM Responder.
   4. Return charge information to FTP Client.
   5. Translate FTAM Responder <Action Result> and <Diagnostic>
      parameters to equivalent FTP reply code(s) and send reply
      code(s) to FTP Client.
   6. Translate FTP Client reply codes to equivalent FTAM <Action
      Result> and <Diagnostic> parameters and send parameters to
      FTAM Responder.

8.1.19. REIN

   1. Flush all I/O and account information.
   2. Allow all transfers in progress to be completed.
   3. Set all parameters to default values.
   4. Send F-CANCEL to FTAM Responder.
   5. Send the following grouped request to FTAM Responder.
      F-BEGIN-GROUP
      F-CLOSE
      F-DESELECT
      F-END-GROUP
   6. Leave the control connection open.
   7. Translate FTAM Responder <Action Result> and <Diagnostic>
      parameters to equivalent FTP reply code(s) and send reply

              code(s) to FTP Client.
         8. Translate FTP Client reply codes to equivalent FTAM <Action
            Result> and <Diagnostic> parameters and send parameters to
            FTAM Responder.

         Note:
         a. Typically followed by a USER command.

   8.1.20. REST

         1. Send F-CHECK to FTAM Responder.
         2. Send F-RESTART to FTAM Responder.
         3. Translate FTAM Responder <Action Result> and <Diagnostic>
            parameters to equivalent FTP reply code(s) and send reply
            code(s) to FTP Client.
         4. Translate FTP Client reply codes to equivalent FTAM <Action
            Result> and <Diagnostic> parameters and send parameters to
            FTAM Responder.

         Notes:
         a. Will only have affect on FTAM Responder if the restart
            functional unit is negotiated on F-INITIALIZE.
         b. Refer to ISO 8571-3 for additional subtleties of FTAM
            checkpoint and restart.

   8.1.21. RETR

         1. Save current pathname by appending saved CWD string with
            <pathname> argument.  If no saved CWD string, proceed to
            step 9.
         2. Set <Contents Type> parameter to appropriate type of file.
         3. Send the following grouped request to the FTAM Responder.
              F-BEGIN-GROUP
              F-SELECT
              F-OPEN
              F-END-GROUP
         4. If file does not exist, proceed to step 9.
         5. Send F-READ to FTAM Responder.
         6. Loop reading F-DATA until F-DATA-END.  As data is received,
            write it to the FTP data connection.
         7. Send F-TRANSFER-END to FTAM Responder.
         8. Send the following grouped request to the FTAM Responder.
              F-BEGIN-GROUP
              F-CLOSE
              F-DESELECT
              F-END-GROUP
         9. Translate FTAM Responder <Action Result> and <Diagnostic>
            parameters to equivalent FTP reply code(s) and send reply

code(s) to FTP Client.
10. Translate FTP Client reply codes to equivalent FTAM <Action
    Result> and <Diagnostic> parameters and send parameters to
    FTAM Responder.

Note:
a. <pathname> argument is assumed to be a filename, relative
   to the currently saved CWD.
b. CWD of the FTAM system must be defined prior to issuance of
   RETR.

8.1.22. RMD

   1. Return a 502 reply code (Command not implemented) to the
      FTP Client.

Note:
a. As indicated in the NIST Stable Implementation Agreements
   for FTAM [NIST92], creation or deletion of NBS-9 files is
   outside the scope of the agreements.

8.1.23. RNFR

   1. Save current pathname by appending saved CWD string with
      <pathname> argument.  If no saved CWD string, proceed to
      step 3.
   2. Send the following grouped request to the FTAM Responder.
      F-BEGIN-GROUP
      F-SELECT
          Get <Filename> parameter value from RNFR <pathname>
      argument.
      F-DESELECT
      F-END-GROUP
   3. Translate FTAM Responder <Action Result> and <Diagnostic>
      parameters to equivalent FTP reply code(s) and send reply
      code(s) to FTP Client.
   4. Translate FTP Client reply codes to equivalent FTAM <Action
      Result> and <Diagnostic> parameters and send parameters to
      FTAM Responder.

Note:
a. <pathname> argument is assumed to be a filename, relative
   to the currently saved CWD.
b. Together with RNTO, this command causes a file to be
   renamed.
c. CWD of the FTAM system must be defined prior to issuance of
   RNFR.

8.1.24. RNTO

> 1. Save current pathname by appending saved CWD string with
>    <pathname> argument.  If no saved CWD string, proceed to
>    step 3.
> 2. Send the following grouped request to the FTAM Responder.
>    F-BEGIN-GROUP
>    F-SELECT
>    F-CHANGE-ATTRIBUTES
>        Get <Filename> parameter from arguments provided by
>        RNTO and previous RNFR.
>    F-DESELECT
>    F-END-GROUP
> 3. Translate FTAM Responder <Action Result> and <Diagnostic>
>    parameters to equivalent FTP reply code(s) and send reply
>    code(s) to FTP Client.
> 4. Translate FTP Client reply codes to equivalent FTAM <Action
>    Result> and <Diagnostic> parameters and send parameters to
>    FTAM Responder.
>
> Note:
> a. <pathname> argument is assumed to be a filename, relative
>    to the currently saved CWD.
> b. Together with RNFR, this command causes a file to be
>    renamed.
> c. CWD of the FTAM system must be defined prior to issuance of
>    RNTO.

8.1.25. SITE

> 1. Save the specified destination address information.
> 2. Set the <Called Presentation Address> parameter value equal
>    to the <string> argument.  This parameter will be used when
>    the F-INITIALIZE is sent to the FTAM Responder.
> 3. Translate FTAM Responder <Action Result> and <Diagnostic>
>    parameters to equivalent FTP reply code(s) and send reply
>    code(s) to FTP Client.
> 4. Translate FTP Client reply codes to equivalent FTAM <Action
>    Result> and <Diagnostic> parameters and send parameters to
>    FTAM Responder.
>
> Note:
> a. The <string> argument to the SITE command may include a
>    Distinguished Name or a User Friendly Name.

8.1.26. SMNT

    1. Return a 502 reply code to FTP Client.

    Note:
    a. Argument is ignored.

8.1.27. STAT

    1. Provide the gateway session status to the FTP Client.
    2. Return a 211 reply code to FTP Client.

    Note:
    a. Argument is ignored.

8.1.28. STOR

    1. Save current pathname by appending saved CWD string with
       <pathname> argument.  If no saved CWD string, proceed to
       step 11.
    2. Send the following grouped request to FTAM Responder.
       F-BEGIN-GROUP
       F-SELECT
       F-READ-ATTRIBUTES
           Save <Contents Type> parameter value
       F-DESELECT
       F-END-GROUP
    3. If the <Contents Type> parameter returned with the F-READ-
       ATTRIBUTES indicates a directory,  proceed to step 11.
    4. Send the following grouped request to the FTAM responder.
       F-BEGIN-GROUP
       F-CREATE
           Set the <Override> parameter in the F-CREATE to
           "Delete and create with new attributes.".
       F-OPEN
       F-END-GROUP
    5. If the file existed, set the <Contents Type> parameter in
       the F-CREATE to match the F-READ-ATTRIBUTES.  If the file
       did not exist, set the <Contents Type> parameter to
       "FTAM-1".  If TYPE "Image" was previously requested, set
       the <Contents Type> parameter to "FTAM-3".
    6. Send F-WRITE, with <Bulk Data Transfer Specification, FADU
       Operation> parameter set to "File Extend", to FTAM Responder.
    7. Loop reading data from FTP data connection, sending the
       data in F-DATA PDUs until end-of-file on the FTP
       connection.
    8. Send F-DATA-END to FTAM Responder.
    9. Send F-TRANSFER-END to FTAM Responder.

10. Send the following grouped request to the FTAM Responder.
    F-BEGIN-GROUP
    F-CLOSE
    F-DESELECT
    F-END-GROUP
11. Translate FTAM Responder <Action Result> and <Diagnostic>
    parameters to equivalent FTP reply code(s) and send reply
    code(s) to FTP Client.
12. Translate FTP Client reply codes to equivalent FTAM
    <Action Result> and <Diagnostic> parameters and send
    parameters to FTAM Responder.

Note:
a. <pathname> argument is assumed to be a filename, relative
   to the currently saved CWD.
b. CWD of the FTAM system must be defined prior to issuance of
   STOR.

8.1.29. STOU

1. Save current pathname by appending saved CWD string with
   <pathname> argument.  If no saved CWD string, proceed to
   step 11.
2. Send the following grouped request to FTAM Responder.
   F-BEGIN-GROUP
   F-SELECT
   F-READ-ATTRIBUTES
       Save <Contents Type> parameter value
   F-DESELECT
   F-END-GROUP
3. If the file already exists, proceed to step 12.
4. If the <Contents Type> parameter returned with the F-READ-
   ATTRIBUTES indicates a directory, proceed to step 11.
5. Send the following grouped request to the FTAM responder.
   F-BEGIN-GROUP
   F-CREATE
       Set the <Override> parameter in the F-CREATE to
       "Delete and create with new attributes.".
   F-OPEN
   F-END-GROUP
6. If the file existed, set the <Contents Type> parameter in
   the F-CREATE to match the F-READ-ATTRIBUTES.  If the file
   did not exist, set the <Contents Type> parameter to
   "FTAM-1".  If TYPE "Image" was previously requested, set
   the <Contents Type> parameter to "FTAM-3".
7. Send F-WRITE, with <Bulk Data Transfer Specification, FADU
   Operation> parameter set to "File Extend", to FTAM Responder.
8. Loop reading data from FTP data connection, sending the

     data in F-DATA PDUs until end-of-file on the FTP
     connection.
 9. Send F-DATA-END to FTAM Responder.
10. Send F-TRANSFER-END to FTAM Responder.
11. Send the following grouped request to the FTAM Responder.
     F-BEGIN-GROUP
     F-CLOSE
     F-DESELECT
     F-END-GROUP
12. Translate FTAM Responder <Action Result> and <Diagnostic>
     parameters to equivalent FTP reply code(s) and send reply
     code(s) to FTP Client.
13. Translate FTP Client reply codes to equivalent FTAM
     <Action Result> and <Diagnostic> parameters and send
     parameters to FTAM Responder.

     Note:
     a. <pathname> argument is assumed to be a filename, relative
        to the currently saved CWD.
     b. Same as STOR, except the name of the created file must be
        unique in that directory.
     c. CWD of the FTAM system must be defined prior to issuance of
        STOU.

8.1.30. STRU

     1. If <structure code> argument is not "File", return 504
        reply code to FTP Client; Otherwise return 200 reply code
        to FTP Client.

8.1.31. SYST

     1. Return 502 reply code to FTP client.

8.1.32. TYPE

     1. If no <type code> argument is provided, set <Contents Type>
        parameter equal to "FTAM-1".
     2. If argument is provided, and equal to "ASCII", set <Contents
        Type> parameter to "FTAM-1".
     3. If argument is provided, and equal to "Image", set <Contents
        Type> parameter to "FTAM-3".
     4. Translate FTAM Responder <Action Result> and <Diagnostic>
        parameters to equivalent FTP reply code(s) and send reply
        code(s) to FTP Client.
     5. Translate FTP Client reply codes to equivalent FTAM <Action
        Result> and <Diagnostic> parameters and send parameters to
        FTAM Responder.

Note:
a. Default to ASCII if no <type code> argument is provided.

8.1.33. USER

1. Set <Initiator Identity> parameter for issuing F-INITIALIZE
   to FTAM Responder.
2. If the destination address was specified in the Domain Name
   used to attach to the gateway, use it to set the value of
   the <Called Presentation Address> parameter of the
   to-be-issued F-INITIALIZE command.
3. If the destination address is not known, check if it was
   specified in a previously issued SITE command.  If
   available, set <Called Presentation Address> parameter for
   issuing F-INITIALIZE to FTAM Responder.
4. If the destination address is still not available, check if
   it is encoded in the user identity (e.g., user@host). If
   encoded, set <Called Presentation Address> parameter for
   issuing F-INITIALIZE to FTAM Responder using the "host"
   portion.
5. If no destination address is available, proceed to step 7.
6. Prompt user for password.
7. Translate FTAM Responder <Action Result> and <Diagnostic>
   parameters to equivalent FTP reply code(s) and send reply
   code(s) to FTP Client.
8. Translate FTP Client reply codes to equivalent FTAM <Action
   Result> and <Diagnostic> parameters and send parameters to
   FTAM Responder.

Note:
a. A USER command should be acceptable in any state.
b. Multiple mechanisms are available for specifying the
   destination address: 1) Domain Name used in connecting to
   gateway (see section 4, Use of Gateway Services); 2) SITE
   command argument; and 3) user@host format.

8.2. FTAM-Initiated Gateway Service

The protocol mapping between FTP and FTAM may be one-to-zero (i.e.,
not mappable), one-to-one, or one-to-many.

The general steps taken by the FTP-FTAM gateway to provide the FTAM-
Initiated service are:

1. Accept an FTAM Initiator request at the FTAM Responder side
   of the gateway.

2. Map the request to the (set of) corresponding FTP Client

function(s).

3. Acting as an FTP Client, send the FTP Client function(s) to
   the FTP Server.

4. Accept information returned to the FTP Client side of the
   gateway.  This information originated at the FTP Server.

5. Map this returned information to a form understood by the
   FTAM Responder side of the gateway.

6. Send this returned information from the FTAM Responder side
   of the gateway to the FTAM Initiator.

For each FTAM protocol function, the FTP protocol functions required
to map it are identified:

```
FTAM                    FTP

--------------------------------------------------------------------

F-BEGIN-GROUP           none

F-CANCEL                ABOR

F-CHANGE-ATTRIBUTE      RNFR, RNTO

F-CHECK                 none

F-CLOSE                 none

F-CREATE                STOR

F-DATA                  ALLO, STOR or RETR or APPE

F-DATA-END              none

F-DELETE                DELE

F-DESELECT              none

F-END-GROUP             STAT

F-ERASE                 DELE

F-INITIALIZE            ACCT, PASS, USER

F-LOCATE                none
```

| F-OPEN | MODE, STRU, TYPE |
|---|---|
| F-READ | MODE, NLST, RETR, TYPE |
| F-READ-ATTRIBUTE | LIST |
| F-RECOVER | REST |
| F-RESTART | ABOR, REST |
| F-SELECT | LIST |
| F-TERMINATE | QUIT |
| F-TRANSFER | none |
| F-P-ABORT | QUIT |
| F-U-ABORT | QUIT |
| F-WRITE | APPE or STOR, NOOP |

The remainder of this section presents detailed mapping procedures for each of the FTAM protocol functions. Where appropriate, each FTAM service primitive is followed by those parameters that are relevant to the mapping. Gateway support for these mappings is required.

8.2.1. F-BEGIN-GROUP REQ

   1. Send F-BEGIN-GROUP RESP PDU to FTAM Initiator signifying that processes are available to handle concatenated requests.

8.2.2. F-CANCEL REQ

   1. Close FTP data connection.
   2. Send ABOR to FTP Server.
   3. Translate FTP Server reply code to equivalent FTAM Responder action and diagnostic parameters and send parameters to FTAM Initiator via F-CANCEL RESP PDU.
   4. Translate FTAM Initiator action and diagnostic parameters to equivalent FTP reply codes and send reply codes to FTP Server.

   Note:
   a. F-U-ABORT REQ is a viable alternative to F-CANCEL REQ.
   b. Note that since ABOR is not implemented by all FTP Servers,

the remote file may be corrupted, though accessible.

8.2.3. F-CHANGE-ATTRIBUTE REQ

1. Get original filename from <Filename> parameter and send it
   with an RNFR to the FTP Server.
2. Get new filename from <Filename> parameter and send it with
   an RNTO to the FTP Server.
3. Translate FTP Server reply code to equivalent FTAM
   Responder action and diagnostic parameters and send
   parameters to FTAM Initiator via F-CHANGE-ATTRIBUTE RESP
   PDU.
4. Translate FTAM Initiator action and diagnostic parameters
   to equivalent FTP reply codes and send reply codes to FTP
   Server.

Note:
a. Allow for processing an arbitrary number attributes at one
   time.
b. Allow for responses of "Attribute currently unavailable for
   change" and "Attribute not currently supported".
c. At a minimum, support the <Filename>, <Permitted Actions>,
   and <Contents Type> parameters.

8.2.4. F-CHECK REQ

1. Send an F-CHECK RESP PDU to the FTAM Initiator.

8.2.5. F-CLOSE REQ

1. Send F-CLOSE RESP PDU , with <Action Result> parameter
   value of "Success", to FTAM Initiator.

Note:
a. If an error had occurred during transfer, it would have
   been noted before the F-CLOSE REQ.

8.2.6. F-CREATE REQ

1. Send STOR and zero data bytes to FTP Server.
2. Translate FTP Server reply code to equivalent FTAM
   Responder <Action Result> and <Diagnostic> parameters and
   send parameters to FTAM Initiator.
3. Translate FTAM Initiator <Action Result> and <Diagnostic>
   parameters to equivalent FTP reply codes and send reply
   codes to FTP Server.

8.2.7. F-DATA PDU

    1. If necessary, send ALLO command to FTP Server.
    2. Depending on whether reading or writing, send STOR, RETR, or APPE command to FTP Server.
    3. Translate FTP Server reply code to equivalent FTAM Responder <Action Result> and <Diagnostic> parameters and send parameters to FTAM Initiator.
    4. Translate FTAM Initiator <Action Result> and <Diagnostic> parameters to equivalent FTP reply codes and send reply codes to FTP Server.

    Note:
    a. The use of an FTP command may be unnecessary.  Sending the data on the data connection may be adequate.

8.2.8. F-DATA-END REQ

    1. Close the data connection.
    2. Save mandatory Diagnostic parameter for later use.
    3. Translate FTP Server reply code to equivalent FTAM Responder <Action Result> and <Diagnostic> parameters and send parameters to FTAM Initiator.
    4. Translate FTAM Initiator <Action Result> and <Diagnostic> parameters to equivalent FTP reply codes and send reply codes to FTP Server.

8.2.9. F-DELETE REQ

    1. Send DELE to FTP server.
    2. Translate FTP Server reply code to equivalent FTAM Responder <Action Result> and <Diagnostic> parameters and send parameters to FTAM Initiator via F-DELETE RESP PDU.
    3. Translate FTAM Initiator <Action Result> and <Diagnostic> parameters to equivalent FTP reply codes and send reply codes to FTP Server.

8.2.10. F-DESELECT REQ

    1. Return F-DESELECT RESP PDU, with <Action Result> parameter value of "Success", to FTAM Initiator.

8.2.11. F-END-GROUP REQ

    1. Send STAT command sequence to FTP Server.
    2. Translate FTP Server reply code to equivalent FTAM Responder <Action Result> and <Diagnostic> parameters and send parameters to FTAM Initiator via F-END

GROUP RESP.

3. Translate FTAM Initiator <Action Result> and <Diagnostic>
   parameters to equivalent FTP reply codes and send reply
   codes to FTP Server.

8.2.12. F-ERASE REQ

1. Send DELE to FTP Server.
2. Translate FTP Server reply code to equivalent FTAM
   Responder <Action Result> and <Diagnostic> parameters and
   send parameters to FTAM Initiator via F-ERASE RESP PDU.
3. Translate FTAM Initiator <Action Result> and <Diagnostic>
   parameters to equivalent FTP reply codes and send reply
   codes to FTP Server.

8.2.13. F-INITIALIZE REQ

1. Establish initial area for activity attributes.
2. Save <Responding Presentation Address>, <Initiator
   Identity>, and <Filestore Password> parameter values
   received from FTAM Initiator.
3. If the destination address was specified in the
   Distinguished Name (or User Friendly Name) used to attach
   to the gateway, save it as the ultimate destination
   address.
4. If the ultimate destination address is not yet known, look
   at the "@host" portion of the <Initiator Identity>
   parameter for the ultimate destination parameter.
5. If the ultimate destination address is still not known,
   check if it is available in the <Responding Presentation
   Address> parameter.
6. Get userid from <Initiator Identity> and send it with USER
   command to FTP Server.
7. Get password from <Filestore Password> and send it with
   PASS command to FTP Server.
8. If necessary, send ACCT command to FTP Server.
9. Negotiate acceptance of mandatory functional units, service
   classes, service types, presentation contexts, and
   attribute groups.
10. Accept context management functional unit passed by
    Presentation service provider.
11. Translate FTP Server reply code to equivalent FTAM
    Responder <Action Result> and <Diagnostic> parameters and
    send parameters to FTAM Initiator via F-INIT RESP PDU.
12. Translate FTAM Initiator <Action Result> and <Diagnostic>
    parameters to equivalent FTP reply codes and send reply
    codes to FTP Server.

Note:

a. Multiple mechanisms are available for specifying the destination address: 1) Distinguished Name, or User Friendly Name, used in connecting to the gateway (see section 4, Use of Gateway Services); 2) user@host format; and 3) Inclusion as <Responding Presentation Address> parameter value.

8.2.14. F-LOCATE REQ

Note:

a. Not supported since FTAM-1 and FTAM-3 don't support this primitive.

8.2.15. F-OPEN REQ

1. Get <Contents Type> and <Processing Mode> parameter values from FTAM Initiator.
2. Send TYPE command to FTP Server.
3. Send MODE command to FTP Server.
4. Send STRU command to FTP Server.
5. Translate FTP Server reply code to equivalent FTAM Responder <Action Result> and <Diagnostic> parameters and send parameters to FTAM Initiator via F-OPEN RESP PDU.
6. Translate FTAM Initiator <Action Result> and <Diagnostic> parameters to equivalent FTP reply codes and send reply codes to FTP Server.

Note:

a. Establishes definite value for presentation context name parameter for this data transfer.
b. Assumes that the <Requested Access> parameter is permitted.

8.2.16. F-READ REQ

1. If requested file type and file mode are different than current settings, send TYPE and MODE to FTP Server.
2. If <Contents Type> is FTAM-1 or FTAM-3, then send RETR to FTP Server.
3. If <Contents Type> is "NBS-9", then send NLST to FTP Server.
4. If reply code from FTP Server is 1xx, open FTP data connection and loop until End-of-File is read on FTP data connection.  Inside loop, read block from FTP data connection, format FTAM DATA PDU, and send FTAM PDU to FTAM Initiator.  At End-of-File on FTP data connection, send F-DATA-END and return.

5. If reply code from FTP Server is not 1xx, send F-CANCEL REQ
   to FTAM Initiator.
6. Translate FTP Server reply code to equivalent FTAM
   Responder <Action Result> and <Diagnostic> parameters and
   send parameters to FTAM Initiator via F-READ RESP PDU.
7. Translate FTAM Initiator <Action Result> and <Diagnostic>
   parameters to equivalent FTP reply codes and send reply
   codes to FTP Server.

Note:
a. To send NLST response, TYPE must be ASCII.

## 8.2.17. F-READ-ATTRIBUTE REQ

1. Send LIST to FTP Server.
2. Translate returned information into the <Filename>,
   <Contents Type>, and <Permitted Actions> parameter values
   and return them to the FTAM Initiator.
3. Translate FTP Server reply code to equivalent FTAM
   Responder <Action Result> and <Diagnostic> parameters and
   send parameters to FTAM Initiator via F-READ-ATTRIBUTE RESP
   PDU.
4. Translate FTAM Initiator <Action Result> and <Diagnostic>
   parameters to equivalent FTP reply codes and send reply
   codes to FTP Server.

## 8.2.18. F-RECOVER REQ

1. Send REST command to FTP Server.
2. Translate FTP Server reply code to equivalent FTAM
   Responder <Action Result> and <Diagnostic> parameters and
   send parameters to FTAM Initiator.
3. Translate FTAM Initiator <Action Result> and <Diagnostic>
   parameters to equivalent FTP reply codes and send reply
   codes to FTP Server.

Note:
a. Regime recovery is only possible if the <Recovery
   Functional Unit> parameter was negotiated previously by an
   F-INITIALIZE.

## 8.2.19. F-RESTART REQ

1. To interrupt any bulk data transfer in progress, send ABOR
   to FTP Server.
2. To negotiate the point at which data transfer is to be
   restarted, get <Checkpoint Identifier> parameter from FTAM
   Initiator and send it with REST to FTP Server.

3. Translate FTP Server reply code to equivalent FTAM
   Responder <Action Result> and <Diagnostic> parameters and
   send parameters to FTAM Initiator via F-RESTART RESP PDU.
4. Translate FTAM Initiator <Action Result> and <Diagnostic>
   parameters to equivalent FTP reply codes and send reply
   codes to FTP Server.

8.2.20. F-SELECT REQ

1. Get <Filename> parameter and send with LIST command to FTP
   Server to determine whether  or not the file exists.
2. If file exists, compare the POSIX file access rights with
   the <Requested Access> parameter sent by the FTAM
   Initiator.  If the access rights match, return <Action
   Result> parameter value of "Success", otherwise return
   <Action Result> parameter value of "Failure".
3. Translate FTP Server reply code to equivalent FTAM
   Responder <Action Result> and <Diagnostic> parameters and
   send parameters to FTAM Initiator via F-SELECT RESP PDU.
4. Translate FTAM Initiator <Action Result> and <Diagnostic>
   parameters to equivalent FTP reply codes and send reply
   codes to FTP Server.

Note:
a. The specified file is binary/text file if one record is
   received or is a directory file if multiple records are
   received.

8.2.21. F-TERMINATE REQ

1. Send QUIT to FTP Server.
2. Translate FTP Server reply code to equivalent FTAM
   Responder <Action Result> and <Diagnostic> parameters and
   send parameters to FTAM Initiator via F-TERMINATE RESP PDU.
3. Translate FTAM Initiator <Action Result> and <Diagnostic>
   parameters to equivalent FTP reply codes and send reply
   codes to FTP Server.

8.2.22. F-TRANSFER-END

1. Get <Action Result> parameter value from last F-DATA-END
   and return it to FTAM Initiator as <Action Result>
   parameter of this F-TRANSFER-END.

8.2.23. F-P-ABORT REQ

1. Send QUIT to FTP Server.
2. Return <Action Result> parameter value of "Permanent Error"

to FTAM Initiator.
3. Translate FTP Server reply code to equivalent FTAM
   Responder <Action Result> and <Diagnostic> parameters and
   send parameters to FTAM Initiator.
4. Translate FTAM Initiator <Action Result> and <Diagnostic>
   parameters to equivalent FTP reply codes and send reply
   codes to FTP Server.

8.2.24. F-U-ABORT REQ

1. Send QUIT to FTP Server.
2. Return <Action Result> parameter value of "Permanent Error"
   to FTAM Initiator.
3. Translate FTP Server reply code to equivalent FTAM
   Responder <Action Result> and <Diagnostic> parameters and
   send parameters to FTAM Initiator.
4. Translate FTAM Initiator <Action Result> and <Diagnostic>
   parameters to equivalent FTP reply codes and send reply
   codes to FTP Server.

8.3. F-WRITE REQ

1. Save bulk transfer specification parameter from PDU.
2. Send NOOP to FTP Server to receive status information.
3. If the <Bulk Data Transfer Specification, FADU Operation>
   parameter has a value of "File Extend", then send an APPE
   to the FTP Server, otherwise send a STOR to the FTP Server.
4. If reply code from FTP Server is 200, then accept FTP data
   connection; otherwise send F-CANCEL REQ to FTAM Initiator.
5. Translate FTP Server reply code to equivalent FTAM Responder
   <Action Result> and <Diagnostic> parameters and send
   parameters to FTAM Initiator.
6. Translate FTAM Initiator <Action Result> and <Diagnostic>
   parameters to equivalent FTP reply codes and send reply
   codes to FTP Server.

9.  Mapping between FTP Reply Codes and FTAM Parameters

   The focus of the protocol function and representation mappings,
   presented in the previous sections, is on non-error encumbered
   processing.  Though appropriate responses are designated in many
   cases, it is intended that a more thorough use of responses will be
   incorporated into gateway implementations.

   The purpose of this section is to provide a set of mappings between
   FTAM responses (<Action Result> and <Diagnostic>) and FTP responses
   (reply codes).

The <Action Result> parameter of the FTAM File Service primitives
conveys information which summarizes that available in the
<Diagnostic> parameter.  The value is never less than the most severe
diagnostic value.  The valid values of this parameter are "Success",
"Transient Error", and "Permanent Error".  The FTP response text
should be supplied in the <Further Details> field of the
<Diagnostics> sequence in the FTAM response and abort messages.

An FTAM <Action Result> "Success" may be accompanied by a
<Diagnostic> with value of "Informative Error Type".  These "Success"
diagnostic messages are associated with error type 0 in the table
below (and in [ISO8571-3]).  Error type 1 indicates a transient
error, while type 2 indicates a permanent error.

An FTP reply consists of a three digit number followed by some text.
The number is defined as a 3-digit code, each digit of which has a
special significance.  The first digit conveys approximately the same
information as the FTAM <Action Result> parameter; i.e., positive,
transient negative, or permanent negative.

The FTP specification document [RFC959] explicitly states that the
list of reply codes should not be expanded beyond that which is
presented in [RFC959].  This requirement is adhered to in the
mappings presented in this document.

9.1.  FTP Reply Codes to FTAM Parameters

This section presents the set of mappings between FTP reply codes and
their equivalent FTAM action and diagnostic parameters.  Gateway
support for these mappings is recommended, but not required.  The
following abbreviations are used for FTAM action parameter values:

```
         trans   =    transient error
         perman  =    permanent error

      FTP Reply                                  |FTAM Diagnostic
                                                 |
                                                 |
         Code     Text                           |Result   Type Id
      -------------------------------------------+-----------------
         110      Restart marker reply           |success  0    0
         120      Service ready in nnn minutes   |success  0    0
         125      Data connection open, transfer |
                  starting                        |success  0    0
         150      File status okay; about to open|
                  data connection                |success  0    0
         200      Command okay                   |success  0    0
         202      Command not implemented;       |
```

| | | | | |
|-----|-----|-----|-----|-----|
| | superfluous | \|success | 0 | 0 |
| 211 | System status, or system help reply | \| \|success | 0 | 0 |
| 212 | Directory status | \|success | 0 | 0 |
| 213 | File status | \|success | 0 | 0 |
| 214 | Help message | \|success | 0 | 0 |
| 215 | NAME system type | \|success | 0 | 0 |
| 220 | Service ready for new user | \|success | 0 | 0 |
| 221 | Service closing control connection | \|success | 0 | 0 |
| 225 | Data connection; no transfer in progress | \| \|success | 0 | 0 |
| 226 | Closing data connection | \|success | 0 | 0 |
| 227 | Entering passive mode (h1,h2,..) | \|success | 0 | 0 |
| 230 | User logged in, proceed | \|success | 0 | 0 |
| 250 | Requested file action okay, completed | \| \|success | 0 | 0 |
| 257 | "PATHNAME" created | \|success | 0 | 0 |
| 331 | User name okay, need password | \|success | 0 | 0 |
| 332 | Need account for logon | \|success | 0 | 0 |
| 350 | Requested file action pending further information | \| \|success | 0 | 0 |
| 421 | Service not available, closing control connection | \| \|trans | 1 | 1 |
| 425 | Can't open data connection | \|trans | 1 | 3 |
| 426 | Connection closed, transfer aborted | \| \|trans | 1 | 1014 |
| 450 | Requested file action not taken, file unavailable (e.g., file busy) | \| \|trans | 1 | 5041 |
| 451 | Requested file action aborted, local error in processing | \| \|trans | 1 | 5028 |
| 452 | Requested action not taken, insufficient storage space | \| \|trans | 1 | 9 |
| 500 | Syntax error, command unrecognized | \|perman | 2 | 5015 |
| 501 | Syntax error in parameters or arguments | \| \|perman | 2 | 4004 |
| 502 | Command not implemented | \|perman | 2 | 5016 |
| 503 | Bad sequence of commands | \|perman | 2 | 1015 |
| 504 | Command not implemented for that parameter | \| \|perman | 2 | 4003 |
| 530 | Not logged in | \|perman | 2 | 2020 |
| 532 | Need account for storing files | \|perman | 2 | 2008 |
| 550 | Requested action not taken; file unavailable (e.g., file not found, no access) | \| \| \|perman | 2 | 3013 |
| 551 | Requested action aborted, page type | \| \|perman | 2 | 5002 |
| 552 | Requested file action aborted, exceeded storage allocation | \| \|perman | 2 | 9 |

```
      553       Requested file action not taken,   |
                file name not allowed              |perman   2    3024
```

## 9.2.  FTAM Parameters to FTP Reply Codes

This section presents the set of mappings between FTAM diagnostic
parameters and their equivalent FTP reply codes.  Gateway support for
these mappings is recommended, but not required.  As previously
mentioned, type 0 is an informative error type that may be returned
with a "Success" action result, type 1 is a transient error type, and
type 2 is a permanent error type.

```
      FTAM Diagnostic                                     |FTP Reply Code
                                                          |
      Type     Id   Reason                                |
      ----------------------------------------------------+--------
                                                          |
      1,2      0    No reason                             |   421
      0        1    Responder error                       |   211
      1,2      1    Responder error                       |   421
      1,2      2    System shutdown                       |   421
      0        3    FTAM mgmt problem, unspecific         |   211
      1,2      3    FTAM mgmt problem, unspecific         |   425
      0        4    FTAM mgmt, bad account                |   221
      2        4    FTAM mgmt, bad account                |   532
      0        5    FTAM mgmt, security not passed        |   211
      2        5    FTAM mgmt, security not passed        |   530
      0        6    Delay may be encountered              |   211
      0        7    Initiator error, unspecific           |   211
      1,2      7    Initiator error, unspecific           |   421
      0        8    Subsequent error                      |   211
      1,2      8    Subsequent error                      |   421
      0        9    Temporal insufficiency of resources|   211
      1,2      9    Temporal insufficiency of resources|   452
      1,2      10   Access req. violates VFS security   |   550
      1,2      11   Access req. violates local security|   550
      2        1000 Conflicting parameter values         |   504
      2        1001 Unsupported parameter values         |   504
      2        1002 Mandatory parameter not set          |   504
      2        1003 Unsupported parameter                |   504
      2        1004 Duplicated parameter                 |   504
      2        1005 Illegal parameter type               |   504
      2        1006 Unsupported parameter types          |   504
      2        1007 FTAM protocol err., unspecific       |   426
      2        1008 FTAM protocol err., procedure err    |   426
      2        1009 FTAM protocol err., funct. unit err|   426
      2        1010 FTAM protocol err., corruption err.|   426
```

```
2          1011 Lower layer failure            |   426
1,2        1012 Lower layer addressing error   |   426
1,2        1013 Timeout                         |   426
1,2        1014 System shutdown                 |   426
2          1015 Illegal grouping sequence       |   503
2          1016 Grouping threshold violation    |   503
2          1017 Inconsistent PDU request        |   503
2          2000 Association with user not allowed |  532
2          2002 Unsupported service class       |   504
0          2003 Unsupported functional unit     |   211
2          2003 Unsupported functional unit     |   502
0          2004 Attribute group error, unspecific |  211
1,2        2004 Attribute group error, unspecific |  504
2          2005 Attribute group not supported   |   504
0          2006 Attribute group not allowed     |   211
2          2006 Attribute group not allowed     |   504
0          2007 Bad account                     |   211
2          2007 Bad account                     |   532
0          2008 Association management, unspecific | 211
1,2        2008 Association management, unspecific | 532
2          2009 Association management, bad address| 532
1,2        2010 Association management, bad account| 532
0          2011 Checkpoint window error, too large | 211
2          2011 Checkpoint window error, too large | 426
0          2012 Checkpoint window error, too small | 211
2          2012 Checkpoint window error, too small | 426
0          2013 Checkpoint window error, unsupp. |   211
2          2013 Checkpoint window error, unsupp. |   504
0          2014 Communications QoS not supported |   211
1,2        2014 Communications QoS not supported |   504
2          2015 Initiator identity unacceptable |   532
0          2016 Context management refused       |   211
0          2017 Rollback not available           |   211
0          2018 Contents type list cut by        |
                responder                        |   211
0          2019 Contents type list by            |
                Presentation Service             |   211
2          2020 Invalid filestore password       |   530
2          2021 Incompatible service classes      |   530
1,2        3000 Filename not found                |   550
1,2        3001 Selection attributes not matched  |   550
2          3002 Initial attributes not possible   |   550
2          3003 Bad attribute name                |   550
1,2        3004 Non-existent file                 |   550
1,2        3005 File already exists               |   553
1,2        3006 File cannot be created            |   553
1,2        3007 File cannot be deleted            |   553
0          3008 Concurrency control not available |   211
```

| 2   | 3008 Concurrency control not available | | 503 |
|-----|------------------------------------------|---|-----|
| 0   | 3009 Concurrency control not supported | | 211 |
| 2   | 3009 Concurrency control not supported | | 502 |
| 0   | 3010 Concurrency control not possible | | 211 |
| 2   | 3010 Concurrency control not possible | | 503 |
| 0   | 3011 More restrictive lock | | 211 |
| 1   | 3011 More restrictive lock | | 450 |
| 1,2 | 3012 File busy | | 450 |
| 1,2 | 3013 File not available | | 450 |
| 0   | 3014 Access control not available | | 211 |
| 1,2 | 3014 Access control not available | | 503 |
| 0   | 3015 Access control not supported | | 211 |
| 1,2 | 3015 Access control not supported | | 502 |
| 0   | 3016 Access control inconsistent | | 211 |
| 1,2 | 3016 Access control inconsistent | | 503 |
| 0   | 3017 Filename truncated | | 211 |
| 0   | 3018 Initial attributes altered | | 211 |
| 1,2 | 3019 Bad account | | 532 |
| 0   | 3020 Override selected existing file | | 211 |
| 0   | 3021 Override deleted and recreated | | 211 |
| 0   | 3022 Create override deleted and recreate file with new attributes | | 211 |
| 1,2 | 3023 Create override, not possible | | 553 |
| 1,2 | 3024 Ambiguous file specification | | 553 |
| 2   | 3025 Invalid create password | | 550 |
| 2   | 3026 Invalid delete password on override | | 550 |
| 2   | 3027 Bad attribute value | | 550 |
| 2   | 3028 Requested access violation | | 550 |
| 2   | 3029 Functional unit not available for requested access | | 550 |
| 0   | 3030 File created but not selected | | 211 |
| 1   | 3030 Invalid create password | | 550 |
| 0   | 4000 Attribute non-existent | | 211 |
| 1,2 | 4000 Attribute non-existent | | 501 |
| 1,2 | 4001 Attribute cannot be read | | 504 |
| 1,2 | 4002 Attribute cannot be changed | | 504 |
| 1,2 | 4003 Attribute not supported | | 504 |
| 2   | 4004 Bad attribute name | | 501 |
| 2   | 4005 Bad attribute value | | 501 |
| 0   | 4006 Attribute partially supported | | 211 |
| 0   | 4007 Additional set attribute value not distinct | | 211 |
| 1,2 | 5000 Bad FADU, unspecific | | 550 |
| 2   | 5001 Bad FADU, size error | | 501 |
| 2   | 5002 Bad FADU, type error | | 551 |
| 2   | 5003 Bad FADU, poorly specified | | 501 |
| 2   | 5004 Bad FADU, bad location | | 550 |
| 0   | 5005 FADU does not exist | | 550 |

```
1            5005 FADU does not exist              |    550
0            5006 FADU not available, unspecific   |    550
1,2          5006 FADU not available, unspecific   |    550
1,2          5007 FADU not available for reading   |    550
1,2          5008 FADU not available for writing   |    550
1,2          5009 FADU not available for location  |    550
1,2          5010 FADU not available for erasure   |    550
1,2          5011 FADU cannot be inserted          |    550
1,2          5012 FADU cannot be replaced          |    550
0            5013 FADU cannot be located           |    550
1,2          5013 FADU cannot be located           |    550
2            5014 Bad data element type            |    550
1,2          5015 Operation not available          |    500
1,2          5016 Operation not supported          |    502
0            5017 Operation inconsistent           |    211
2            5017 Operation inconsistent           |    503
0            5018 Concurrency control not available |   211
1,2          5018 Concurrency control not available |   503
0            5019 Concurrency control not supported |   211
2            5019 Concurrency control not supported |   502
0            5020 Concurrency control inconsistent |    211
2            5020 Concurrency control inconsistent |    503
0            5021 Processing mode not available    |    211
1,2          5021 Processing mode not available    |    503
0            5022 Processing mode not supported    |    211
2            5022 Processing mode not supported    |    504
0            5023 Processing mode inconsistent     |    211
2            5023 Processing mode inconsistent     |    503
0            5024 Access context not available     |    211
2            5024 Access context not available     |    503
0            5025 Access context not supported     |    211
2            5025 Access context not supported     |    504
1,2          5026 Bad write, unspecific            |    550
1,2          5027 Bad read, unspecific             |    550
0            5028 Local failure, unspecific        |    211
1,2          5028 Local failure, unspecific        |    451
0            5029 Local failure, filespace exhausted |  211
1,2          5029 Local failure, filespace exhausted |  552
0            5030 Local failure, data corrupted    |    211
1,2          5030 Local failure, data corrupted    |    451
0            5031 Local failure, data corrupted    |    211
1,2          5031 Local failure, data corrupted    |    451
2            5032 Future file size exceeded        |    451
0            5034 Future file size increased       |    211
0            5035 Functional unit invalid in       |
                  processing mode                   |    211
2            5035 Functional unit invalid in       |
                  processing mode                   |    503
```

| 0   | 5036 Contents type inconsistent          | | 211 |
| 2   | 5036 Contents type inconsistent          | | 503 |
| 0   | 5037 Contents type simplified            | | 211 |
| 0   | 5038 Duplicate FADU name                 | | 211 |
| 1,2 | 5039 Damage to select/open regime        | | 553 |
| 1,2 | 5040 FADU locking not available on file  | | 450 |
| 1,2 | 5041 FADU locked by another user         | | 450 |

9.3.  Future Mapping Problem

At some point in the future, the FTAM <Responding Presentation
Address> parameter may be used for purposes other than the current
use of passing the final destination address in the FTAM-Initiated
gateway service [NIST86].  If this happens, the destination address
will have to be passed in another location, such as in the "@host"
portion of the <Initiator Identity>.  Currently, the FTP-FTAM gateway
specification permits either mechanism for storage of the ultimate
destination address.

9.4.  Error Handling

The minimal acceptable solution for FTAM-Initiated service errors is
to map FTP failures to FTAM "Unrecoverable error" and return the FTP
diagnostic string in the FTAM <Further Details> field.  Similarly for
FTP-Initiated service errors, the minimal acceptable solution is to
return reply code 221, "Service closing control connection, Logged
out if appropriate".  While this minimal solution is acceptable, the
recommended approach for Gateway developers is to implement the
mappings presented in Section 9.1, FTP Reply Codes to FTAM
Parameters, and Section 9.2, FTAM Parameters to FTP Reply Codes.

10.  Implementation and Configuration Guidelines

The intent of this specification is to specify the required
characteristics and functions of an FTP-FTAM gateway.  The specific
approach taken to realize these specifications in an operational
gateway are left to the discretion of the implementor.  We do take
the liberty, however, of suggesting several ideas concerning the
configuration and implementation of such gateways.

10.1.  Robustness

The gateway should be robust enough to handle situations where a
subset of the FTP and/or FTAM protocols are implemented on a host.

The gateway should support multiple concurrent FTP and FTAM
connections.

These are requirements for gateway implementations.

10.2.  Well-Known TCP/IP Port

It is recommended that the FTP-Initiated gateway process listen on
TCP/IP port 21, the well-known port for FTP listener processes.  As
the gateway computer is primarily intended to provide gateway
services,  use of this port will alleviate the need for gateway users
to specify the desired port when they connect to the gateway.  The
standard FTP server listener process can then be moved to another
port that is known to those users (e.g., System Administrators)
requiring FTP-to-FTP access to the gateway computer.

10.3.  Gateway Listener Processes

To simplify the administrative overhead on the gateway computer
system, it is recommended that the FTP-Initiated service and FTAM-
Initiated gateway listener processes be merged into a single
executable module.  This single daemon will act as the one and only
gateway listener processes.  As connections were established with
hosts, other processes would be created.

10.4.  Implementation Testing

To assist in the development and evaluation of FTP-FTAM gateway
prototypes, NIST has developed a test system to evaluate a gateway's
conformance to the protocol standards [NIST88].

10.5.  POSIX File Naming and Organization

The OSI profiles do not define a standard manner for an FTAM
Responder to return file names.

To avoid unnecessary complexity, proprietary file systems are not
addressed in these mappings.  Gateway support for POSIX file naming
and organization conventions is required; i.e., files are assumed to
be organized in a hierarchical structure in which all of the non-
terminal nodes are directories and all of the terminal nodes are any
other type of file.

11.  Security Considerations

The gateway system may place the burden of authentication on the
destination system.  However, the gateway must accommodate the
passing through of all authentication parameters.  The authentication
parameters of each protocol are applied at the destination and no
additional parameters are needed for authentication at the gateway.
As such, no gateway password file is required to support gateway

functions.

It is anticipated that the requirement for a strong authentication
mechanism will soon replace the most currently used, userid and
password mechanism.  The U.S. National Security Agency (NSA) has
already prototyped and has plans field a Message Secure Protocol
(MSP) as part of the Defense Message System (DMS) Program which will
soon become the Department of Defense (DoD) mandatory messaging
system.  MSP utilizes a public key encryption-like mechanism which
will be used to authenticate users and allow signed operations.  The
current philosophy is to use this same mechanism for all
authentication and access control situations, such as logging onto
remote hosts or gateways.  Detailed specifications for Pre-MSP, used
in the unclassified though sensitive arena, are scheduled to be
published in the first quarter of 1993.  The requirement for gateways
to process PMSP and MSP strong authentication mechanisms will be part
of all future DoD procurements.

12.  References

   [ISO8571-1]   Information processing systems - Open Systems
                 Interconnection - File Transfer, Access and
                 Management, Part 1: General Introduction, International
                 Standards Organization for Standards, First Edition,
                 October 1988.

   [ISO8571-2]   Information processing systems - Open Systems
                 Interconnection - File Transfer, Access and Management,
                 Part 2: Virtual Filestore Definition, International
                 Standards Organization for Standards, First Edition,
                 October 1988.

   [ISO8571-3]   Information processing systems - Open Systems
                 Interconnection - File Transfer, Access and Management,
                 Part 3: File Service Definition, International Standards
                 Organization for Standards, First Edition, October 1988.

   [ISO8571-4]   Information processing systems - Open Systems
                 Interconnection - File Transfer, Access and Management,
                 Part 4: File Protocol Specification, International
                 Standards Organization for Standards, First Edition,
                 October 1988.

   [ISO8571-5]   Information processing systems - Open Systems
                 Interconnection - File Transfer, Access and Management,
                 Part 5: Protocol Implementation Conformance Statement,
                 International Standards Organization for Standards,
                 First Edition.

[KILLE92]  Hardcastle-Kille, S., "Using the OSI Directory to achieve
           User Friendly Naming", OSI-DS 24 (v1.1), October 1992.

[MITRE87]  Scott, J., "An FTP/FTAM Application Bridge, An FTAM/FTAM
           (MTR-87W00186)", The MITRE Corporation, July 1987.

[NETWRX90a]  Mindel, J., "Gateway Technical Specification" Open
             Networks, Inc. (formerly NetWorks One), 28 February 1990.

[NETWRX90b]  Mindel, J., "FTP Gateway User's Guide", Open
             Networks, Inc. (formerly NetWorks One), 28 February 1990.

[NIST86]   Wallace, M, et. al., "A Gateway Architecture Between FTP
           and FTAM (ICST/SNA86-6)", National Institute of Standards
           and Technology, U.S. Department of Commerce, July 1986.

[NIST88]   A Test System for Implementations of FTAM/FTP Gateways:
           Final Report Part 1, National Institute of Standards and
           Technology, U.S. Chamber of Commerce, October 1988.

[NIST91]   CSL Bulletin: File Transfer, Access, and Management,
           National Institute of Standards and Technology, U.S.
           Chamber of Commerce, July 1991.

[NIST92]   Stable Implementation Agreements for Open Systems
           Interconnection Protocols: Part 9 - FTAM Phase 2, Output
           from the March 1992 Open Systems Environment Implementors'
           Workshop (OIW), March 1992.

[RFC959]   Postel, J., and J. Reynolds, "File Transfer  Protocol
           (FTP), STD 9, RFC 959, USC/Information Sciences Institute,
           October 1985.

[RFC1101]  Mockapetris, P., "DNS Encoding of Network Names and other
           Types",  RFC 1101, USC/Information Sciences Institute,
           April 1989.

[RFC1279]  Hardcastle-Kille, S., "X.500 and Domain", RFC 1279,
           University College London, November 1991.

[ROSE90]   Rose, M., "The Open Book: A Practical Perspective on OSI",
           Prentice-Hall Inc., 1990.

13.   Authors' Addresses

Joshua L. Mindel
Open Networks, Inc.
11490 Commerce Park Dr., Suite 205
Reston, Virginia 22091  USA

Phone:   (703) 648-0013
Email: mindel@netwrx1.nw1.com


Robert L. Slaski
Open Networks, Inc.
11490 Commerce Park Dr., Suite 205
Reston, Virginia 22091  USA

Phone:   (703) 648-0013
Email: slaski@netwrx1.nw1.com

Network Working Group                                    S. Bellovin
Request for Comments: 1579                      AT&T Bell Laboratories
Category: Informational                               February 1994

Firewall-Friendly FTP

Status of this Memo

Abstract

   This memo describes a suggested change to the behavior of FTP client
   programs.  No protocol modifications are required, though we outline
   some that might be useful.

Overview and Rational

   The FTP protocol [1] uses a secondary TCP connection for actual
   transmission of files.  By default, this connection is set up by an
   active open from the FTP server to the FTP client.  However, this
   scheme does not work well with packet filter-based firewalls, which
   in general cannot permit incoming calls to random port numbers.

   If, on the other hand, clients use the PASV command, the data channel
   will be an outgoing call through the firewall.  Such calls are more
   easily handled, and present fewer problems.

The Gory Details

   The FTP specification says that by default, all data transfers should
   be over a single connection.  An active open is done by the server,
   from its port 20 to the same port on the client machine as was used
   for the control connection.  The client does a passive open.

   For better or worse, most current FTP clients do not behave that way.
   A new connection is used for each transfer; to avoid running afoul of
   TCP's TIMEWAIT state, the client picks a new port number each time
   and sends a PORT command announcing that to the server.

   Neither scenario is firewall-friendly.  If a packet filter is used
   (as, for example, provided by most modern routers), the data channel
   requests appear as incoming calls to unknown ports.  Most firewalls
   are constructed to allow incoming calls only to certain believed-to-
   be-safe ports, such as SMTP.  The usual compromise is to block only

the "server" area, i.e., port numbers below 1024.  But that strategy
is risky; dangerous services such as X Windows live at higher-
numbered ports.

Outgoing calls, on the other hand, present fewer problems, either for
the firewall administrator or for the packet filter.  Any TCP packet
with the ACK bit set cannot be the packet used to initiate a TCP
connection; filters can be configured to pass such packets in the
outbound direction only.  We thus want to change the behavior of FTP
so that the data channel is implemented as a call from the client to
the server.

Fortunately, the necessary mechanisms already exist in the protocol.
If the client sends a PASV command, the server will do a passive TCP
open on some random port, and inform the client of the port number.
The client can then do an active open to establish the connection.

There are a few FTP servers in existence that do not honor the PASV
command.  While this is unfortunate (and in violation of STD 3, RFC
1123 [2]), it does not pose a problem.  Non-conforming
implementations will return a "500 Command not understood" message;
it is a simple matter to fall back to current behavior.  While it may
not be possible to talk to such sites through a firewall, that would
have been the case had PASV not been adopted.

Recommendation

We recommend that vendors convert their FTP client programs
(including FTP proxy agents such as Gopher [3] daemons) to use PASV
instead of PORT.  There is no reason not to use it even for non-
firewall transfers, and adopting it as standard behavior will make
the client more useful in a firewall environment.

STD 3, RFC 1123 notes that the format of the response to a PASV
command is not well-defined.  We therefore recommend that FTP clients
and servers follow the recommendations of that RFC for solving this
problem.

Discussion

Given the behavior of most current FTP clients, the use of PASV does
not cause any additional messages to be sent.  In all cases, a
transfer operation is preceded by an extra exchange between the
client and the server; it does not matter if that exchange involves a
PORT command or a PASV command.

There is some extra overhead with Gopher-style clients; since they
transfer exactly one file per control channel connection, they do not

need to use PORT commands.  If this is a serious concern, the Gopher
proxy should be located on the outside of the firewall, so that it is
not hampered by the packet filter's restrictions.

If we accept that clients should always perform active opens, it
might be worthwhile enhancing the FTP protocol to eliminate the extra
exchange entirely.  At startup time, the client could send a new
command APSV ("all passive"); a server that implements this option
would always do a passive open.  A new reply code 151 would be issued
in response to all file transfer requests not preceded by a PORT or
PASV command; this message would contain the port number to use for
that transfer.  A PORT command could still be sent to a server that
had previously received APSV; that would override the default
behavior for the next transfer operation, thus permitting third-party
transfers.

Implementation Status

At least two independent implementations of the modified clients
exist.  Source code to one is freely available.  To our knowledge,
APSV has not been implemented.

Security Considerations

Some people feel that packet filters are dangerous, since they are
very hard to configure properly.  We agree.  But they are quite
popular.  Another common complaint is that permitting arbitrary
outgoing calls is dangerous, since it allows free export of sensitive
data through a firewall.  Some firewalls impose artificial bandwidth
limits to discourage this.  While a discussion of the merits of this
approach is beyond the scope of this memo, we note that the sort of
application-level gateway necessary to implement a bandwidth limiter
could be implemented just as easily using PASV as with PORT.

Using PASV does enhances the security of gateway machines, since they
no longer need to create ports that an outsider might connect to
before the real FTP client.  More importantly, the protocol between
the client host and the firewall can be simplified, if there is no
need to specify a "create" operation.

Concerns have been expressed that this use of PASV just trades one
problem for another.  With it, the FTP server must accept calls to
random ports, which could pose an equal problem for its firewall.  We
believe that this is not a serious issue, for several reasons.

First, there are many fewer FTP servers than there are clients.  It
is possible to secure a small number of special-purpose machines,
such as gateways and organizational FTP servers.  The firewall's

filters can be configured to allow access to just these machines. Further precautions can be taken by modifying the FTP server so that it only uses very high-numbered ports for the data channel. It is comparatively easy to ensure that no dangerous services live in a given port range. Again, this is feasible because of the small number of servers.

References

    [1] Postel, J., and J. Reynolds, "File Transfer Protocol", STD 1, RFC
        959, USC/Information Sciences Institute, October 1985.

    [2] Braden, R., Editor, "Requirements for Internet Hosts -
        Application and Support", STD 3, RFC 1123, USC/Information
        Sciences Institute, October 1989.

    [3] Anklesaria, F., McCahill, M., Lindner, P., Johnson, D., Torrey,
        D., and B. Alberti, "The Internet Gopher Protocol (a distributed
        document search and retrieval protocol)", RFC 1436, University of
        Minnesota, March 1993.

Author's Address

        Steven M. Bellovin
        AT&T Bell Laboratories
        600 Mountain Avenue
        Murray Hill, NJ   07974

        Phone: (908) 582-5886
        EMail: smb@research.att.com

**RFC 1579**

**4**

Network Working Group                                          P. Deutsch
Request for Comments: 1635                                     A. Emtage
FYI: 24                                                          Bunyip
Category: Informational                                        A. Marine
                                                               NASA NAIC
                                                                May 1994

How to Use Anonymous FTP

Status of this Memo

Abstract

   This document provides information for the novice Internet user about
   using the File Transfer Protocol (FTP).  It explains what FTP is,
   what anonymous FTP is, and what an anonymous FTP archive site is.  It
   shows a sample anonymous FTP session.  It also discusses common ways
   files are packaged for efficient storage and transmission.

Acknowledgements

   This document is the result of work done in the Internet Anonymous
   FTP Archives (IAFA) working group of the IETF.  Special thanks are
   due to Mark Baushke (Cisco), John Curran (BBN), Aydin Edguer (CWRU),
   Rafal Maszkowski (Onsala Space Observatory), Marsha Perrott
   (PREPnet), Bob Peterson (Texas Instruments), Nathan Torkington
   (Victoria University of Wellington), and Stephen Tihor (NYU) for
   excellent comments and contributions.

What is FTP?

   FTP refers to the File Transfer Protocol [1], one of the protocols
   within the TCP/IP protocol suite used on the Internet.  The File
   Transfer Protocol makes it possible to transfer files from one
   computer (or host) on the Internet to another.  There are many FTP
   implementations built on the specification of the FTP protocol.  A
   user of an FTP program must log in to both hosts in order to transfer
   a file from one to the other.

   It is common for a user with files on more than one host to use the
   FTP program to transfer files from one host to another.  In this
   case, the user has an account on both hosts involved, so he has
   passwords for both hosts.

However, Internet users may also take advantage of a wealth of
information available from archive sites by using a general purpose
account called "anonymous FTP".

What is an Archive Site?

An archive site is a host that acts as a repository of information,
much like a conventional library.  Information stored on these
Internet hosts is made available for users to transfer to their local
sites.  Users run software to identify this information and transfer
it to their own hosts.  Such a transfer is done with a program that
implements the File Transfer Protocol (FTP).

What is Anonymous FTP?

Anonymous FTP is a means by which archive sites allow general access
to their archives of information.  These sites create a special
account called "anonymous".  User "anonymous" has limited access
rights to the archive host, as well as some operating restrictions.
In fact, the only operations allowed are logging in using FTP,
listing the contents of a limited set of directories, and retrieving
files.  Some sites limit the contents of a directory listing an
anonymous user can see as well.  Note that "anonymous" users are not
usually allowed to transfer files TO the archive site, but can only
retrieve files from such a site.

Traditionally, this special anonymous user account accepts any string
as a password, although it is common to use either the password
"guest" or one's electronic mail (e-mail) address.  Some archive
sites now explicitly ask for the user's e-mail address and will not
allow login with the "guest" password.  Providing an e-mail address
is a courtesy that allows archive site operators to get some idea of
who is using their services.

What Information Do You Need to Know?

To retrieve a specific file, a user needs to know what host it is on,
and the pathname of the file.  A pathname tells the directory (and
possibly subdirectories) that house the file, and the name of the
file.  Often discussions of available files will not specifically
say, "This file is available for anonymous FTP from X host with Y
pathname".  However, if a file is publicly announced as available and
referred to as something like pub/good-stuff on nisc.sri.com, it is a
good assumption that you can try to transfer it.

You may also need to know if your machine uses an ASCII, EBCDIC, or
other character set to know how likely a transfer of binary
information will work, or whether such a transfer will require other

keywords, such as is true for TENEX.

In the general case, you may assume that an ASCII transfer will
always do the right thing for plain text files. However, more and
more information is being stored in various compressed formats (which
are discussed later in this document), so knowing the binary
characteristics of your machine may be important.

A Sample Session

To start an FTP session on a UNIX or VMS host, you type "ftp" and the
host name or host IP address of the machine to which you want to
connect. For example, if you wish to access the NASA Network
Applications and Information Center archive site, you would normally
execute one of the following commands at the UNIX prompt:

              ftp naic.nasa.gov
     or
              ftp 128.102.128.6

Observe that the first form uses the fully-qualified domain name and
the second uses the Internet address for the same host.

The following is an example of connecting to the naic.nasa.gov host
to retrieve STD 9, RFC 959, "File Transfer Protocol (FTP)" [1].

Note several things about the session.

  1. Every response the FTP program at the archive site gives
     is preceded by a number. These numbers are called
     Reply Codes and are defined in the FTP specification,
     RFC 959. The text that accompanies these reply codes
     can vary in different FTP implementations, and usually does.

     Also note that some FTP client implementations (e.g., MVS
     systems) may not echo the reply codes or text as
     transmitted from the remote host. They may generate their
     own status lines or just hide the non-fatal replies
     from you. For the purposes of this document, the more
     popular UNIX interface to the FTP client will be
     presented.

  2. The password you type is never shown on your screen.

  3. It is possible to "browse" in archives, but most often users
     already know the pathname of the file they want. The pathname
     for RFC 959 on this host is files/rfc/rfc959.txt. In the

example, we first connect to the 'files/rfc' directory (cd
files/rfc), then get the specific file we know we want.  If you
do not know the name of the file you want, a file called README
or something similar (00README.1ST, AAREAD.ME, INDEX, etc.) is
probably the one to retrieve first.

```
atlas.arc.nasa.gov% ftp naic.nasa.gov
Connected to naic.nasa.gov.
220 naic.nasa.gov FTP server (Wed May 4 12:15:15 PDT 1994) ready.
Name (naic.nasa.gov:amarine): anonymous
331 Guest login ok, send your complete e-mail address as password.
Password:
230-------------------------------------------------------------------
230-Welcome to the NASA Network Applications and Info Center Archive
230-
230-      Access to NAIC's online services is also available through:
230-
230-          Gopher          - naic.nasa.gov (port 70)
230-      World-Wide-Web - http://naic.nasa.gov/naic/naic-home.html
230-
230-          If you experience any problems please send email to
230-
230-                          naic@nasa.gov
230-
230-                      or call +1 (800) 858-9947
230-------------------------------------------------------------------
230-
230-Please read the file README
230-  it was last modified on Fri Dec 10 13:06:33 1993 - 165 days ago
230 Guest login ok, access restrictions apply.
ftp> cd files/rfc
250-Please read the file README.rfc
250-  it was last modified on Fri Jul 30 16:47:29 1993 - 298 days ago
250 CWD command successful.
ftp> get rfc959.txt
200 PORT command successful.
150 Opening ASCII mode data connection for rfc959.txt (147316 bytes).
226 Transfer complete.
local: rfc959.txt remote: rfc959.txt
151249 bytes received in 0.9 seconds (1.6e+02 Kbytes/s)
ftp> quit
221 Goodbye.
atlas.arc.nasa.gov%
```

Variations

   The above example is of the FTP program available on UNIX systems.
   Other operating systems also make FTP programs available.  The actual
   commands you type may vary somewhat with other programs.  However, in
   general, you will do the following with every FTP program:

      - Log in to your local host, and invoke the FTP program.

      - Open a connection to the host (using either the host name
        or its IP address)

      - Once connected to the remote host, log in with username
        "anonymous".

      - Provide either the password "guest" or whatever the password the
        site requests.

      - Issue whatever FTP commands you require, such as those to
        change directories or to retrieve a file.

      - When finished, exit the FTP program, which will close your
        connection to the archive host.

Friendly Servers

   These days, many sites are using a form of FTP that allows them to
   display several lines of explanatory text that help direct users
   through their archive.  The listing of alternative services on
   naic.nasa.gov is an example.  If these effusive servers confuse the
   client you are using, try typing a hyphen ( - ) before your password
   when you log in.  That should disable the verbose mode of the server.

Other FTP Commands

   We have demonstrated some of the commands available with FTP
   programs.  Many others are possible.  For example, once you have
   logged in to a remote host:

      - You may ask the FTP program to display a list of available
        commands, typically by invoking the FTP program without
        arguments and typing "help".

      - You may view the contents of the directory to which you are
        connected.  Type "dir" or "ls" to do so.

      - You may rename a file by using the "get" command's
        optional local file name, which follows the remote file

name on the command line.  You probably should rename a
file when the remote file name exceeds your local file
system's naming constraints, e.g., if the remote file
name is too long.  An example of using the "get" command
to rename a file when transferring it might be "get
really-long-named-file.txt short.txt".

- You may set BINARY mode to transfer executable programs or files
  of data.  Type "binary" to do so.  Usually
  FTP programs assume files use only 7 bits per byte, the norm for
  standard ASCII-encoded files.  The BINARY command allows you to
  transfer files that use the full 8 bits per byte without error,
  but this may have implications on how the file is transferred
  to your local system.

  If you are not sure what format a file is in, you may need to
  transfer it a second time in the other mode (BINARY or ASCII)
  if your first guess is wrong.  The extension at the end of the
  file name may give you a clue.  File name extensions are
  described below.

  Because some machines store text files differently than others,
  you may have to try your luck if you're not sure what format
  a file is in.  A good guess is to try ASCII mode first, if
  you have grounds to suspect the file is a text file.  Otherwise,
  try BINARY mode.  Try TENEX mode as a last resort.

- You may transfer multiple files at the same time.  To set this
  mode, type "mget".  You then supply a file name pattern that
  the remote system understands and it tries to transfer each
  file in turn.  If your local FTP user agent cannot transform
  the remote file names into legal local file names, or if there
  are some files that must be transferred in ASCII mode and others
  that must be transferred in BINARY mode, you may not be able to
  take advantage of this facility.

Full details on the commands and options available are in the FTP
documentation that comes with your system.  You can also type "help"
at the FTP command prompt for a list of command options.

A copy of the UNIX version of the FTP documentation is available from
the online manual.  If your UNIX site has the manuals installed, type
the following at the UNIX prompt:

        % man ftp

The Packaging and Naming of Files

   Several widely used conventions allow for efficient storage and
   transmission of information stored at archive sites.

   Information stored on archive sites is often "transformed" in three
   common ways.  "Compressing" (reducing the size of) the stored
   information makes more space available on the archive, and reduces
   the amount of data actually transferred across the network.
   "Bundling" several files into one larger file maintains the internal
   directory structure of the components, and allows users to transfer
   only one larger object rather than several (sometimes hundreds) of
   smaller files.

   In addition, binary data is often converted into an ASCII format for
   transmission, a process referred to in this document as
   "transformation".  Traditionally, Internet RFC 822-based electronic
   mail and USENET protocols did not allow the transmission of "binary"
   (8-bit) data; therefore, files in binary format had to be transformed
   into printable 7-bit ASCII before being transmission.

   On many systems, various file naming conventions are used to help the
   remote user to determine the format of the stored information without
   first having to retrieve the files.  Below we list the more common
   compression, bundling, and transformation conventions used on the
   Internet.  This list is not intended to be exhaustive.  In all cases
   public domain or freely-available implementations of the programs
   associated with these mechanisms are available on the network.

   1) compress/uncompress

   Filenames terminating in ".Z" normally signify files that have been
   compressed by the standard UNIX Lempel-Ziv "compress" utility.
   There is an equivalent program called "uncompress" to reverse the
   process and return the file to its original state.  No bundling
   mechanism is provided, and the resulting files are always in binary
   format, regardless of the original format of the input data.

   2) atob/btoa

   Performs a transformation of ASCII to binary (atob) and the reverse
   (btoa) in a standard format.  Files so transformed often have
   filenames terminated with ".atob".  No bundling or compression
   mechanisms are used.

3) atox/xtoa

A data transformation standard used to convert binary
files to transferable ASCII format.  Sometimes used in
preference to other similar mechanisms because it is more
space efficient; however, it is not a compression
mechanism per se.  It is just more efficient in the
transformation from one format to the other.  Filenames of
files in this format often have the ".atox" extension.

4) uuencode/uudecode

Transforms binary to ASCII ("uuencode") and the reverse
("uudecode") transformation in a standard manner.
Originally used in the UUCP ("Unix to Unix CoPy")
mail/USENET system.  No bundling or compression mechanisms
are used.  Naming conventions often add a .uu at the end
of the file name.

5) tar/untar

Originally a UNIX based utility for bundling (and
unbundling) several files and directories into (and from)
a single file (the acronym stands for "Tape ARchive").
Standard format provides no compression mechanism.  The
resulting bundled file is always in binary format
regardless of whether the constituent files are binary or
not.  Naming conventions usually hold that the filename of
a "tarfile" contain the sequence ".tar" or "-tar".

6) zip/unzip

Often used in IBM PC environments, these complementary programs
provide both bundling and compression mechanisms.  The resulting
files are always in binary format.  Files resulting from the "zip"
program are by convention terminated with the ".zip" filename
extension.

7) arc/unarc

Often used in IBM PC environments, these complementary programs
provide both bundling and compression mechanisms.  The resulting
files are always in binary format.  Files stored in this format
often have a ".arc" filename extension.

8) binhex

Used in the Apple MacIntosh environment, the binhex
process provides bundling as well as binary to ASCII data
transformations.  Files in this format by convention have
a filename extension of ".hqx".

9) shar

Bourse shell archives package text or binary files into a
single longer file which, when executed, will create the
component files.  Because this format is vulnerable to
misuse, most users use a special tool called unshar to
decode these archives.  By convention, files in this
format have a filename extension of ".shar".

10) VMS_SHARE

DCL archives package text or binary files into a single
longer file which, when executed, will created the
component files.  Because this format is vulnerable to
misuse, care must be take to examine such an archive
before executing it.  By convention, files in this format
have a filename extension of ".shar".

11) Multipart shar/vms_share files

Sometimes these shell archive files are broken into
multiple small parts to simplify their transfer over other
forms of fileservers that share the same archive tree.  In
such cases, the parts of the files are usually suffixed
with a part number (e.g., xyz.01 xyz.02 xyz.03 ... or even
.01-of-05).  Collect all the parts, concatenate them on
your local system, and then apply the procedure listed
above for a simple shar or vms_share file to the
concatenated file you just made.

12) zoo

The zoo program implements compression/decompression and
bundling/unbundling in a single program.  Utilities
supporting the zoo format exist on a wide variety of
systems, including Unix, MS-DOS, Macintosh, OS/2, Atari
ST, and VAX VMS.  Files created by the "zoo" programs by
convention end with the ".zoo" filename extension.  Zoo is
a popular distribution format due to the availability of
free implementations (both source and executable code) on
a wide variety of operating systems.

13) gzip/gunzip

The Free Software Foundation GNU project adopted a variant
of the zip compression mechanism as a substitute for the
compress/uncompress commands.  The resulting files are
always in binary format.  Files resulting from the "gzip"
program are by convention terminated with the ".z" or
".gz" filename extensions.  The gunzip program also
recognizes ".tgz" and ".taz" as shorthands for ".tar.z" or
".tar.Z".  Also, gunzip can recognize and decompress files
created by the gzip, zip, compress, or pack commands.

The GNU project recently began distributing and using the
gzip/gunzip utilities.  Even more recently they changed
the default suffix from .z to .gz, in an attempt to (1)
reduce confusion with .Z, and (2) eliminate a problem with
case-insensitive file systems such as MS-DOS.  The gzip
software is freely redistributable and has been ported to
most UNIX systems, as well as Amiga, Atari, MSDOS, OS2,
and VMS systems.

In some cases, a series of the above processes are performed to
produce the final file as stored on the archive.  In cases where
multiple transformation processes have been used, tradition holds
that the original (base) filename be changed to reflect these
processes, and that the associated filename extensions be added in
the order in which the processes were performed.  For example, a
common procedure is first to bundle the original files and
directories using the "tar" process, then to "compress" the bundled
file.  Starting with a base file name of "foobar", the file name in
the archive would become "foobar.tar.Z".  As this is a binary file,
it would require a further transformation into printable ASCII by a
program such as "uuencode" in order to be transmitted over
traditional email or USENET facilities, so it might finally be called
"foobar.tar.Z.uu."

Some operating systems can not handle multiple periods; in such cases
they are often replaced by hyphen ( - ), underscore ( _ ), or by
detailed instructions in the "read me" files in the directories.

Compress and Tar

Here is an example of the use of the "compress/uncompress" and
"tar/untar" programs.

Suppose "patch" is a useful public domain program for applying
program patches and updates.  You find this file at an archive site
as "patch.tar.Z".  Now you know that the ".Z" indicates that the file

was compressed with the UNIX "compress" command, and the ".tar"
indicates that it was tar'ed using the UNIX "tar" tape archive
command.

First retrieve the file onto your machine using anonymous FTP.  To
unpack this program, you would first  uncompress it by typing:

    uncompress patch.tar.Z

This will uncompress the file, and in the process, rename it to
"patch.tar".  You can then execute the "tar" command to extract the
individual files.

In the example of patch.tar, you could invoke the command as:

    %tar xvf patch.tar

The files would be extracted (that's the 'x' argument to tar) from
the file patch.tar (that's the 'f' argument).  Because we use the 'v'
(for verbose) argument, the name of each file is printed as it is
extracted.  When tar is complete you should have all the files that
make up the "patch" program in your working directory.

Etiquette

   Not every site that supports FTP permits anonymous tranfers.  It is
   wrong to try to get files from systems that have not advertised the
   availability of such a service.

   Remember that Internet site administrators for archive sites have
   made their systems available out of a sense of community.  Rarely are
   they fully compensated for the time and effort it takes to administer
   such a site.  There are some things users can do to make their jobs
   somewhat easier, such as checking with local support personnel first
   if problems occur before asking the archive administrator for help.

   Most archive machines perform other functions as well.  Please
   respect the needs of their primary users and restrict your FTP access
   to non-prime hours (generally between 1900 and 0600 hours local time
   for that site) whenever possible.  It is especially important to
   remember this for sites located on another continent or across a
   significant body of water because most such links are relatively slow
   and heavily loaded.

In addition, some sites offering anonymous FTP limit the number of concurrent anonymous FTP logins.  If your attempt to log onto such a site results in an error message to the effect that too many anonymous FTP users are online, you should wait a while before attempting another connection rather than retrying immediately.

To reduce redundant storage, you should find out how to make useful the files you fetch using FTP available to your entire organization. If you retrieve and test a program that turns out to be useful, you should probably ask your administrator to consider making the program generally available, which will reduce the redundant effort and disk space resulting from multiple individuals installing the same package in their personal directories.

If you find an interesting file or program on an archive site, tell others about it.  You should not copy the file or program to your own archive unless you are willing to keep your copy current.

References

[1] Postel, J., and J. Reynolds, "File Transfer Protocol (FTP)", STD
    9, RFC 959, USC/Information Sciences Institute, October 1985.

Security Considerations

   Security issues are not discussed in this memo.

Authors' Addresses

    Peter Deutsch
    Bunyip Information Systems
    266 Blvd. Neptune
    Dorval, Quebec, H9S 2L4
    Canada

    Phone: (514) 398-3709
    EMail: peterd@bunyip.com


    Alan Emtage
    Bunyip Information Systems
    266 Blvd. Neptune
    Dorval, Quebec, H9S 2L4
    Canada

    Phone: (514) 398-3709
    EMail: bajan@bunyip.com


    April N. Marine
    NASA NAIC
    M/S 204-14
    Ames Research Center
    Moffett Field, CA 94035-1000

    Phone: (415) 604-0762
    EMail: amarine@atlas.arc.nasa.gov

Network Working Group                              D. Piscitello
Request for Comments: 1639                    Core Competence, Inc.
Obsoletes: 1545                                        June 1994
Category: Experimental

FTP Operation Over Big Address Records (FOOBAR)

Status of this Memo

Abstract

   This paper describes a convention for specifying address families
   other than the default Internet address family in FTP commands and
   replies.

Introduction

   In the File Transfer Protocol (STD 9, RFC 959), the PORT command
   argument <host-port> specifies the data port to be used to establish
   a data connection for FTP (STD 9, RFC 959).  This argument is also
   used in the PASV reply to request the server-DTP to listen on a data
   port other than its default data port.  This RFC specifies a method
   for assigning addresses other than 32-bit IPv4 addresses to data
   ports through the specification of a "long Port (LPRT)" command and
   "Long Passive (LPSV)" reply, each having as its argument a <long-
   host-port>, which allows for additional address families, variable
   length network addresses and variable length port numbers.

   This is a general solution, applicable for all "next generation" IP
   alternatives, as well as for other network protocols than IP.  This
   revision also extends FTP to allow for its operation over transport
   interfaces other than TCP.

Acknowledgments

   Many thanks to all the folks in the IETF who casually mentioned how
   to do this, but who left it to me to write this RFC.  Special thanks
   to Rich Colella, Bob Ullmann, Steve Lunt, Jay Israel, Jon Postel,
   Shawn Ostermann, and Tae Kyong Song, who contributed to this work.

1.  Background

The PORT command of File Transfer Protocol allows users to specify an
address other than the default data port for the transport connection
over which data are transferred. The PORT command syntax is:

    PORT <SP> <host-port> <CRLF>

The <host-port> argument is the concatenation of a 32-bit internet
<host-address> and a 16-bit TCP <port-address>. This address
information is broken into 8-bit fields and the value of each field
is transmitted as a decimal number (in character string
representation).  The fields are separated by commas.  A PORT command
is thus of the general form "PORT h1,h2,h3,h4,p1,p2", where h1 is the
high order 8 bits of the internet host address.

The <host-port> argument is also used by the PASV reply, and in
certain negative completion replies.

To accommodate larger network addresses anticipated for all IP "next
generation" alternatives, and to accommodate FTP operation over
network and transport protocols other than IP, new commands and reply
codes are needed for FTP.

2.  The LPRT Command

The LPRT command allows users to specify a "long" address for the
transport connection over which data are transferred. The LPRT
command syntax is:

    LPRT <SP> <long-host-port> <CRLF>

The <long-host-port> argument is the concatenation of the following
fields;

o   an 8-bit <address-family> argument (af)

o   an 8-bit <host-address-length> argument (hal)

o   a <host-address> of <host-address-length> (h1, h2, ...)

o   an 8-bit <port-address-length> (pal)

o   a <port-address> of <port-address-length> (p1, p2, ...)

The initial values assigned to the <address-family> argument take the
value of the version number of IP (see Assigned Numbers, STD 2, RFC
1340); values in the range of 0-15 decimal are thus reserved for IP

and assigned by IANA.  Values in the range 16-255 are available for
the IANA to assign to all other network layer protocols over which
FTP may be operated.

Relevant assigned <address-family> numbers for FOOBAR are:

```
    Decimal           Keyword
    ------            -------
    0                 reserved
    1-3               unassigned
    4                 Internet Protocol (IP)
    5                 ST Datagram Mode
    6                 SIP
    7                 TP/IX
    8                 PIP
    9                 TUBA
    10-14             unassigned
    15                reserved
    16                Novell IPX
```

The value of each field is broken into 8-bit fields and the value of
each field is transmitted as an unsigned decimal number (in character
string representation, note that negative numbers are explicitly not
permitted). The fields are separated by commas.

A LPRT command is thus of the general form

    LPRT af,hal,h1,h2,h3,h4...,pal,p1,p2...

where h1 is the high order 8 bits of the internet host address, and
p1 is the high order 8 bits of the port number (transport address).

3.   The LPSV Command

The L(ONG) PASSIVE command requests the server-DTP to listen on a
data port other than its default data port and to wait for a
connection rather than initiate one upon receipt of a transfer
command. The response to this command includes the address family,
host address length indicator, host address, port address length, and
port address of the listener process at the server. The reply code
and text for entering the passive mode using a long address is 228
(Interpretation according to FTP is: positive completion reply 2yz,
connections x2z, passive mode entered using long address xy8).

The suggested text message to accompany this reply code is:

 228 Entering Long Passive Mode
     (af, hal, h1, h2, h3,..., pal, p1, p2...)

4.  Permanent Negative Completion Reply Codes

The negative completion reply codes that are associated with syntax errors in the PORT and PASV commands are appropriate for the LPRT and LPSV commands (500, 501). An additional negative completion reply code is needed to distinguish the case where a host supports the LPRT or LPSV command, but does not support the address family specified.

Of the FTP function groupings defined for reply codes (syntax, information, connections, authentication and accounting, and file system), "connections" seems the most logical choice; thus, an additional negative command completion reply code, 521 is added, with the following suggested textual message:

    521 Supported address families are (af1, af2, ..., afn)

Where (af1, af2, ..., afn) are the values of the version numbers of the "next generation" or other protocol families supported. (Note: it has been suggested that the families could also be represented by ASCII strings.)

5.  Rationale

An explicit address family argument in the LPRT command and LPSV reply allows the Internet community to experiment with a variety of "next generation IP" and other network layer protocol alternatives within a common FTP implementation framework. (It also allows the use of a different address family on the command and data connections.) An explicit length indicator for the host address is necessary because some of the IPNG alternatives make use of variable length addresses. An explicit host address is necessary because FTP says it's necessary.

The decision to provide a length indicator for the port number is not as obvious, and certainly goes beyond the necessary condition of having to support TCP port numbers.

Currently, at least one IPng alternative (TP/IX) supports longer port addresses. And given the increasingly "multi-protocol" nature of the Internet, it seems reasonable that someone, somewhere, might wish to operate FTP operate over Appletalk, IPX, and OSI networks as well as TCP/IP networks.  (In theory, FTP should operate over *any* transport protocol that offers the same service as TCP.)  Since some of these transport protocols may offer transport selectors or port numbers that exceed 16 bits, a length indicator may be desirable. If FTP must indeed be changed to accommodate larger network addresses, it may be prudent to determine at this time whether the same flexibility is useful or necessary with respect to transport addresses.

6. Conclusions

   The mechanism defined here is simple, extensible, and meets both IPNG
   and multi-protocol internet needs.

7. References

   STD 9, RFC 959  Postel, J., and J. Reynolds, "File Transfer Protocol",
                   STD 9, RFC 959, USC/Information Sciences Institute,
                   October 1985.

   STD 2, RFC 1340 Reynolds, J., and J. Postel, "Assigned Numbers",
                   STD 2, RFC 1340, USC/Information Sciences Institute,
                   July 1992.  (Does not include recently assigned IPv7
                   numbers).

   STD 3, RFC 1123 Braden, R., Editor, "Requirements for Internet
                   Hosts - Application and Support", STD 3, RFC 1123,
                   USC/Information Sciences Institute, October 1989.

8. Security Considerations

   Security issues are not discussed in this memo.

9. Author's Address

   David M. Piscitello
   Core Competence, Inc.
   1620 Tuckerstown Road
   Dresher, PA 19025

   EMail: dave@corecom.com

Network Working Group                                      G. Malkin
Request for Comments: 1785                            Xylogics, Inc.
Updates: 1350                                             A. Harkin
Category: Informational                          Hewlett Packard Co.
                                                         March 1995

TFTP Option Negotiation Analysis

Status of this Memo

Abstract

   The TFTP option negotiation mechanism, proposed in [1], is a
   backward-compatible extension to the TFTP protocol, defined in [2].
   It allows file transfer options to be negotiated prior to the
   transfer using a mechanism which is consistent with TFTP's Request
   Packet format.  The mechanism is kept simple by enforcing a request-
   respond-acknowledge sequence, similar to the lock-step approach taken
   by TFTP itself.

   This document was written to allay concerns that the presence of
   options in a TFTP Request packet might cause pathological behavior on
   servers which do not support TFTP option negotiation.

Test Results

   A TFTP client, modified to send TFTP options, was tested against five
   unmodified servers:

        DEC   DEC 3000/400 alpha   OSF1 V3.0
        SGI   IP17 mips            IRIX 5.2
        SUN   sun4c sparc          SunOS 5.1
        IBM   RS/6000 Model 320    AIX 3.4
        SUN   sun4m                SunOS 4.1.3

   In each case, the servers ignored the option information in the
   Request packet and the transfer proceeded as though no option
   negotiation had been attempted.  In addition, the standard BSD4.3
   source for TFTPD, the starting point for many implementations, was
   examined.  The code clearly ignores any extraneous information in
   Request packets.

   From these results and examinations, it is clear that the TFTP option

negotiation mechanism is fully backward-compatible with unmodified
TFTP servers.

Security Considerations

   Security issues are not discussed in this memo.

References

   [1] Malkin, G., and A. Harkin, "TFTP Option Extension", RFC 1782,
       Xylogics, Inc., Hewlett Packard Co., March 1995.

   [2] Sollins, K., "The TFTP Protocol (Revision 2)", STD 33, RFC 1350,
       MIT, July 1992.

Related Documents

   Malkin, G., and A. Harkin, "TFTP Blocksize Option", RFC 1783,
       Xylogics, Inc., Hewlett Packard Co., March 1995.

   Malkin, G., and A. Harkin, "TFTP Timeout Interval and Transfer Size
       Options", RFC 1784, Xylogics, Inc., Hewlett Packard Co., March
       1995.

Authors' Addresses

         Gary Scott Malkin
         Xylogics, Inc.
         53 Third Avenue
         Burlington, MA   01803

         Phone:   (617) 272-8140
         EMail:   gmalkin@xylogics.com


         Art Harkin
         Internet Services Project
         Information Networks Division
         19420 Homestead Road MS 43LN
         Cupertino, CA   95014

         Phone: (408) 447-3755
         EMail: ash@cup.hp.com

Network Working Group                                    W. Polites
Request for Comments: 1986                               W. Wollman
Category: Experimental                                      D. Woo
                                               The MITRE Corporation
                                                         R. Langan
                                                    U.S. ARMY CECOM
                                                      August 1996

        Experiments with a Simple File Transfer Protocol for Radio Links
               using Enhanced Trivial File Transfer Protocol (ETFTP)


Status of this Memo

   This memo defines an Experimental Protocol for the Internet
   community.  This memo does not specify an Internet standard of any
   kind.  Discussion and suggestions for improvement are requested.
   Distribution of this memo is unlimited.

1. INTRODUCTION SECTION

   This document is a description of the Enhanced Trivial File Transfer
   Protocol (ETFTP). This protocol is an experimental implementation of
   the NETwork BLock Transfer Protocol (NETBLT), RFC 998 [1], as a file
   transfer application program. It uses the User Datagram Protocol
   (UDP), RFC 768 [2], as its transport layer. The two protocols are
   layered to create the ETFTP client server application. The ETFTP
   program is named after Trivial File Transfer Protocol (TFTP), RFC
   1350 [3], because the source code from TFTP is used as the building
   blocks for the ETFTP program. This implementation also builds on but
   differs from the work done by the National Imagery Transmission
   Format Standard [4].

   This document is published for discussion and comment on improving
   the throughput performance of data transfer utilities over Internet
   Protocol (IP) compliant, half duplex, radio networks.

   There are many file transfer programs available for computer
   networks.  Many of these programs are designed for operations through
   high-speed, low bit error rate (BER) cabled networks. In tactical
   radio networks, traditional file transfer protocols, such as File
   Transfer Protocol (FTP) and TFTP, do not always perform well. This is
   primarily because tactical half duplex radio networks typically
   provide slow-speed, long delay, and high BER communication links.
   ETFTP is designed to allow a user to control transmission parameters
   to optimize file transfer rates through half-duplex radio links.

The tactical radio network used to test this application was
developed by the Survivable Adaptive Systems (SAS) Advanced
Technology Demonstration (ATD). Part of the SAS ATD program was to
address the problems associated with extending IP networks across
tactical radios.  Several tactical radios, such as, SINgle Channel
Ground and Airborne Radio Systems (SINCGARS), Enhanced Position
Location Reporting Systems (EPLRS), Motorola LST-5C, and High
Frequency (HF) radios have been interfaced to the system.  This
document will discuss results obtained from using ETFTP across a
point-to-point LST-5C tactical SATellite COMmunications (SATCOM)
link. The network includes a 25 Mhz 486 Personal Computer (PC) called
the Army Lightweight Computer Unit (LCU), Cisco 2500 routers,
Gracilis PackeTen Network switches, Motorola Sunburst Cryptographic
processors, a prototype forward error correction (FEC) device, and
Motorola LST-5C tactical Ultra High Frequency (UHF) satellite
communications (SATC! OM) radio. Table 1, "Network Trans fer Rates,"
describes the equipment network connections and the bandwidth of the
physical media interconnecting the devices.

Table 1: Network Transfer Rates

| Equipment | Rate (bits per second) |
|---|---|
| Host Computer (486 PC) | 10,000,000 Ethernet |
| Cisco Router | 10,000,000 Ethernet to 19,200 Serial Line Internet Protocol (SLIP) |
| Gracilis PackeTen | 19,200 SLIP to 16,000 Amateur Radio (AX.25) |
| FEC | half rate or quarter rate |
| Sunburst Crypto | 16,000 |
| LST-5C Radio | 16,000 |

During 1993, the MITRE team collected data for network configurations
that were stationary and on-the-move. This network configuration did
not include any Forward Error Correction (FEC) at the link layer.
Several commercially available implementations of FTP were used to
transfer files through a 16 kbps satellite link. FTP relies upon the
Transmission Control Protocol (TCP) for reliable communications.  For
a variety of file sizes, throughput measurements ranged between 80
and 400 bps. At times, TCP connections could be opened, however, data

transfers would be unsuccessful. This was most likely due to the
smaller TCP connection synchronization packets, as compared to the
TCP data packets.  Because of the high bit error rate of the link,
the smaller packets were much more likely to be received without
error. In most cases, satellite channel utilization was less than 20
percent.  Very often a file transfer would fail because FTP
implementations would curtail the transfer due to the poor
conditions of the communication link.

The current focus is to increase the throughput and channel
utilization over a point to point, half duplex link. Follow on
experiments will evaluate ETFTP's ability to work with multiple hosts
in a multicast scenario. Evaluation of the data collected helped to
determine that several factors limited data throughput. A brief
description of those limiting factors, as well as, solutions that can
reduce these networking limitations is provided below.

Link Quality

The channel quality of a typical narrow-band UHF satellite link does
not sufficiently support data communications without the addition of
a forward error correction (FEC) capability.  From the data
collected, it was determined that the UHF satellite link supports, on
average, a 10e-3 bit error rate.

Solution: A narrow-band UHF satellite radio FEC prototype was
developed that improves data reliability, without excessively
increasing synchronization requirements. The prototype FEC increased
synchronization requirements by less than 50 milliseconds (ms). The
FEC implementation will improve an average 10e-3 BER channel to an
average 10e-5 BER channel.

Delays

Including satellite propagation delays, the tactical satellite radios
require approximately 1.25 seconds for radio synchronization prior to
transmitting any data across the communication channel.  Therefore,
limiting the number of channel accesses required will permit data
throughput to increase. This can be achieved by minimizing the number
of acknowledgments required during the file transfer.  FTP generates
many acknowledgments which decreases throughput by increasing the
number of satellite channel accesses required.

To clarify, when a FTP connection request is generated, it is sent
via Ethernet to the router and then forwarded to the radio network
controller (RNC).  The elapsed time is less than 30 ms. The RNC keys
the crypto unit and 950 ms later modem/crypto synchronization occurs.
After synchronization is achieved, the FTP connection request is

transmitted. The transmitting terminal then drops the channel and the modem/crypto synchronization is lost. Assuming that the request was received successfully, the receiving host processes the request and sends an acknowledgment. Again the modem/crypto have to synchronize prior to transmitting the acknowledgment. Propagation delays over a UHF satellite also adds roughly 500 ms to the total round trip delay.

Solution: When compared to FTP, NETBLT significantly reduces the number of acknowledgments required to complete a file transfer. Therefore, leveraging the features available within an implementation of NETBLT will significantly improve throughput across the narrow-band UHF satellite communication link.

To reduce the number of channel accesses required, a number of AX.25 parameters were modified. These included the value of p for use within the p-persistence link layer protocol, the slot time, the transmit tail time, and the transmit delay time. The p-persistence is a random number threshold between 0 and 255. The slot time is the time to wait prior to attempting to access the channel. The transmit tail increases the amount of time the radio carrier is held on, prior to dropping the channel. Transmit delay is normally equal to the value of the radio synchronization time. By adjusting these parameters to adapt to the tactical satellite environment, improved communication performance can be achieved.

First, in ETFTP, several packets within a buffer are transmitted within one burst. If the buffer is partitioned into ten packets, each of 1024 bytes, then 10,240 bytes of data is transmitted with each channel access. It is possible to configure ETFTP's burstsize to equal the number of packets per buffer. Second, the transmit tail time was increased to hold the key down on the transmitter long enough to insure all of the packets within the buffer are sent in a single channel access. These two features, together, allow the system to transmit an entire file (example, 100,000 bytes) with only a single channel access by adjusting buffer size. Thirdly, the ETFTP protocol only acknowledges each buffer, not each packet. Thus, a single acknowledgment is sent from the receiving terminal containing a request for the missing packets within each buffer, reducing the number of acknowledgment packets sent. Which in turn, reduced the number of times the channel has to be turned around.

To reduce channel access time, p-persistence was set to the maximum value and slot time to a minimum value. These settings support operations for a point-to-point communication link between two users. This value of p would not be used if more users were sharing the satellite channel.

Backoffs

   TCP's slow start and backoff algorithms implemented in most TCP
   packages assume that packet loss is due to network congestion.  When
   operating across a tactical half duplex communication channel
   dedicated to two users, packet loss is primarily due to poor channel
   quality, not network congestion. A linear backoff at the transport
   layer is recommended. In a tactical radio network there are numerous
   cases where a single host is connected to multiple radios. In a
   tactical radio network, layer two will handle channel access.
   Channel access will be adjusted through parameters like p-persistence
   and slot time. The aggregate effect of the exponential backoff from
   the transport layer added to the random backoff of the data link
   layer, will in most cases, cause the radio network to miss many
   network access opportunities. A linear backoff will reduce the number
   missed data link network access opportunities

   Solution: Tunable parameters and timers have been modified to
   resemble those suggested by NETBLT.

Packet Size

   In a tactical environment, channel conditions change rapidly.
   Continuously transmitting large packets under 10e-3 BER conditions
   reduces effective throughput.

   Solution: Packet sizes are dynamically adjusted based upon the
   success of the buffer transfers. If 99 percent of all packets within
   a buffer are received successfully, packet size can be increased to a
   negotiated value.  If 50 percent or more of all packets within a
   buffer are not successfully delivered, the packet size can be
   decreased to a negotiated value.

2. PROTOCOL DESCRIPTION

   Throughout this document the term packet is used to describe a
   datagram that includes all network overhead. A block is used to
   describe information, without any network encapsulation.

   The original source files for TFTP, as downloaded from ftp.uu.net,
   were modified to implement the ETFTP/NETBLT protocol. These same
   files are listed in "UNIX Network Programming" [5].

   ETFTP was implemented for operations under the Santa Cruz Operations
   (SCO) UNIX. In the service file, "/etc/services", an addition was
   made to support "etftp" at a temporary well known port of "1818"
   using "UDP" protocol. The file, "/etc/inetd.conf", was modified so
   the "inetd" program could autostart the "etftpd" server when a

connection request came in on the well known port.

As stated earlier, the transport layer for ETFTP is UDP, which will
not be discussed further here. This client server application layer
protocol is NETBLT, with four notable differences.

The first change is that this NETBLT protocol is implemented on top
of the UDP layer. This allowed the NETBLT concepts to be tested
without modifying the operating system's transport or network layers.
Table 2, "Four Layer Protocol Model," shows the protocol stack for
FTP, TFTP and ETFTP.

Table 2: Four Layer Protocol Model

```
+----------------------------------------------------------------+
|                        PROTOCOL STACK                          |
+---------------+---------------+---------------+---------------+
|APPLICATION    |FTP            |TFTP           |ETFTP/NETBLT   |
+---------------+---------------+---------------+---------------+
|TRANSPORT      |TCP            |UDP            |UDP            |
+---------------+---------------+---------------+---------------+
|NETWORK        |IP                                             |
+---------------+---------------+---------------+---------------+
|LINK           |Ethernet, SLIP, AX.25                          |
+---------------+---------------+---------------+---------------+
```

The second change is a carryover from TFTP, which allows files to be
transferred in netascii or binary modes. A new T bit flag is assigned
to the reserved field of the OPEN message type.

The third change is to re-negotiate the DATA packet size. This change
affects the OPEN, NULL-ACK, and CONTROL_OK message types.  A new R
bit is assigned to the reserved field of the OPEN message type.

The fourth change is the addition of two new fields to the OPEN
message type. The one field is a two byte integer for radio delay in
seconds, and the next field is two bytes of padding.

The ETFTP data encapsulation is shown in Table 3, "ETFTP Data
Encapsulation,". The Ethernet, SLIP, and AX.25 headers are mutually
exclusive. They are stripped off and added by the appropriate
hardware layer.

Table 3: ETFTP Data Encapsulation

```
+------------+------------+------------+------------+-----------+
|Ethernet(14)|            |            |ETFTP/      |           |
|SLIP(2)     |IP(20)      |UDP(8)      |NETBLT(24)  |DATA(1448) |
|AX.25(20)   |            |            |            |           |
+------------+------------+------------+------------+-----------+
```

## 2.1    MESSAGE TYPES AND FORMATS

Here are the ETFTP/NETBLT message types and formats.

```
MESSAGES         VALUES
OPEN     0  Client request to open a new connection
RESPONSE     1  Server positive acknowledgment for OPEN
KEEPALIVE    2  Reset the timer
QUIT     3  Sender normal Close request
QUITACK  4  Receiver acknowledgment of QUIT
ABORT    5  Abnormal close
DATA     6  Sender packet containing data
LDATA    7  Sender last data block of a buffer
NULL-ACK     8  Sender confirmation of CONTROL_OK changes
CONTROL  9  Receiver request to
         GO      0 Start transmit of next buffer
         OK      1 Acknowledge complete buffer
         RESEND  2 Retransmit request
REFUSED 10 Server negative acknowledgment of OPEN
DONE    11 Receiver acknowledgment of QUIT.
```

Packets are "longword-aligned", at four byte word boundaries.
Variable length strings are NULL terminated, and padded to the four
byte boundary. Fields are listed in network byte order. All the
message types share a common 12 byte header. The common fields are:

```
Checksum      IP compliant checksum
Version Current version ID
Type    NETBLT message type
Length  Total byte length of packet
Local Port     My port ID
Foreign Port    Remote port ID
Padding Pad as necessary to 4 byte boundary
```

The OPEN and RESPONSE messages are similar and shown in Table 4,
"OPEN and RESPONSE Message Types,". The client string field is used
to carry the filename to be transferred.

Table 4: OPEN and RESPONSE Message Types

```
                         1                   2                   3
   1 2 3 4 5 6 7 8 9 0 1 2 3 4 5 6 7 8 9 0 1 2 3 4 5 6 7 8 9 0 1 2
  +---------------+---------------+---------------+---------------+
  |Checksum                       |Version        |Type           |
  +---------------+---------------+---------------+---------------+
  |Length                         |Local Port                     |
  +---------------+---------------+---------------+---------------+
  |Foreign Port                   |Longword Alignment Padding     |
  +---------------+---------------+---------------+---------------+
  |Connection ID                                                  |
  +---------------+---------------+---------------+---------------+
  |Buffer size                                                    |
  +---------------+---------------+---------------+---------------+
  |Transfer size                                                  |
  +---------------+---------------+---------------+---------------+
  |DATA Packet size               |Burstsize                      |
  +---------------+---------------+---------------+---------------+
  |Burstrate                      |Death Timer Value              |
  +---------------+---------------+---------------+---------------+
  |Reserved(MBZ)          |R|T|C|M|Maximum # Outstanding Buffers  |
  +---------------+---------------+---------------+---------------+
  |*Radio Delay                   |*Padding                       |
  +---------------+---------------+---------------+---------------+
  |Client String . . .            |Longword Alignment Padding     |
  +---------------+---------------+---------------+---------------+
```

```
Connection ID    The unique connection number
Buffer size      Bytes per buffer
Transfer size    The length of the file in bytes
DATA Packet size          Bytes per ETFTP block
Burstsize        Concatenated packets per burst
Burstrate        Milliseconds per burst
Death Timer      Seconds before closing idle links
Reserved         M bit is mode: 0=read/put, 1=write/get
         C bit is checksum: 0=header, 1=all
         *T bit is transfer: 0=netascii, 1=binary
         *R bit is re-negotiate: 0=off, 1=on
Max # Out Buffs Maximum allowed un-acknowledged buffers
Radio Delay      *Seconds of delay from send to receive
Padding *Unused
Client String    Filename.
```

The KEEPALIVE, QUITACK, and DONE messages are identical to the common
header, except for the message type values. See Table 5, "KEEPALIVE,
QUITACK, and DONE Message Types,".

Table 5: KEEPALIVE, QUITACK, and DONE Message Types

```
                  1                   2                   3
 1 2 3 4 5 6 7 8 9 0 1 2 3 4 5 6 7 8 9 0 1 2 3 4 5 6 7 8 9 0 1 2
+---------------+---------------+---------------+---------------+
|Checksum                       |Version        |Type           |
+---------------+---------------+---------------+---------------+
|Length                         |Local Port                     |
+---------------+---------------+---------------+---------------+
|Foreign Port                   |Longword Alignment Padding     |
+---------------+---------------+---------------+---------------+
```

The QUIT, ABORT, and REFUSED messages allow a string field to carry
the reason for the message. See Table 6, "QUIT, ABORT, and REFUSED
Message Types,".

Table 6: QUIT, ABORT, and REFUSED Message Types

```
                  1                   2                   3
 1 2 3 4 5 6 7 8 9 0 1 2 3 4 5 6 7 8 9 0 1 2 3 4 5 6 7 8 9 0 1 2
+---------------+---------------+---------------+---------------+
|Checksum                       |Version        |Type           |
+---------------+---------------+---------------+---------------+
|Length                         |Local Port                     |
+---------------+---------------+---------------+---------------+
|Foreign Port                   |Longword Alignment Padding     |
+---------------+---------------+---------------+---------------+
|Reason for QUIT/ABORT/REFUSED . . .                            |
+---------------+---------------+---------------+---------------+
|. . .                          |Longword Alignment Padding     |
+---------------+---------------+---------------+---------------+
```

The DATA and LDATA messages make up the bulk of the messages
transferred. The last packet of each buffer is flagged as an LDATA
message. Each and every packet of the last buffer has the reserved L
bit set. The highest consecutive sequence number is used for the
acknowledgment of CONTROL messages. It should contain the ID number
of the current CONTROL message being processed. Table 7, "DATA and
LDATA Message Types,", shows the DATA and LDATA formats.

Table 7: DATA and LDATA Message Types

```
                    1                   2                   3
 1 2 3 4 5 6 7 8 9 0 1 2 3 4 5 6 7 8 9 0 1 2 3 4 5 6 7 8 9 0 1 2
+---------------+---------------+---------------+---------------+
|Checksum                       |Version        |Type           |
+---------------+---------------+---------------+---------------+
|Length                         |Local Port                     |
+---------------+---------------+---------------+---------------+
|Foreign Port                   |Longword Alignment Padding     |
+---------------+---------------+---------------+---------------+
|Buffer Number                                                  |
+---------------+---------------+---------------+---------------+
|High Consecutive Seq Num Rcvd  |Packet Number                  |
+---------------+---------------+---------------+---------------+
|Data Area Checksum Value       |Reserved (MBZ)               |L|
+---------------+---------------+---------------+---------------+
```

```
Buffer Number    The first buffer number starts at 0
Hi Con Seq Num   The acknowledgment for CONTROL messages
Packet Number    The first packet number starts at 0
Data Checksum    Checksum for data area only
Reserved         L: the last buffer bit: 0=false, 1=true
```

The NULL-ACK message type is sent as a response to a CONTROL_OK
message that modifies the current packet size, burstsize, or
burstrate. In acknowledging the CONTROL_OK message, the sender is
confirming the change request to the new packet size, burstsize, or
burstrate. If no modifications are requested, a NULL-ACK message is
unnecessary. See Table 8, "NULL-ACK Message Type," for further
details.

Table 8: NULL-ACK Message Type

```
                    1                   2                   3
 1 2 3 4 5 6 7 8 9 0 1 2 3 4 5 6 7 8 9 0 1 2 3 4 5 6 7 8 9 0 1 2
+---------------+---------------+---------------+---------------+
|Checksum                       |Version        |Type           |
+---------------+---------------+---------------+---------------+
|Length                         |Local Port                     |
+---------------+---------------+---------------+---------------+
|Foreign Port                   |Longword Alignment Padding     |
+---------------+---------------+---------------+---------------+
|High Consecutive Seq Num Rcvd  |New Burstsize                  |
+---------------+---------------+---------------+---------------+
|New Burstrate                  |*New DATA Packet size          |
+---------------+---------------+---------------+---------------+
```

The CONTROL messages have three subtypes: GO, OK, and RESEND as shown
in Tables 9-12. The CONTROL message common header may be followed by
any number of longword aligned subtype messages.

Table 9: CONTROL Message Common Header

```
                    1                   2                   3
 1 2 3 4 5 6 7 8 9 0 1 2 3 4 5 6 7 8 9 0 1 2 3 4 5 6 7 8 9 0 1 2
+---------------+---------------+---------------+---------------+
|Checksum                       |Version        |Type           |
+---------------+---------------+---------------+---------------+
|Length                         |Local Port                     |
+---------------+---------------+---------------+---------------+
|Foreign Port                   |Longword Alignment Padding      |
+---------------+---------------+---------------+---------------+
```

Table 10: CONTROL_GO Message Subtype

```
                    1                   2                   3
 1 2 3 4 5 6 7 8 9 0 1 2 3 4 5 6 7 8 9 0 1 2 3 4 5 6 7 8 9 0 1 2
+---------------+---------------+---------------+---------------+
|Subtype        |Padding        |Sequence Number                |
+---------------+---------------+---------------+---------------+
|Buffer Number                                                   |
+---------------+---------------+---------------+---------------+
```

Table 11: CONTROL_OK Message Subtype

```
                    1                   2                   3
 1 2 3 4 5 6 7 8 9 0 1 2 3 4 5 6 7 8 9 0 1 2 3 4 5 6 7 8 9 0 1 2
+---------------+---------------+---------------+---------------+
|Subtype        |Padding        |Sequence Number                |
+---------------+---------------+---------------+---------------+
|Buffer Number                                                   |
+---------------+---------------+---------------+---------------+
|New Offered Burstsize          |New Offered Burstrate           |
+---------------+---------------+---------------+---------------+
|Current Control Timer Value    |*New DATA Packet size           |
+---------------+---------------+---------------+---------------+
```

Table 12: CONTROL_RESEND Message Subtype

```
                         1                   2                   3
     1 2 3 4 5 6 7 8 9 0 1 2 3 4 5 6 7 8 9 0 1 2 3 4 5 6 7 8 9 0 1 2
    +---------------+---------------+---------------+---------------+
    |Subtype        |Padding        |Sequence Number                |
    +---------------+---------------+---------------+---------------+
    |Buffer Number                                                  |
    +---------------+---------------+---------------+---------------+
    |Number of Missing Packets      |Longword Alignment Padding      |
    +---------------+---------------+---------------+---------------+
    |Packet Number (2 bytes)        |. . .                          |
    +---------------+---------------+---------------+---------------+
    |. . .                          |Longword Alignment Padding      |
    +---------------+---------------+---------------+---------------+
```

## 2.2 ETFTP COMMAND SET

Being built from TFTP source code, ETFTP shares a significant portion
of TFTP's design. Like TFTP, ETFTP does NOT support user password
validation. The program does not support changing directories (i.e.
cd), neither can it list directories, (i.e. ls). All filenames must
be given in full paths, as relative paths are not supported. The
internal finite state machine was modified to support NETBLT message
types.

The NETBLT protocol is implemented as closely as possible to what is
described in RFC 998, with a few exceptions. The client string field
in the OPEN message type is used to carry the filename of the file to
be transferred. Netascii or binary transfers are both supported. If
enabled, new packet sizes, burstsizes, and burstrates are re-
negotiated downwards when half or more of the blocks in a buffer
require retransmission. If 99% of the packets in a buffer is
successfully transferred without any retransmissions, packet size is
re-negotiated upwards.

The interactive commands supported by the client process are similar
to TFTP. Here is the ETFTP command set. Optional parameters are in
square brackets. Presets are in parentheses.

```
?         help, displays command list
ascii     mode ascii, appends CR-LF per line
autoadapt         toggles backoff function (on)
baudrate baud     baud rate (16000 bits/sec)
binary    mode binary, image transfer
blocksize bytes packet size in bytes (512 bytes/block)
bufferblock blks        buffer size in blocks (128 blocks/buff)
burstsize packets       burst size in packets (8 blocks/burst)
```

```
connect host [p]          establish connection with host at port p
exit     ends program
get rfile lfile copy remote file to local file
help     same as ?
mode choice      set transfer mode (binary)
multibuff num    number of buffers (2 buffers)
put lfile rfile copy local file to remote file
quit     same as exit
radiodelay sec  transmission delay in seconds (2 sec)
status  display network parameters
trace   toggles debug display (off).
```

2.3 DATA TRANSFER AND FLOW CONTROL

This is the scenario between client and server transfers:

Client sends OPEN for connection, blocksize, buffersize, burstsize, burstrate, transfer mode, and get or put. See M bit of reserved field.

Server sends a RESPONSE with the agreed parameters.

Receiver sends a CONTROL_GO request sending of first buffer.

Sender starts transfer by reading the file into multiple memory buffers. See Figure 1, "File Segmentation,". Each buffer is divided according to the number of bytes/block. Each block becomes a DATA packet, which is concatenated according to the blocks/burst. Bursts are transmitted according to the burstrate. Last data block is flagged as LDATA type.

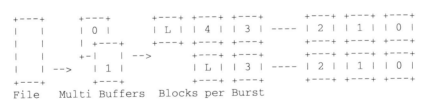

```
+---+      +---+       +---+ +---+ +---+      +---+ +---+ +---+
|   |      | 0 |       | L | | 4 | | 3 | ---- | 2 | | 1 | | 0 |
|   |      | +---+     +---+ +---+ +---+      +---+ +---+ +---+
|   |      +-|   | -->       +---+ +---+      +---+ +---+ +---+
|   | -->  | 1 |           | L | | 3 | ---- | 2 | | 1 | | 0 |
+---+      +---+           +---+ +---+      +---+ +---+ +---+
File   Multi Buffers  Blocks per Burst
```

Figure 1. File Segmentation

Receiver acknowledges buffer as CONTROL_OK or CONTROL_RESEND.

If blocks are missing, a CONTROL_RESEND packet is transmitted. If half or more of the blocks in a buffer are missing, an adaptive algorithm is used for the next buffer transfer. If no blocks are missing, a CONTROL_OK packet is transmitted.

Sender re-transmits blocks until receipt of a CONTROL_OK. If the
adaptive algorithm is set, then new parameters are offered, in the
CONTROL_OK message. The priority of the adaptive algorithm is:

-           Reduce packetsize by half (MIN = 16 bytes/packet)
-           Reduce burstsize by one (MIN = 1 packet/burst)
-           Reduce burstrate to actual tighttimer rate

If new parameters are valid, the sender transmits a NULL-ACK packet,
to confirm the changes.

Receiver sends a CONTROL_GO to request sending next buffer.

At end of transfer, sender sends a QUIT to close the connection.

Receiver acknowledges the close request with a DONE packet.

## 2.4 TUNABLE PARAMETERS

These parameters directly affect the throughput rate of ETFTP.

Packetsize       The packetsize is the number of 8 bit bytes per
packet. This number refers to the user data bytes in a block, (frame),
exclusive of any network overhead. The packet size has a valid range
from 16 to 1,448 bytes. The Maximum Transfer Unit (MTU) implemented in
most commercial network devices is 1,500 bytes. The de-facto industry
standard is 576 byte packets.

Bufferblock      The bufferblock is the number of blocks per buffer.
Each implementation may have restrictions on available memory, so the
buffersize is calculated by multiplying the packetsize times the
bufferblocks.

Baudrate         The baudrate is the bits per second transfer rate of
the slowest link (i.e., the radios). The baudrate sets the speed of
the sending process. The sending process cannot detect the actual
speed of the network, so the user must set the correct baudrate.

Burstsize        The burstsize in packets per burst sets how many
packets are concatenated and burst for transmission efficiency. The
burstsize times the packetsize must not exceed the available memory of
any intervening network devices. On the Ethernet portion of the
network, all the packets are sent almost instantaneously. It is
necessary to wait for the network to drain down its memory buffers,
before the next burst is sent. The sending process needs to regulate
the rate used to place packets into the network.

Radiodelay      The radiodelay is the time in seconds per burst it takes to synchronize with the radio controllers. Any additional hardware delays should be set here. It is the aggregate delay of the link layer, such as transmitter key-up, FEC, crypto synchronization, and propagation delays.

These parameters above are used to calculate a burstrate, which is the length of time it takes to transmit one burst. The ov is the overhead of 72 bytes per packet of network encapsulation. A byte is defined as 8 bits. The burstrate value is:

burstrate = (packetsize+ov)*burstsize*8/baudrate

In a effort to calculate the round trip time, when data is flowing in one direction for most of the transfer, the OPEN and RESPONSE message types are timed, and the tactical radio delays are estimated. Using only one packet in each direction to estimate the rate of the link is statistically inaccurate. It was decided that the radio delay should be a constant provided by the user interface.  However, a default value of 2 seconds is used. The granularity of this value is in seconds because of two reasons. The first reason is that the UNIX supports a sleep function in seconds only. The second reason is that in certain applications, such as deep space probes, a 16-bit integer maximum of 32,767 seconds would suffice.

## 2.5 DELAYS AND TIMERS

From these parameters, several timers are derived. The control timer is responsible for measuring the per buffer rate of transfer. The SENDER copy is nicknamed the loosetimer.

loosetimer = (burstrate+radiodelay)*bufferblock/burstsize

The RECEIVER copy of the timer is nicknamed the tighttimer, which measures the elapsed time between CONTROL_GO and CONTROL_OK packets. The tighttimer is returned to the SENDER to allow the protocol to adjust for the speed of the network.

The retransmit timer is responsible for measuring the network receive data function. It is used to set an alarm signal (SIGALRM) to interrupt the network read. The retransmit timer (wait) is initially set to be the greater of twice the round trip or 4 times the radiodelay, plus a constant 5 seconds.

```
wait = MAX ( 2*roundtriptime,  4*radiodelay ) + 5 seconds
```

and

```
alarm timeout = wait.
```

Each time the same read times out, a five second backoff is added to the next wait. The backoff is necessary because the initial user supplied radiodelay, or the initial measured round trip time may be incorrect.

The retransmit timer is set differently for the RECEIVER during a buffer transfer. Before the arrival of the first DATA packet, the original alarm time out is used. Once the DATA packets start arriving, and for the duration of each buffer transfer, the RECEIVER alarm time out is reset to the expected arrival time of the last DATA packet (blockstogo) plus the delay (wait). As each DATA packet is received, the alarm is decremented by one packet interval. This same algorithm is used for receiving missing packets, during a RESEND.

```
alarmtimeout = blockstogo*burstrate/burstsize + wait
```

The death timer is responsible for measuring the idle time of a connection. In the ETFTP program, the death timer is set to be equal to the accumulated time of ten re-transmissions plus their associated backoffs. As such, the death timer value in the OPEN and RESPONSE message types is un-necessary. In the ETFTP program, this field could be used to transfer the radio delay value instead of creating the two new fields.

The keepalive timer is responsible for resetting the death timer. This timer will trigger the sending of a KEEPALIVE packet to prevent the remote host from closing a connection due to the expiration of its death timer. Due to the nature of the ETFTP server process, a keepalive timer was not necessary, although it is implemented.

2.6 TEST RESULTS

The NETBLT protocol has been tested on other high speed networks before, see RFC 1030 [6]. These test results in Tables 13 and 14, "ETFTP Performance," were gathered from files transferred across the network and LST-5C TACSAT radios.  The radios were connected together via a coaxial cable to provide a "clean" link. A clean link is defined to a BER of 10e-5. The throughput rates are defined to be the file size divided by the elapsed time resulting in bits per second (bps).  The elapsed time is measured from the time of the "get" or "put" command to the completion of the transfer. This is an all inclusive time measurement based on user perspective. It includes the

connection time, transfer time, error recovery time, and disconnect
time. The user concept of elapsed time is the length of time it takes
to copy a file from disk to disk. These results show only the average
performances, including the occasional packet re-transmissions. The
network configuration was set as:

ETFTP Parameters:

Filesize                  101,306 bytes
Radiodelay      2 seconds
Buffersize      16,384-131,072 bytes
Packetsize      512-2048 bytes
Burstsize                 8-16 packets/burst

Gracilis PackeTen Parameters:

0 TX Delay      400 milliseconds
1 P Persist     255 [range 1-255]
2 Slot Time     30 milliseconds
3 TX Tail                 300 milliseconds
4 Rcv Buffers   8 2048 bytes/buffer
5 Idle Code     Flag

Radio Parameters:

Baudrate                  16,000 bps
Encryption      on

Table 13: ETFTP Performance at 8 Packets/Burst in Bits/Second

| buffersize (bytes) | packetsize 2,048 bytes | packetsize 1,448 bytes | packetsize 1,024 bytes | packetsize 512 bytes |
|---|---|---|---|---|
| 16,384 | 7,153 | 6,952 | 6,648 | 5,248 |
| 32,768 | 7,652 | 7,438 | 7,152 | 4,926 |
| 65,536 | 8,072 | 8,752 | 8,416 | 5,368 |
| 131,072 | 8,828 | 9,112 | 7,888 | 5,728 |

Table 14: ETFTP Performance at 16 Packets/Burst in Bits/Second

| buffersize (bytes) | packetsize 2,048 bytes | packetsize 1,448 bytes | packetsize 1,024 bytes | packetsize 512 bytes |
|---|---|---|---|---|
| 16,384 | 5,544 | 5,045 | 4,801 | 4,570 |
| 32,768 | 8,861 | 8,230 | 8,016 | 7,645 |
| 65,536 | 9,672 | 9,424 | 9,376 | 8,920 |
| 131,072 | 10,432 | 10,168 | 9,578 | 9,124 |

2.7 PERFORMANCE CONSIDERATIONS

These tests were performed across a tactical radio link with a maximum data rate of 16000 bps. In testing ETFTP, it was found that the delay associated with the half duplex channel turnaround time was the biggest factor in throughput performance. Therefore, every attempt was made to minimize the number of times the channel needed to be turned around. Obviously, the easiest thing to do is to use as big a buffer as necessary to read in a file, as acknowledgments occurred only at the buffer boundaries. This is not always feasible, as available storage on disk could easily exceed available memory. However, the current ETFTP buffersize is set at a maximum of 524,288 bytes.

The larger packetsizes also improved performance. The limit on packetsize is based on the 1500 byte MTU of network store and forward devices. In a high BER environment, a large packetsize could be detrimental to success. By reducing the packetsize, even though it negatively impacts performance, reliability is sustained. When used in conjunction with FEC, both performance and reliability can be maintained at an acceptable level.

The burstsize translates into how long the radio transmitters are keyed to transmit. In ETFTP, the ideal situation is to have the first packet of a burst arrive in the radio transmit buffer, as the last packet of the previous burst is just finished being sent. In this way, the radio transmitter would never be dropped for the duration of one buffer. In a multi-user radio network, a full buffer transmission would be inconsiderate, as the transmit cycle could last for several minutes, instead of seconds. In measuring voice communications, typical transmit durations are on the order of five to twenty seconds. This means that the buffersize and burstsize could be adjusted to have similar transmission durations.

3. REFERENCE SECTION

    [1] Clark, D., Lambert, M., and L. Zhang,
        "NETBLT: A Bulk Data Transfer Protocol", RFC 998, MIT,
        March 1987.

    [2] Postel, J., "User Datagram Protocol" STD 6, RFC 768,
        USC/Information Sciences Institute, August 1980.

    [3] Sollins, K., "Trivial File Transfer Protocol", STD 33,
        RFC 1350, MIT, July 1992.

    [4] MIL-STD-2045-44500, 18 June 1993, "Military Standard Tactical
        Communications Protocol 2 (TACO 2) fot the National Imagery
        Transmission Format Standard", Ft. Monmouth, New Jersey.

    [5] Stevens, W. Richard, 1990, "UNIX Network Programming",
        Prentice-Hall Inc., Englewood, New Jersey, Chapter 12.

    [6] Lambert, M., "On Testing the NETBLT Protocol over
        Divers Networks", RFC 1030, MIT, November 1987.

4. SECURITY CONSIDERATIONS

The ETFTP program is a security loophole in any UNIX environment.
There is no user/password validation. All the problems associated to
TFTP are repeated in ETFTP. The server program must be owned by root
and setuid to root in order to work. As an experimental prototype
program, the security issue was overlooked. Since this protocol has
proven too be a viable solution in tactical radio networks, the
security issues will have to be addressed, and corrected.

RFC 1986
19

5.  AUTHORS' ADDRESSES

William J. Polites
The Mitre Corporation
145 Wyckoff Rd.
Eatontown, NJ 07724

Phone: (908) 544-1414
EMail:wpolites@mitre.org


William Wollman
The Mitre Corporation
145 Wyckoff Rd.
Eatontown, NJ 07724

Phone: (908) 544-1414
EMail:wwollman@mitre.org


David Woo
The Mitre Corporation
145 Wyckoff Rd.
Eatontown, NJ 07724

Phone: (908) 544-1414
EMail: dwoo@mitre.org


Russ Langan
U.S. Army Communications Electronics Command (CECOM)
AMSEL-RD-ST-SP
ATTN: Russell Langan
Fort Monmouth, NJ 07703

Phone: (908) 427-2064
Fax: (908) 427-2822
EMail: langanr@doim6.monmouth.army.mil

6.  GLOSSARY

| | |
|---|---|
| ATD | Advanced Technology Demonstration |
| AX.25 | Amateur Radio X.25 Protocol |
| BER | Bit Error Rate |
| EPLRS | Enhanced Position Location Reporting Systems |
| ETFTP | Enhanced Trivial File Transfer Protocol |
| FEC | Forward Error Correction |
| FTP | File Transfer Protocol |
| HF | High Frequency |
| LCU | Lightweight Computer Unit |
| ms | milliseconds |
| MTU | Maximum Transfer Unit |
| NETBLT | NETwork Block Transfer protocol |
| NITFS | National Imagery Transmission Format Standard |
| PC | Personal Computer |
| RNC | Radio Network Controller |
| SAS | Survivable Adaptive Systems |
| SATCOM | SATellite COMmunications |
| SCO | Santa Cruz Operations |
| SINCGARS | SINgle Channel Ground and Airborne Radio Systems |
| SLIP | Serial Line Internet Protocol |
| TACO2 | Tactical Communications Protocol 2 |
| TCP | Transmission Control Protocol |
| TFTP | Trivial File Transfer Protocol |
| UDP | User Datagram Protocol |
| UHF | Ultra High Frequency |

* Modification from NETBLT RFC 998.
* The new packet size is a modification to the NETBLT RFC 998.
* The new packet size is a modification to the NETBLT RFC 998.

Network Working Group                                    A. Emberson
Request for Comments: 2090                   Lanworks Technologies Inc.
Category: Experimental                                  February 1997

TFTP Multicast Option

Status of this Memo

Abstract

   The Trivial File Transfer Protocol [1] is a simple, lock-step, file
   transfer protocol which allows a client to get or put a file onto a
   remote host.

   This document describes a new TFTP option. This new option will allow
   the multiple clients to receive the same file concurrently through
   the use of Multicast packets. The TFTP Option Extension mechanism is
   described in [2].

   Often when similar computers are booting remotely they will each
   download the same image file. By adding multicast into the TFTP
   option set, two or more computers can download a file
   concurrently, thus increasing network efficiency.

   This document assumes that the reader is familiar with the
   terminology and notation of both [1] and [2].

Multicast Option Specification

   The TFTP Read Request packet is modified to include the multicast
   option as follows:

```
   +--------+----~-----+---+--~~---+---+----------+---+---+
   | opc=1 | filename | 0 | mode | 0 | multicast | 0 | 0 |
   +--------+----~-----+---+--~~---+---+----------+---+---+
```

opc
   The opcode field contains a 1, for Read Requests, as defined
   in [1].

filename
    The name of the file to be read, as defined in [1]. This is a
    NULL-terminated field.

mode
    The mode of the file transfer: "netascii", "octet", or
    "mail", as defined in [1]. This is a NULL-terminated field.

multicast
    Request for multicast transmission of the file option,
    "multicast" (case insensitive). This is a NULL-terminated
    field. The value for this option request is a string of zero
    length.

If the server is willing to accept the multicast option, it
sends an Option Acknowledgment (OACK) to the client including
the multicast option, as defined in [2]. The OACK to the client
will specify the multicast address and flag to indicate whether
that client should send block acknowledgments (ACK).

```
+-------+-----------+---+-------~~-------+---+
|  opc  | multicast | 0 | addr, port, mc | 0 |
+-------+-----------+---+-------~~-------+---+
```

opc
    The opcode field contains the number 6, for Option
    Acknowledgment, as defined in [2].

multicast
    Acknowledges the multicast option. This is a NULL-terminated
    field.

addr
    The addr field contains the multicast IP address. This field
    is terminated with a comma.

port
    The port field contains the destination port of the multicast
    packets. The use of Registered Port number 1758 (tftp-mcast)
    is recommended. This field is terminated with a comma.

mc
    This field will be either 0 or 1, to tell the client whether
    it is the master client, that is, it is responsible for
    sending ACKs to the server. This is NULL-terminated field.

Data Transfer

After the OACK is received by the client it will send an ACK for
packet zero, as in [2]. With the multicast option being accepted this
ACK will indicate to the server that the client wants the first
packet. In other words the ACKs may now be seen as a request for the
n+1th block of data. This enables each a client to request any block
within the file that it may be missing.

To manage the data transfer the server will maintain a list of
clients. Typically the oldest client on the list, from here on
referred to as the Master Client, will be responsible for sending
ACKs. When the master client is finished, the server will send
another OACK to the next oldest client, telling it to start sending
ACKs. Upon receipt of this OACK the new master client will send an
ACK for the block immediately before the first block required to
complete its download.

Any subsequent clients can start receiving blocks of a file during a
transfer and then request any missing blocks when that client becomes
the master client. When the current master client is finished, the
server will notify the next client with an OACK making it the new
master client. The new master client can start requesting  missed
packets.  Each  client  must  terminate  the transfer by sending an
acknowledgment of the last packet or by sending an error message to
server. This termination can occur even if the client is not the
master client.

Any subsequent OACKs to a client may have an empty multicast address
and port fields, since this information will already be held by that
client. In the event a client fails to respond in a timely manner to
a OACK enabling it as the master client, the server shall select the
next oldest client to be the master client. The server shall
reattempt to send a OACK to the non- responding client when the new
master client is finished. The server may cease communication with a
client after a reasonable number of attempts.

Each transfer will be given a multicast address for use to distribute
the data packets. Since there can be multiple servers on a given
network or a limited number of addresses available to a given server,
it is possible that their might be more than one transfer using a
multicast address. To ensure that a client only accepts the correct
packets, each transfer must use a unique port on the server. The
source IP address and port number will identify the data packets for
the transfer. Thus the server must send the unicast OACK packet to
the client using the same port as will be used for sending the
multicast data packets.

At any point if a client, other than the master client, sends a ACK
to the server, the server will respond with another OACK with the mc
field holding a value of zero. If this client persists in sending
erroneous ACKs, the server may send an error packet to the client,
discontinuing the file transfer for that client.

The server may also send unicast packets to a lone client to reduce
adverse effects on other machines. As it is possible that machines
may be forced to process many extraneous multicast packets when
attempting to receive a single multicast address.

Example

```
              clients                                    server  message
          -------------------------------------------------------------
    1  C1  |1|afile|0|octet|0|multicast|0|0| ->              RRQ
    2            C1 <- |6|multicast|224.100.100.100,1758,1|  OACK
    3  C1  |4|0| ->                                          ACK
    4                        M <- |3|1|1| 512 octets of data|  DATA
    5  C1  |4|1| ->                                          ACK
    6                        M <- |3|2|1| 512 octets of data|  DATA
    7  C2  |1|afile|0|octet|0|multicast|0|0| ->              RRQ
    8            C2 <- |6|multicast|224.100.100.100,1758,0|  OACK
    9  C2  |4|0| ->                                          ACK
   10  C1  |4|2| ->                                          ACK
   11                        M <- |3|3|1| 512 octets of data|  DATA
   12  C3  |1|afile|0|octet|0|multicast|0|0| ->              RRQ
   13            C3 <- |6|multicast|224.100.100.100,1758,0|  OACK
   14  C1  |4|3| ->                                          ACK
   15  C2  |4|0| ->                                          ACK
   16          M (except C2) <- |3|4|1| 512 octets of data|  DATA
   17  C1  |4|4| ->                                          ACK
   18                        M <- |3|5|1| 512 octets of data|  DATA
   19  C1  |4|5| ->                                          ACK
   20                        M <- |3|6|1| 100 octets of data|  DATA
   21  C1  |4|6| ->                                          ACK
   22                          C2 <- |6|multicast|,,1|       OACK
   23  C2  |4|0| ->                                          ACK
   24                        M <- |3|1|1| 512 octets of data|  DATA
   25  C2  |4|1| ->                                          ACK
   26                        M <- |3|2|1| 512 octets of data|  DATA
   27  C2  |4|3| ->                                          ACK
   28                        M <- |3|4|1| 512 octets of data|  DATA
   29  C2  |4|6| ->                                          ACK
   30                          C3 <- |6|multicast|,,1|       OACK
   31  C3  |4|2| ->                                          ACK
   32                        M <- |3|3|1| 512 octets of data|  DATA
   33  C3  |4|6| ->                                          ACK
```

Comments:
    1  request from client 1
    2  option acknowledgment
    3  acknowledgment for option acknowledgment,
       or request for first block of data
    4  first data packet sent to the multicast address
    7  request from client 2
    8  option acknowledgment to client 2,
       send no acknowledgments
    9  OACK acknowledgment from client 2
   15  OACK acknowledgment from client 3
   16  client 2 fails to receive a packet
   21  client 1 acknowledges receipt of the last block,
       telling the server it is done
   23  option acknowledgment to client 2,
       now the master client
   25  client 2 acknowledging with request for first block
   27  client 2 acknowledges with request for missed block
   29  client 2 signals it is finished
   31  client 3 is master client and asks for missing blocks
   33  client 3 signals it is finished

Conclusion

   With the use of the multicast and blocksize[3] options TFTP will be
   capable of fast and efficient downloads of data. Using TFTP with the
   multicast option will maintain backward compatibility for both
   clients and servers.

Security Considerations

   Security issues are not discussed in this memo.

References

   [1] Sollins, K., "The TFTP Protocol (Revision 2)", STD 33, RFC
       1350, MIT, July 1992.

   [2] Malkin, G., and A. Harkin, "TFTP Option Extension", RFC
       1782, Xylogics, Inc., Hewlett Packard Co., March 1995.

   [3] Malkin, G., and A. Harkin, "TFTP Blocksize Option", RFC
       1783, Xylogics, Inc., Hewlett Packard Co., March 1995.

RFC 2090
5

Author's Address

    A. Thomas Emberson
    Lanworks Technologies, Inc.
    2425 Skymark Avenue
    Mississauga, Ontario
    Canada L4W 4Y6


    Phone: (905) 238-5528
    EMail: tom@lanworks.com

Network Working Group                                    M. Horowitz
Request for Comments: 2228                          Cygnus Solutions
Updates: 959                                               S. Lunt
Category: Standards Track                                  Bellcore
                                                      October 1997

                        FTP Security Extensions

Status of this Memo

Copyright Notice

Abstract

   This document defines extensions to the FTP specification STD 9, RFC
   959, "FILE TRANSFER PROTOCOL (FTP)" (October 1985).  These extensions
   provide strong authentication, integrity, and confidentiality on both
   the control and data channels with the introduction of new optional
   commands, replies, and file transfer encodings.

   The following new optional commands are introduced in this
   specification:

      AUTH (Authentication/Security Mechanism),
      ADAT (Authentication/Security Data),
      PROT (Data Channel Protection Level),
      PBSZ (Protection Buffer Size),
      CCC (Clear Command Channel),
      MIC (Integrity Protected Command),
      CONF (Confidentiality Protected Command), and
      ENC (Privacy Protected Command).

   A new class of reply types (6yz) is also introduced for protected
   replies.

   None of the above commands are required to be implemented, but
   interdependencies exist.  These dependencies are documented with the
   commands.

   Note that this specification is compatible with STD 9, RFC 959.

1.  Introduction

   The File Transfer Protocol (FTP) currently defined in STD 9, RFC 959
   and in place on the Internet uses usernames and passwords passed in
   cleartext to authenticate clients to servers (via the USER and PASS
   commands).  Except for services such as "anonymous" FTP archives,
   this represents a security risk whereby passwords can be stolen
   through monitoring of local and wide-area networks.  This either aids
   potential attackers through password exposure and/or limits
   accessibility of files by FTP servers who cannot or will not accept
   the inherent security risks.

   Aside from the problem of authenticating users in a secure manner,
   there is also the problem of authenticating servers, protecting
   sensitive data and/or verifying its integrity.  An attacker may be
   able to access valuable or sensitive data merely by monitoring a
   network, or through active means may be able to delete or modify the
   data being transferred so as to corrupt its integrity.  An active
   attacker may also initiate spurious file transfers to and from a site
   of the attacker's choice, and may invoke other commands on the
   server.  FTP does not currently have any provision for the encryption
   or verification of the authenticity of commands, replies, or
   transferred data.  Note that these security services have value even
   to anonymous file access.

   Current practice for sending files securely is generally either:

      1.  via FTP of files pre-encrypted under keys which are manually
          distributed,

      2.  via electronic mail containing an encoding of a file encrypted
          under keys which are manually distributed,

      3.  via a PEM message, or

      4.  via the rcp command enhanced to use Kerberos.

   None of these means could be considered even a de facto standard, and
   none are truly interactive.  A need exists to securely transfer files
   using FTP in a secure manner which is supported within the FTP
   protocol in a consistent manner and which takes advantage of existing
   security infrastructure and technology.  Extensions are necessary to
   the FTP specification if these security services are to be introduced
   into the protocol in an interoperable way.

Although the FTP control connection follows the Telnet protocol, and Telnet has defined an authentication and encryption option [TELNET-SEC], [RFC-1123] explicitly forbids the use of Telnet option negotiation over the control connection (other than Synch and IP).

Also, the Telnet authentication and encryption option does not provide for integrity protection only (without confidentiality), and does not address the protection of the data channel.

2.  FTP Security Overview

At the highest level, the FTP security extensions seek to provide an abstract mechanism for authenticating and/or authorizing connections, and integrity and/or confidentiality protecting commands, replies, and data transfers.

In the context of FTP security, authentication is the establishment of a client's identity and/or a server's identity in a secure way, usually using cryptographic techniques.  The basic FTP protocol does not have a concept of authentication.

Authorization is the process of validating a user for login.  The basic authorization process involves the USER, PASS, and ACCT commands.  With the FTP security extensions, authentication established using a security mechanism may also be used to make the authorization decision.

Without the security extensions, authentication of the client, as this term is usually understood, never happens.  FTP authorization is accomplished with a password, passed on the network in the clear as the argument to the PASS command.  The possessor of this password is assumed to be authorized to transfer files as the user named in the USER command, but the identity of the client is never securely established.

An FTP security interaction begins with a client telling the server what security mechanism it wants to use with the AUTH command.  The server will either accept this mechanism, reject this mechanism, or, in the case of a server which does not implement the security extensions, reject the command completely.  The client may try multiple security mechanisms until it requests one which the server accepts.  This allows a rudimentary form of negotiation to take place.  (If more complex negotiation is desired, this may be implemented as a security mechanism.)  The server's reply will indicate if the client must respond with additional data for the security mechanism to interpret.  If none is needed, this will usually mean that the mechanism is one where the password (specified by the PASS command) is to be interpreted differently, such as with a token or one-time password system.

If the server requires additional security information, then the client and server will enter into a security data exchange.  The client will send an ADAT command containing the first block of security data.  The server's reply will indicate if the data exchange is complete, if there was an error, or if more data is needed.  The server's reply can optionally contain security data for the client to interpret.  If more data is needed, the client will send another ADAT command containing the next block of data, and await the server's reply.  This exchange can continue as many times as necessary.  Once this exchange completes, the client and server have established a security association.  This security association may include authentication (client, server, or mutual) and keying information for integrity and/or confidentiality, depending on the mechanism in use.

The term "security data" here is carefully chosen.  The purpose of the security data exchange is to establish a security association, which might not actually include any authentication at all, between the client and the server as described above.  For instance, a Diffie-Hellman exchange establishes a secret key, but no authentication takes place.  If an FTP server has an RSA key pair but the client does not, then the client can authenticate the server, but the server cannot authenticate the client.

Once a security association is established, authentication which is a part of this association may be used instead of or in addition to the standard username/password exchange for authorizing a user to connect to the server.  A username specified by the USER command is always required to specify the identity to be used on the server.

In order to prevent an attacker from inserting or deleting commands on the control stream, if the security association supports integrity, then the server and client must use integrity protection on the control stream, unless it first transmits a CCC command to turn off this requirement.  Integrity protection is performed with the MIC and ENC commands, and the 63z reply codes.  The CCC command and its reply must be transmitted with integrity protection.  Commands and replies may be transmitted without integrity (that is, in the clear or with confidentiality only) only if no security association is established, the negotiated security association does not support integrity, or the CCC command has succeeded.

Once the client and server have negotiated with the PBSZ command an
acceptable buffer size for encapsulating protected data over the data
channel, the security mechanism may also be used to protect data
channel transfers.

Policy is not specified by this document.  In particular, client and
server implementations may choose to implement restrictions on what
operations can be performed depending on the security association
which exists.  For example, a server may require that a client
authorize via a security mechanism rather than using a password,
require that the client provide a one-time password from a token,
require at least integrity protection on the command channel, or
require that certain files only be transmitted encrypted.  An
anonymous ftp client might refuse to do file transfers without
integrity protection in order to insure the validity of files
downloaded.

No particular set of functionality is required, except as
dependencies described in the next section.  This means that none of
authentication, integrity, or confidentiality are required of an
implementation, although a mechanism which does none of these is not
of much use.  For example, it is acceptable for a mechanism to
implement only integrity protection, one-way authentication and/or
encryption, encryption without any authentication or integrity
protection, or any other subset of functionality if policy or
technical considerations make this desirable.  Of course, one peer
might require as a matter of policy stronger protection than the
other is able to provide, preventing perfect interoperability.

3.  New FTP Commands

The following commands are optional, but dependent on each other.
They are extensions to the FTP Access Control Commands.

The reply codes documented here are generally described as
recommended, rather than required.  The intent is that reply codes
describing the full range of success and failure modes exist, but
that servers be allowed to limit information presented to the client.
For example, a server might implement a particular security
mechanism, but have a policy restriction against using it.  The
server should respond with a 534 reply code in this case, but may
respond with a 504 reply code if it does not wish to divulge that the
disallowed mechanism is supported.  If the server does choose to use
a different reply code than the recommended one, it should try to use
a reply code which only differs in the last digit.  In all cases, the
server must use a reply code which is documented as returnable from
the command received, and this reply code must begin with the same
digit as the recommended reply code for the situation.

AUTHENTICATION/SECURITY MECHANISM (AUTH)

The argument field is a Telnet string identifying a supported
mechanism.  This string is case-insensitive.  Values must be
registered with the IANA, except that values beginning with "X-"
are reserved for local use.

If the server does not recognize the AUTH command, it must respond
with reply code 500.  This is intended to encompass the large
deployed base of non-security-aware ftp servers, which will
respond with reply code 500 to any unrecognized command.  If the
server does recognize the AUTH command but does not implement the
security extensions, it should respond with reply code 502.

If the server does not understand the named security mechanism, it
should respond with reply code 504.

If the server is not willing to accept the named security
mechanism, it should respond with reply code 534.

If the server is not able to accept the named security mechanism,
such as if a required resource is unavailable, it should respond
with reply code 431.

If the server is willing to accept the named security mechanism,
but requires security data, it must respond with reply code 334.

If the server is willing to accept the named security mechanism,
and does not require any security data, it must respond with reply
code 234.

If the server is responding with a 334 reply code, it may include
security data as described in the next section.

Some servers will allow the AUTH command to be reissued in order
to establish new authentication.  The AUTH command, if accepted,
removes any state associated with prior FTP Security commands.
The server must also require that the user reauthorize (that is,
reissue some or all of the USER, PASS, and ACCT commands) in this
case (see section 4 for an explanation of "authorize" in this
context).

AUTHENTICATION/SECURITY DATA (ADAT)

> The argument field is a Telnet string representing base 64 encoded
> security data (see Section 9, "Base 64 Encoding"). If a reply
> code indicating success is returned, the server may also use a
> string of the form "ADAT=base64data" as the text part of the reply
> if it wishes to convey security data back to the client.

> The data in both cases is specific to the security mechanism
> specified by the previous AUTH command. The ADAT command, and the
> associated replies, allow the client and server to conduct an
> arbitrary security protocol. The security data exchange must
> include enough information for both peers to be aware of which
> optional features are available. For example, if the client does
> not support data encryption, the server must be made aware of
> this, so it will know not to send encrypted command channel
> replies. It is strongly recommended that the security mechanism
> provide sequencing on the command channel, to insure that commands
> are not deleted, reordered, or replayed.

> The ADAT command must be preceded by a successful AUTH command,
> and cannot be issued once a security data exchange completes
> (successfully or unsuccessfully), unless it is preceded by an AUTH
> command to reset the security state.

> If the server has not yet received an AUTH command, or if a prior
> security data exchange completed, but the security state has not
> been reset with an AUTH command, it should respond with reply code
> 503.

> If the server cannot base 64 decode the argument, it should
> respond with reply code 501.

> If the server rejects the security data (if a checksum fails, for
> instance), it should respond with reply code 535.

> If the server accepts the security data, and requires additional
> data, it should respond with reply code 335.

> If the server accepts the security data, but does not require any
> additional data (i.e., the security data exchange has completed
> successfully), it must respond with reply code 235.

> If the server is responding with a 235 or 335 reply code, then it
> may include security data in the text part of the reply as
> specified above.

If the ADAT command returns an error, the security data exchange
will fail, and the client must reset its internal security state.
If the client becomes unsynchronized with the server (for example,
the server sends a 234 reply code to an AUTH command, but the
client has more data to transmit), then the client must reset the
server's security state.

PROTECTION BUFFER SIZE (PBSZ)

The argument is a decimal integer representing the maximum size,
in bytes, of the encoded data blocks to be sent or received during
file transfer.  This number shall be no greater than can be
represented in a 32-bit unsigned integer.

This command allows the FTP client and server to negotiate a
maximum protected buffer size for the connection.  There is no
default size; the client must issue a PBSZ command before it can
issue the first PROT command.

The PBSZ command must be preceded by a successful security data
exchange.

If the server cannot parse the argument, or if it will not fit in
32 bits, it should respond with a 501 reply code.

If the server has not completed a security data exchange with the
client, it should respond with a 503 reply code.

Otherwise, the server must reply with a 200 reply code.  If the
size provided by the client is too large for the server, it must
use a string of the form "PBSZ=number" in the text part of the
reply to indicate a smaller buffer size.  The client and the
server must use the smaller of the two buffer sizes if both buffer
sizes are specified.

DATA CHANNEL PROTECTION LEVEL (PROT)

The argument is a single Telnet character code specifying the data
channel protection level.

This command indicates to the server what type of data channel
protection the client and server will be using.  The following
codes are assigned:

    C - Clear
    S - Safe
    E - Confidential
    P - Private

The default protection level if no other level is specified is
Clear.  The Clear protection level indicates that the data channel
will carry the raw data of the file transfer, with no security
applied.  The Safe protection level indicates that the data will
be integrity protected.  The Confidential protection level
indicates that the data will be confidentiality protected.  The
Private protection level indicates that the data will be integrity
and confidentiality protected.

It is reasonable for a security mechanism not to provide all data
channel protection levels.  It is also reasonable for a mechanism
to provide more protection at a level than is required (for
instance, a mechanism might provide Confidential protection, but
include integrity-protection in that encoding, due to API or other
considerations).

The PROT command must be preceded by a successful protection
buffer size negotiation.

If the server does not understand the specified protection level,
it should respond with reply code 504.

If the current security mechanism does not support the specified
protection level, the server should respond with reply code 536.

If the server has not completed a protection buffer size
negotiation with the client, it should respond with a 503 reply
code.

The PROT command will be rejected and the server should reply 503
if no previous PBSZ command was issued.

If the server is not willing to accept the specified protection
level, it should respond with reply code 534.

If the server is not able to accept the specified protection
level, such as if a required resource is unavailable, it should
respond with reply code 431.

Otherwise, the server must reply with a 200 reply code to indicate
that the specified protection level is accepted.

CLEAR COMMAND CHANNEL (CCC)

This command does not take an argument.

It is desirable in some environments to use a security mechanism
to authenticate and/or authorize the client and server, but not to
perform any integrity checking on the subsequent commands.  This
might be used in an environment where IP security is in place,
insuring that the hosts are authenticated and that TCP streams
cannot be tampered, but where user authentication is desired.

If unprotected commands are allowed on any connection, then an
attacker could insert a command on the control stream, and the
server would have no way to know that it was invalid.  In order to
prevent such attacks, once a security data exchange completes
successfully, if the security mechanism supports integrity, then
integrity (via the MIC or ENC command, and 631 or 632 reply) must
be used, until the CCC command is issued to enable non-integrity
protected control channel messages.  The CCC command itself must
be integrity protected.

Once the CCC command completes successfully, if a command is not
protected, then the reply to that command must also not be
protected.  This is to support interoperability with clients which
do not support protection once the CCC command has been issued.

This command must be preceded by a successful security data
exchange.

If the command is not integrity-protected, the server must respond
with a 533 reply code.

If the server is not willing to turn off the integrity
requirement, it should respond with a 534 reply code.

Otherwise, the server must reply with a 200 reply code to indicate
that unprotected commands and replies may now be used on the
command channel.

INTEGRITY PROTECTED COMMAND (MIC) and
CONFIDENTIALITY PROTECTED COMMAND (CONF) and
PRIVACY PROTECTED COMMAND (ENC)

The argument field of MIC is a Telnet string consisting of a base
64 encoded "safe" message produced by a security mechanism
specific message integrity procedure.  The argument field of CONF
is a Telnet string consisting of a base 64 encoded "confidential"
message produced by a security mechanism specific confidentiality
procedure.  The argument field of ENC is a Telnet string
consisting of a base 64 encoded "private" message produced by a
security mechanism specific message integrity and confidentiality
procedure.

The server will decode and/or verify the encoded message.

This command must be preceded by a successful security data exchange.

A server may require that the first command after a successful security data exchange be CCC, and not implement the protection commands at all.  In this case, the server should respond with a 502 reply code.

If the server cannot base 64 decode the argument, it should respond with a 501 reply code.

If the server has not completed a security data exchange with the client, it should respond with a 503 reply code.

If the server has completed a security data exchange with the client using a mechanism which supports integrity, and requires a CCC command due to policy or implementation limitations, it should respond with a 503 reply code.

If the server rejects the command because it is not supported by the current security mechanism, the server should respond with reply code 537.

If the server rejects the command (if a checksum fails, for instance), it should respond with reply code 535.

If the server is not willing to accept the command (if privacy is required by policy, for instance, or if a CONF command is received before a CCC command), it should respond with reply code 533.

Otherwise, the command will be interpreted as an FTP command.  An end-of-line code need not be included, but if one is included, it must be a Telnet end-of-line code, not a local end-of-line code.

The server may require that, under some or all circumstances, all commands be protected.  In this case, it should make a 533 reply to commands other than MIC, CONF, and ENC.

4.  Login Authorization

   The security data exchange may, among other things, establish the identity of the client in a secure way to the server.  This identity may be used as one input to the login authorization process.

In response to the FTP login commands (AUTH, PASS, ACCT), the server
may choose to change the sequence of commands and replies specified
by RFC 959 as follows.  There are also some new replies available.

If the server is willing to allow the user named by the USER command
to log in based on the identity established by the security data
exchange, it should respond with reply code 232.

If the security mechanism requires a challenge/response password, it
should respond to the USER command with reply code 336.  The text
part of the reply should contain the challenge.  The client must
display the challenge to the user before prompting for the password
in this case.  This is particularly relevant to more sophisticated
clients or graphical user interfaces which provide dialog boxes or
other modal input.  These clients should be careful not to prompt for
the password before the username has been sent to the server, in case
the user needs the challenge in the 336 reply to construct a valid
password.

5.  New FTP Replies

The new reply codes are divided into two classes.  The first class is
new replies made necessary by the new FTP Security commands.  The
second class is a new reply type to indicate protected replies.

5.1.  New individual reply codes

    232 User logged in, authorized by security data exchange.
    234 Security data exchange complete.
    235 [ADAT=base64data]
        ; This reply indicates that the security data exchange
        ; completed successfully.  The square brackets are not
        ; to be included in the reply, but indicate that
        ; security data in the reply is optional.

    334 [ADAT=base64data]
        ; This reply indicates that the requested security mechanism
        ; is ok, and includes security data to be used by the client
        ; to construct the next command.  The square brackets are not
        ; to be included in the reply, but indicate that
        ; security data in the reply is optional.
    335 [ADAT=base64data]
        ; This reply indicates that the security data is
        ; acceptable, and more is required to complete the
        ; security data exchange.  The square brackets
        ; are not to be included in the reply, but indicate
        ; that security data in the reply is optional.

336 Username okay, need password.  Challenge is "...."
        ; The exact representation of the challenge should be chosen
        ; by the mechanism to be sensible to the human user of the
        ; system.

431 Need some unavailable resource to process security.

533 Command protection level denied for policy reasons.
534 Request denied for policy reasons.
535 Failed security check (hash, sequence, etc).
536 Requested PROT level not supported by mechanism.
537 Command protection level not supported by security mechanism.

  5.2.  Protected replies.

    One new reply type is introduced:

      6yz    Protected reply

          There are three reply codes of this type.  The first, reply
          code 631 indicates an integrity protected reply.  The
          second, reply code 632, indicates a confidentiality and
          integrity protected reply.  the third, reply code 633,
          indicates a confidentiality protected reply.

          The text part of a 631 reply is a Telnet string consisting
          of a base 64 encoded "safe" message produced by a security
          mechanism specific message integrity procedure.  The text
          part of a 632 reply is a Telnet string consisting of a base
          64 encoded "private" message produced by a security
          mechanism specific message confidentiality and integrity
          procedure.  The text part of a 633 reply is a Telnet string
          consisting of a base 64 encoded "confidential" message
          produced by a security mechanism specific message
          confidentiality procedure.

          The client will decode and verify the encoded reply.  How
          failures decoding or verifying replies are handled is
          implementation-specific.  An end-of-line code need not be
          included, but if one is included, it must be a Telnet end-
          of-line code, not a local end-of-line code.

          A protected reply may only be sent if a security data
          exchange has succeeded.

          The 63z reply may be a multiline reply.  In this case, the
          plaintext reply must be broken up into a number of
          fragments.  Each fragment must be protected, then base 64

encoded in order into a separate line of the multiline
reply.  There need not be any correspondence between the
line breaks in the plaintext reply and the encoded reply.
Telnet end-of-line codes must appear in the plaintext of the
encoded reply, except for the final end-of-line code, which
is optional.

The multiline reply must be formatted more strictly than the
continuation specification in RFC 959.  In particular, each
line before the last must be formed by the reply code,
followed immediately by a hyphen, followed by a base 64
encoded fragment of the reply.

For example, if the plaintext reply is

```
123-First line
Second line
  234 A line beginning with numbers
123 The last line
```

then the resulting protected reply could be any of the
following (the first example has a line break only to fit
within the margins):

```
631 base64(protect("123-First line\r\nSecond line\r\n  234 A line
631-base64(protect("123-First line\r\n"))
631-base64(protect("Second line\r\n"))
631-base64(protect("  234 A line beginning with numbers\r\n"))
631 base64(protect("123 The last line"))

631-base64(protect("123-First line\r\nSecond line\r\n  234 A line b"))
631 base64(protect("eginning with numbers\r\n123 The last line\r\n"))
```

6.  Data Channel Encapsulation

   When data transfers are protected between the client and server (in
   either direction), certain transformations and encapsulations must be
   performed so that the recipient can properly decode the transmitted
   file.

   The sender must apply all protection services after transformations
   associated with the representation type, file structure, and transfer
   mode have been performed.  The data sent over the data channel is,
   for the purposes of protection, to be treated as a byte stream.

   When performing a data transfer in an authenticated manner, the
   authentication checks are performed on individual blocks of the file,
   rather than on the file as a whole. Consequently, it is possible for

insertion attacks to insert blocks into the data stream (i.e.,
replays) that authenticate correctly, but result in a corrupted file
being undetected by the receiver. To guard against such attacks, the
specific security mechanism employed should include mechanisms to
protect against such attacks. Many GSS-API mechanisms usable with
the specification in Appendix I, and the Kerberos mechanism in
Appendix II do so.

The sender must take the input byte stream, and break it up into
blocks such that each block, when encoded using a security mechanism
specific procedure, will be no larger than the buffer size negotiated
by the client with the PBSZ command.  Each block must be encoded,
then transmitted with the length of the encoded block prepended as a
four byte unsigned integer, most significant byte first.

When the end of the file is reached, the sender must encode a block
of zero bytes, and send this final block to the recipient before
closing the data connection.

The recipient will read the four byte length, read a block of data
that many bytes long, then decode and verify this block with a
security mechanism specific procedure.  This must be repeated until a
block encoding a buffer of zero bytes is received.  This indicates
the end of the encoded byte stream.

Any transformations associated with the representation type, file
structure, and transfer mode are to be performed by the recipient on
the byte stream resulting from the above process.

When using block transfer mode, the sender's (cleartext) buffer size
is independent of the block size.

The server will reply 534 to a STOR, STOU, RETR, LIST, NLST, or APPE
command if the current protection level is not at the level dictated
by the server's security requirements for the particular file
transfer.

If any data protection services fail at any time during data transfer
at the server end (including an attempt to send a buffer size greater
than the negotiated maximum), the server will send a 535 reply to the
data transfer command (either STOR, STOU, RETR, LIST, NLST, or APPE).

7.  Potential policy considerations

    While there are no restrictions on client and server policy, there
    are a few recommendations which an implementation should implement.

    - Once a security data exchange takes place, a server should require
      all commands be protected (with integrity and/or confidentiality),
      and it should protect all replies.  Replies should use the same
      level of protection as the command which produced them.  This
      includes replies which indicate failure of the MIC, CONF, and ENC
      commands.  In particular, it is not meaningful to require that
      AUTH and ADAT be protected; it is meaningful and useful to require
      that PROT and PBSZ be protected.  In particular, the use of CCC is
      not recommended, but is defined in the interest of
      interoperability between implementations which might desire such
      functionality.

    - A client should encrypt the PASS command whenever possible.  It is
      reasonable for the server to refuse to accept a non-encrypted PASS
      command if the server knows encryption is available.

    - Although no security commands are required to be implemented, it
      is recommended that an implementation provide all commands which
      can be implemented, given the mechanisms supported and the policy
      considerations of the site (export controls, for instance).

8.  Declarative specifications

    These sections are modelled after sections 5.3 and 5.4 of RFC 959,
    which describe the same information, except for the standard FTP
    commands and replies.

    8.1.  FTP Security commands and arguments

        AUTH <SP> <mechanism-name> <CRLF>
        ADAT <SP> <base64data> <CRLF>
        PROT <SP> <prot-code> <CRLF>
        PBSZ <SP> <decimal-integer> <CRLF>
        MIC <SP> <base64data> <CRLF>
        CONF <SP> <base64data> <CRLF>
        ENC <SP> <base64data> <CRLF>

        <mechanism-name> ::= <string>
        <base64data> ::= <string>
                ; must be formatted as described in section 9
        <prot-code> ::= C | S | E | P
        <decimal-integer> ::= any decimal integer from 1 to (2^32)-1

8.2.  Command-Reply sequences

    Security Association Setup
      AUTH
        234
        334
        502, 504, 534, 431
        500, 501, 421
      ADAT
        235
        335
        503, 501, 535
        500, 501, 421
    Data protection negotiation commands
      PBSZ
        200
        503
        500, 501, 421, 530
      PROT
        200
        504, 536, 503, 534, 431
        500, 501, 421, 530
    Command channel protection commands
      MIC
        535, 533
        500, 501, 421
      CONF
        535, 533
        500, 501, 421
      ENC
        535, 533
        500, 501, 421
    Security-Enhanced login commands (only new replies listed)
      USER
        232
        336
    Data channel commands (only new replies listed)
      STOR
        534, 535
      STOU
        534, 535
      RETR
        534, 535

```
LIST
   534, 535
NLST
   534, 535
APPE
   534, 535
```

In addition to these reply codes, any security command can return
500, 501, 502, 533, or 421.  Any ftp command can return a reply
code encapsulated in a 631, 632, or 633 reply once a security data
exchange has completed successfully.

9.  State Diagrams

    This section includes a state diagram which demonstrates the flow of
    authentication and authorization in a security enhanced FTP
    implementation.  The rectangular blocks show states where the client
    must issue a command, and the diamond blocks show states where the
    server must issue a response.

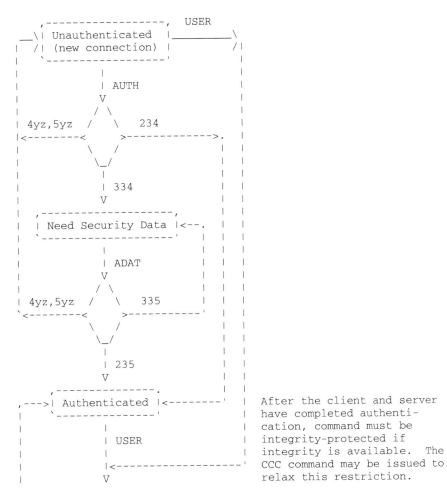

```
            ,----------------, USER
       __\| Unauthenticated |_____\
       | /| (new connection) |          /|
       |  `----------------'             |
       |         |                       |
       |         | AUTH                  |
       |         V                       |
       |        / \                      |
       | 4yz,5yz /   \  234              |
       |<--------<     >------------->.  |
       |         \   /              |  |
       |          \_/               |  |
       |           |                |  |
       |           | 334            |  |
       |           V                |  |
       |  ,------------------,       |  |
       |  | Need Security Data |<--. |  |
       |  `------------------'    | |  |
       |           |               | |  |
       |           | ADAT          | |  |
       |           V               | |  |
       |          / \              | |  |
       | 4yz,5yz /   \  335        | |  |
       `<--------<     >----------' |  |
                 \   /              |  |
                  \_/               |  |
                   |                |  |
                   | 235            |  |
                   V                |  |
          ,---------------.         |  |
      ,--->| Authenticated |<--------'  |
      |    `---------------'            |
      |           |                     |
      |           | USER                |
      |           |                     |
      |           |<--------------------'
      |           V
```

After the client and server
have completed authenti-
cation, command must be
integrity-protected if
integrity is available.  The
CCC command may be issued to
relax this restriction.

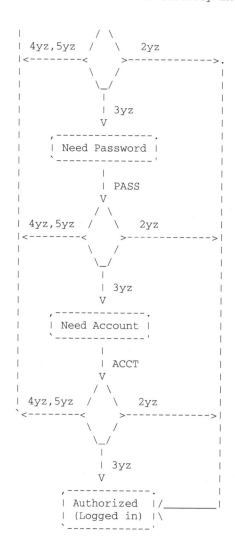

```
            |        / \
            | 4yz,5yz /   \  2yz
            |<--------<     >------------->.
            |         \   /                |
            |          \_/                 |
            |           |                  |
            |           | 3yz              |
            |           V                  |
            |     ,--------------.         |
            |     | Need Password |        |
            |     `--------------'         |
            |           |                  |
            |           | PASS             |
            |           V                  |
            |          / \                 |
            | 4yz,5yz /   \  2yz           |
            |<--------<     >------------->|
            |         \   /                |
            |          \_/                 |
            |           |                  |
            |           | 3yz              |
            |           V                  |
            |     ,--------------.         |
            |     | Need Account |         |
            |     `--------------'         |
            |           |                  |
            |           | ACCT             |
            |           V                  |
            | 4yz,5yz /   \  2yz           |
            `<--------<     >------------->|
                      \   /                |
                       \_/                 |
                        |                  |
                        | 3yz              |
                        V                  |
                  ,--------------.         |
                  | Authorized   |/_____|
                  | (Logged in)  |\
                  `--------------'
```

10.  Base 64 Encoding

   Base 64 encoding is the same as the Printable Encoding described in
   Section 4.3.2.4 of [RFC-1421], except that line breaks must not be
   included. This encoding is defined as follows.

   Proceeding from left to right, the bit string resulting from the
   mechanism specific protection routine is encoded into characters
   which are universally representable at all sites, though not
   necessarily with the same bit patterns (e.g., although the character
   "E" is represented in an ASCII-based system as hexadecimal 45 and as
   hexadecimal C5 in an EBCDIC-based system, the local significance of
   the two representations is equivalent).

   A 64-character subset of International Alphabet IA5 is used, enabling
   6 bits to be represented per printable character.  (The proposed
   subset of characters is represented identically in IA5 and ASCII.)
   The character "=" signifies a special processing function used for
   padding within the printable encoding procedure.

   The encoding process represents 24-bit groups of input bits as output
   strings of 4 encoded characters.  Proceeding from left to right
   across a 24-bit input group output from the security mechanism
   specific message protection procedure, each 6-bit group is used as an
   index into an array of 64 printable characters, namely "[A-Z][a-
   z][0-9]+/".  The character referenced by the index is placed in the
   output string.  These characters are selected so as to be universally
   representable, and the set excludes characters with particular
   significance to Telnet (e.g., "<CR>", "<LF>", IAC).

   Special processing is performed if fewer than 24 bits are available
   in an input group at the end of a message.  A full encoding quantum
   is always completed at the end of a message.  When fewer than 24
   input bits are available in an input group, zero bits are added (on
   the right) to form an integral number of 6-bit groups.  Output
   character positions which are not required to represent actual input
   data are set to the character "=".  Since all canonically encoded
   output is an integral number of octets, only the following cases can
   arise: (1) the final quantum of encoding input is an integral
   multiple of 24 bits; here, the final unit of encoded output will be
   an integral multiple of 4 characters with no "=" padding, (2) the
   final quantum of encoding input is exactly 8 bits; here, the final
   unit of encoded output will be two characters followed by two "="
   padding characters, or (3) the final quantum of encoding input is
   exactly 16 bits; here, the final unit of encoded output will be three
   characters followed by one "=" padding character.

Implementors must keep in mind that the base 64 encodings in ADAT,
MIC, CONF, and ENC commands, and in 63z replies may be arbitrarily
long.  Thus, the entire line must be read before it can be processed.
Several successive reads on the control channel may be necessary.  It
is not appropriate to for a server to reject a command containing a
base 64 encoding simply because it is too long (assuming that the
decoding is otherwise well formed in the context in which it was
sent).

Case must not be ignored when reading commands and replies containing
base 64 encodings.

## 11.  Security Considerations

This entire document deals with security considerations related to
the File Transfer Protocol.

Third party file transfers cannot be secured using these extensions,
since a security context cannot be established between two servers
using these facilities (no control connection exists between servers
over which to pass ADAT tokens).  Further work in this area is
deferred.

## 12.  Acknowledgements

I would like to thank the members of the CAT WG, as well as all
participants in discussions on the "cat-ietf@mit.edu" mailing list,
for their contributions to this document.  I would especially like to
thank Sam Sjogren, John Linn, Ted Ts'o, Jordan Brown, Michael Kogut,
Derrick Brashear, John Gardiner Myers, Denis Pinkas, and Karri Balk
for their contributions to this work.  Of course, without Steve Lunt,
the author of the first six revisions of this document, it would not
exist at all.

## 13.  References

[TELNET-SEC] Borman, D., "Telnet Authentication and Encryption
    Option", Work in Progress.

[RFC-1123] Braden, R., "Requirements for Internet Hosts --
    Application and Support", STD 3, RFC 1123, October 1989.

[RFC-1421] Linn, J., "Privacy Enhancement for Internet Electronic
    Mail: Part I: Message Encryption and Authentication Procedures",
    RFC 1421, February 1993.

14.  Author's Address

Marc Horowitz
Cygnus Solutions
955 Massachusetts Avenue
Cambridge, MA 02139

Phone: +1 617 354 7688
EMail: marc@cygnus.com

Appendix I: Specification under the GSSAPI

In order to maximise the utility of new security mechanisms, it is
desirable that new mechanisms be implemented as GSSAPI mechanisms
rather than as FTP security mechanisms.  This will enable existing
ftp implementations to support the new mechanisms more easily, since
little or no code will need to be changed.  In addition, the
mechanism will be usable by other protocols, such as IMAP, which are
built on top of the GSSAPI, with no additional specification or
implementation work needed by the mechanism designers.

The security mechanism name (for the AUTH command) associated with
all mechanisms employing the GSSAPI is GSSAPI.  If the server
supports a security mechanism employing the GSSAPI, it must respond
with a 334 reply code indicating that an ADAT command is expected
next.

The client must begin the authentication exchange by calling
GSS_Init_Sec_Context, passing in 0 for input_context_handle
(initially), and a targ_name equal to output_name from
GSS_Import_Name called with input_name_type of Host-Based Service and
input_name_string of "ftp@hostname" where "hostname" is the fully
qualified host name of the server with all letters in lower case.
(Failing this, the client may try again using input_name_string of
"host@hostname".) The output_token must then be base 64 encoded and
sent to the server as the argument to an ADAT command.  If
GSS_Init_Sec_Context returns GSS_S_CONTINUE_NEEDED, then the client
must expect a token to be returned in the reply to the ADAT command.
This token must subsequently be passed to another call to
GSS_Init_Sec_Context.  In this case, if GSS_Init_Sec_Context returns
no output_token, then the reply code from the server for the previous
ADAT command must have been 235.  If GSS_Init_Sec_Context returns
GSS_S_COMPLETE, then no further tokens are expected from the server,
and the client must consider the server authenticated.

The server must base 64 decode the argument to the ADAT command and
pass the resultant token to GSS_Accept_Sec_Context as input_token,
setting acceptor_cred_handle to NULL (for "use default credentials"),
and 0 for input_context_handle (initially).  If an output_token is
returned, it must be base 64 encoded and returned to the client by
including "ADAT=base64string" in the text of the reply.  If
GSS_Accept_Sec_Context returns GSS_S_COMPLETE, the reply code must be
235, and the server must consider the client authenticated.  If
GSS_Accept_Sec_Context returns GSS_S_CONTINUE_NEEDED, the reply code
must be 335.  Otherwise, the reply code should be 535, and the text
of the reply should contain a descriptive error message.

The chan_bindings input to GSS_Init_Sec_Context and
GSS_Accept_Sec_Context should use the client internet address and
server internet address as the initiator and acceptor addresses,
respectively.  The address type for both should be GSS_C_AF_INET. No
application data should be specified.

Since GSSAPI supports anonymous peers to security contexts, it is
possible that the client's authentication of the server does not
actually establish an identity.

The procedure associated with MIC commands, 631 replies, and Safe
file transfers is:

    GSS_Wrap for the sender, with conf_flag == FALSE

    GSS_Unwrap for the receiver

The procedure associated with ENC commands, 632 replies, and Private
file transfers is:

    GSS_Wrap for the sender, with conf_flag == TRUE
    GSS_Unwrap for the receiver

CONF commands and 633 replies are not supported.

Both the client and server should inspect the value of conf_avail to
determine whether the peer supports confidentiality services.

When the security state is reset (when AUTH is received a second
time, or when REIN is received), this should be done by calling the
GSS_Delete_sec_context function.

Appendix II:  Specification under Kerberos version 4

The security mechanism name (for the AUTH command) associated with
Kerberos Version 4 is KERBEROS_V4.  If the server supports
KERBEROS_V4, it must respond with a 334 reply code indicating that an
ADAT command is expected next.

The client must retrieve a ticket for the Kerberos principal
"ftp.hostname@realm" by calling krb_mk_req(3) with a principal name
of "ftp", an instance equal to the first part of the canonical host
name of the server with all letters in lower case (as returned by
krb_get_phost(3)), the server's realm name (as returned by
krb_realmofhost(3)), and an arbitrary checksum.  The ticket must then
be base 64 encoded and sent as the argument to an ADAT command.

If the "ftp" principal name is not a registered principal in the
Kerberos database, then the client may fall back on the "rcmd"
principal name (same instance and realm).  However, servers must
accept only one or the other of these principal names, and must not
be willing to accept either.  Generally, if the server has a key for
the "ftp" principal in its srvtab, then that principal only must be
used, otherwise the "rcmd" principal only must be used.

The server must base 64 decode the argument to the ADAT command and
pass the result to krb_rd_req(3).  The server must add one to the
checksum from the authenticator, convert the result to network byte
order (most significant byte first), and sign it using
krb_mk_safe(3), and base 64 encode the result.  Upon success, the
server must reply to the client with a 235 code and include
"ADAT=base64string" in the text of the reply.  Upon failure, the
server should reply 535.

Upon receipt of the 235 reply from the server, the client must parse
the text of the reply for the base 64 encoded data, decode it,
convert it from network byte order, and pass the result to
krb_rd_safe(3).  The client must consider the server authenticated if
the resultant checksum is equal to one plus the value previously
sent.

The procedure associated with MIC commands, 631 replies, and Safe
file transfers is:

    krb_mk_safe(3) for the sender
    krb_rd_safe(3) for the receiver

The procedure associated with ENC commands, 632 replies, and Private
file transfers is:

    krb_mk_priv(3) for the sender
    krb_rd_priv(3) for the receiver

CONF commands and 633 replies are not supported.

Note that this specification for KERBEROS_V4 contains no provision
for negotiating alternate means for integrity and confidentiality
routines.  Note also that the ADAT exchange does not convey whether
the peer supports confidentiality services.

In order to stay within the allowed PBSZ, implementors must take note
that a cleartext buffer will grow by 31 bytes when processed by
krb_mk_safe(3) and will grow by 26 bytes when processed by
krb_mk_priv(3).

Full Copyright Statement

Network Working Group                                    G. Malkin
Request for Commments: 2347                           Bay Networks
Updates: 1350                                            A. Harkin
Obsoletes: 1782                               Hewlett Packard Co.
Category: Standards Track                                May 1998

TFTP Option Extension

Abstract

   The Trivial File Transfer Protocol [1] is a simple, lock-step, file
   transfer protocol which allows a client to get or put a file onto a
   remote host.  This document describes a simple extension to TFTP to
   allow option negotiation prior to the file transfer.

Introduction

   The option negotiation mechanism proposed in this document is a
   backward-compatible extension to the TFTP protocol.  It allows file
   transfer options to be negotiated prior to the transfer using a
   mechanism which is consistent with TFTP's Request Packet format.  The
   mechanism is kept simple by enforcing a request-respond-acknowledge
   sequence, similar to the lock-step approach taken by TFTP itself.

   While the option negotiation mechanism is general purpose, in that
   many types of options may be negotiated, it was created to support
   the Blocksize option defined in [2].  Additional options are defined
   in [3].

Packet Formats

   TFTP options are appended to the Read Request and Write Request
   packets.  A new type of TFTP packet, the Option Acknowledgment
   (OACK), is used to acknowledge a client's option negotiation request.
   A new error code, 8, is hereby defined to indicate that a transfer

should be terminated due to option negotiation.

Options are appended to a TFTP Read Request or Write Request packet
as follows:

```
+-------+---~~---+---+---~~---+---+---~~---+---+---~~---+---+-->
|  opc  |filename| 0 |  mode  | 0 |  opt1  | 0 | value1 | 0 | <
+-------+---~~---+---+---~~---+---+---~~---+---+---~~---+---+-->

 >-------+---+---~~---+---+
<  optN  | 0 | valueN | 0 |
 >-------+---+---~~---+---+
```

opc
    The opcode field contains either a 1, for Read Requests, or 2,
    for Write Requests, as defined in [1].

filename
    The name of the file to be read or written, as defined in [1].
    This is a NULL-terminated field.

mode
    The mode of the file transfer: "netascii", "octet", or "mail",
    as defined in [1].  This is a NULL-terminated field.

opt1
    The first option, in case-insensitive ASCII (e.g., blksize).
    This is a NULL-terminated field.

value1
    The value associated with the first option, in case-
    insensitive ASCII.  This is a NULL-terminated field.

optN, valueN
    The final option/value pair.  Each NULL-terminated field is
    specified in case-insensitive ASCII.

The options and values are all NULL-terminated, in keeping with the
original request format.  If multiple options are to be negotiated,
they are appended to each other.  The order in which options are
specified is not significant.  The maximum size of a request packet
is 512 octets.

The OACK packet has the following format:

```
+-------+---~----+---+---~----+---+---~----+---+---~----+---+
|  opc  |  opt1  | 0 | value1 | 0 |  optN  | 0 | valueN | 0 |
+-------+---~----+---+---~----+---+---~----+---+---~----+---+
```

opc
   The opcode field contains a 6, for Option Acknowledgment.

opt1
   The first option acknowledgment, copied from the original
   request.

value1
   The acknowledged value associated with the first option.  If
   and how this value may differ from the original request is
   detailed in the specification for the option.

optN, valueN
   The final option/value acknowledgment pair.

Negotiation Protocol

   The client appends options at the end of the Read Request or Write
   request packet, as shown above.  Any number of options may be
   specified; however, an option may only be specified once.  The order
   of the options is not significant.

   If the server supports option negotiation, and it recognizes one or
   more of the options specified in the request packet, the server may
   respond with an Options Acknowledgment (OACK).  Each option the
   server recognizes, and accepts the value for, is included in the
   OACK.  Some options may allow alternate values to be proposed, but
   this is an option specific feature.  The server must not include in
   the OACK any option which had not been specifically requested by the
   client; that is, only the client may initiate option negotiation.
   Options which the server does not support should be omitted from the
   OACK; they should not cause an ERROR packet to be generated.  If the
   value of a supported option is invalid, the specification for that
   option will indicate whether the server should simply omit the option
   from the OACK, respond with an alternate value, or send an ERROR
   packet, with error code 8, to terminate the transfer.

   An option not acknowledged by the server must be ignored by the
   client and server as if it were never requested.  If multiple options
   were requested, the client must use those options which were
   acknowledged by the server and must not use those options which were
   not acknowledged by the server.

When the client appends options to the end of a Read Request packet, three possible responses may be returned by the server:

    OACK  - acknowledge of Read Request and the options;

    DATA  - acknowledge of Read Request, but not the options;

    ERROR - the request has been denied.

When the client appends options to the end of a Write Request packet, three possible responses may be returned by the server:

    OACK  - acknowledge of Write Request and the options;

    ACK   - acknowledge of Write Request, but not the options;

    ERROR - the request has been denied.

If a server implementation does not support option negotiation, it will likely ignore any options appended to the client's request.  In this case, the server will return a DATA packet for a Read Request and an ACK packet for a Write Request establishing normal TFTP data transfer.  In the event that a server returns an error for a request which carries an option, the client may attempt to repeat the request without appending any options.  This implementation option would handle servers which consider extraneous data in the request packet to be erroneous.

Depending on the original transfer request there are two ways for a client to confirm acceptance of a server's OACK.  If the transfer was initiated with a Read Request, then an ACK (with the data block number set to 0) is sent by the client to confirm the values in the server's OACK packet.  If the transfer was initiated with a Write Request, then the client begins the transfer with the first DATA packet, using the negotiated values.  If the client rejects the OACK, then it sends an ERROR packet, with error code 8, to the server and the transfer is terminated.

Once a client acknowledges an OACK, with an appropriate non-error response, that client has agreed to use only the options and values returned by the server.  Remember that the server cannot request an option; it can only respond to them.  If the client receives an OACK containing an unrequested option, it should respond with an ERROR packet, with error code 8, and terminate the transfer.

Examples

   Read Request

```
       client                                          server
       -----------------------------------------------------
       |1|foofile|0|octet|0|blksize|0|1432|0|  -->           RRQ
                             <--   |6|blksize|0|1432|0|      OACK
       |4|0|  -->                                            ACK
                           <--   |3|1|  1432 octets of data |  DATA
       |4|1|  -->                                            ACK
                           <--   |3|2|  1432 octets of data |  DATA
       |4|2|  -->                                            ACK
                           <--   |3|3|<1432 octets of data |  DATA
       |4|3|  -->                                            ACK
```

   Write Request

```
       client                                          server
       -----------------------------------------------------
       |2|barfile|0|octet|0|blksize|0|2048|0|  -->           RRQ
                             <--   |6|blksize|0|2048|0|      OACK
       |3|1|  2048 octets of data |  -->                     DATA
                                      <--   |4|1|   ACK
       |3|2|  2048 octets of data |  -->                     DATA
                                      <--   |4|2|   ACK
       |3|3|<2048 octets of data |  -->                     DATA
                                      <--   |4|3|   ACK
```

Security Considerations

   The basic TFTP protocol has no security mechanism.  This is why it
   has no rename, delete, or file overwrite capabilities.  This document
   does not add any security to TFTP; however, the specified extensions
   do not add any additional security risks.

References

   [1] Sollins, K., "The TFTP Protocol (Revision 2)", STD 33, RFC 1350,
       October 1992.

   [2] Malkin, G., and A. Harkin, "TFTP Blocksize Option", RFC 2348,
       May 1998.

   [3] Malkin, G., and A. Harkin, "TFTP Timeout Interval and Transfer
       Size Options", RFC 2349, May 1998.

Authors' Addresses

   Gary Scott Malkin
   Bay Networks
   8 Federal Street
   Billerica, MA  01821

   Phone:  (978) 916-4237
   EMail:  gmalkin@baynetworks.com


   Art Harkin
   Internet Services Project
   Information Networks Division
   19420 Homestead Road MS 43LN
   Cupertino, CA  95014

   Phone: (408) 447-3755
   EMail: ash@cup.hp.com

Full Copyright Statement

Network Working Group                                          G. Malkin
Request for Commments: 2348                                 Bay Networks
Updates: 1350                                                  A. Harkin
Obsoletes: 1783                                      Hewlett Packard Co.
Category: Standards Track                                      May 1998

                          TFTP Blocksize Option

Status of this Memo

   This document specifies an Internet standards track protocol for the
   Internet community, and requests discussion and suggestions for
   improvements.  Please refer to the current edition of the "Internet
   Official Protocol Standards" (STD 1) for the standardization state
   and status of this protocol.  Distribution of this memo is unlimited.

Copyright Notice

Abstract

   The Trivial File Transfer Protocol [1] is a simple, lock-step, file
   transfer protocol which allows a client to get or put a file onto a
   remote host.  One of its primary uses is the booting of diskless
   nodes on a Local Area Network.  TFTP is used because it is very
   simple to implement in a small node's limited ROM space.  However,
   the choice of a 512-octet blocksize is not the most efficient for use
   on a LAN whose MTU may 1500 octets or greater.

   This document describes a TFTP option which allows the client and
   server to negotiate a blocksize more applicable to the network
   medium.  The TFTP Option Extension mechanism is described in [2].

Blocksize Option Specification

   The TFTP Read Request or Write Request packet is modified to include
   the blocksize option as follows.  Note that all fields except "opc"
   are NULL-terminated.

      +-------+---~~---+---+---~~---+---+---~~---+---+---~~---+---+
      | opc  |filename| 0 | mode   | 0 | blksize| 0 | #octets| 0 |
      +-------+---~~---+---+---~~---+---+---~~---+---+---~~---+---+

   opc
      The opcode field contains either a 1, for Read Requests, or 2,
      for Write Requests, as defined in [1].

filename
    The name of the file to be read or written, as defined in [1].

mode
    The mode of the file transfer: "netascii", "octet", or "mail",
    as defined in [1].

blksize
    The Blocksize option, "blksize" (case in-sensitive).

#octets
    The number of octets in a block, specified in ASCII.  Valid
    values range between "8" and "65464" octets, inclusive.  The
    blocksize refers to the number of data octets; it does not
    include the four octets of TFTP header.

For example:

```
+-------+--------+---+--------+---+--------+---+--------+---+
|   1   | foobar | 0 | octet  | 0 | blksize| 0 |  1428  | 0 |
+-------+--------+---+--------+---+--------+---+--------+---+
```

is a Read Request, for the file named "foobar", in octet (binary)
transfer mode, with a block size of 1428 octets (Ethernet MTU, less
the TFTP, UDP and IP header lengths).

If the server is willing to accept the blocksize option, it sends an
Option Acknowledgment (OACK) to the client.  The specified value must
be less than or equal to the value specified by the client.  The
client must then either use the size specified in the OACK, or send
an ERROR packet, with error code 8, to terminate the transfer.

The rules for determining the final packet are unchanged from [1].
The reception of a data packet with a data length less than the
negotiated blocksize is the final packet.  If the blocksize is
greater than the amount of data to be transfered, the first packet is
the final packet.  If the amount of data to be transfered is an
integral multiple of the blocksize, an extra data packet containing
no data is sent to end the transfer.

Proof of Concept

Performance tests were run on the prototype implementation using a
variety of block sizes.  The tests were run on a lightly loaded
Ethernet, between two HP-UX 9000, in "octet" mode, on 2.25MB files.
The average (5x) transfer times for paths with (g-time) and without
(n-time) a intermediate gateway are graphed as follows:

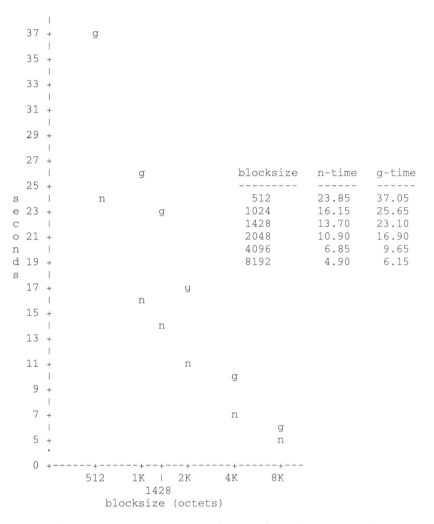

```
      |
  37 +      g
      |
  35 +
      |
  33 +
      |
  31 +
      |
  29 +
      |
  27 +
      |           g               blocksize   n-time   g-time
  25 +                            ---------    ------   ------
 s    |       n                       512      23.85    37.05
 e 23 +              g               1024      16.15    25.65
 c    |                              1428      13.70    23.10
 o 21 +                              2048      10.90    16.90
 n    |                              4096       6.85     9.65
 d 19 +                              8192       4.90     6.15
 s    |
  17 +              g
      |         n
  15 +
      |           n
  13 +
      |
  11 +           n
      |              g
   9 +
      |
   7 +              n
      |               g
   5 +                n
      "
   0 +------+------+--+---+------+------+---
          512    1K  |  2K    4K     8K
                  1428
              blocksize (octets)
```

The comparisons between transfer times (without a gateway) between
the standard 512-octet blocksize and the negotiated blocksizes are:

```
   1024    2x    -32%
   1428    2.8x  -42%
   2048    4x    -54%
   4096    8x    -71%
   8192    16x   -80%
```

As was anticipated, the transfer time decreases with an increase in blocksize.  The reason for the reduction in time is the reduction in the number of packets sent.  For example, by increasing the blocksize from 512 octets to 1024 octets, not only are the number of data packets halved, but the number of acknowledgement packets is also halved (along with the number of times the data transmitter must wait for an ACK).  A secondary effect is the efficiency gained by reducing the per-packet framing and processing overhead.

Of course, if the blocksize exceeds the path MTU, IP fragmentation and reassembly will begin to add more overhead.  This will be more noticable the greater the number of gateways in the path.

Security Considerations

    The basic TFTP protocol has no security mechanism.  This is why it has no rename, delete, or file overwrite capabilities.  This document does not add any security to TFTP; however, the specified extensions do not add any additional security risks.

References

    [1] Sollins, K., "The TFTP Protocol (Revision 2)", STD 33, RFC 1350,
        October 1992.

    [2] Malkin, G., and A. Harkin, "TFTP Option Extension", RFC 2347,
        May 1998.

Authors' Addresses

    Gary Scott Malkin
    Bay Networks
    8 Federal Street
    Billerica, MA  10821

    Phone:  (978) 916-4237
    EMail:  gmalkin@baynetworks.com


    Art Harkin
    Networked Computing Division
    Hewlett-Packard Company
    19420 Homestead Road MS 43LN
    Cupertino, CA  95014

    Phone: (408) 447-3755
    EMail: ash@cup.hp.com

Full Copyright Statement

5

RFC 2348

Network Working Group                                    G. Malkin
Request for Commments: 2349                          Bay Networks
Updates: 1350                                            A. Harkin
Obsoletes: 1784                              Hewlett Packard Co.
Category: Standards Track                                May 1998

         TFTP Timeout Interval and Transfer Size Options

Status of this Memo

Copyright Notice

Abstract

   The Trivial File Transfer Protocol [1] is a simple, lock-step, file
   transfer protocol which allows a client to get or put a file onto a
   remote host.

   This document describes two TFTP options. The first allows the client
   and server to negotiate the Timeout Interval.  The second allows the
   side receiving the file to determine the ultimate size of the
   transfer before it begins.  The TFTP Option Extension mechanism is
   described in [2].

Timeout Interval Option Specification

   The TFTP Read Request or Write Request packet is modified to include
   the timeout option as follows:

```
+-------+---~---+---+---~---+---+---~---+---+---~---+---+
|  opc  |filename| 0 |  mode  | 0 | timeout| 0 |  #secs | 0 |
+-------+---~---+---+---~---+---+---~---+---+---~---+---+
```

   opc
      The opcode field contains either a 1, for Read Requests, or 2,
      for Write Requests, as defined in [1].

filename
    The name of the file to be read or written, as defined in [1].
    This is a NULL-terminated field.

mode
    The mode of the file transfer: "netascii", "octet", or "mail",
    as defined in [1].  This is a NULL-terminated field.

timeout
    The Timeout Interval option, "timeout" (case in-sensitive).
    This is a NULL-terminated field.

#secs
    The number of seconds to wait before retransmitting, specified
    in ASCII.  Valid values range between "1" and "255" seconds,
    inclusive.  This is a NULL-terminated field.

For example:

```
+-------+--------+---+--------+---+--------+---+-------+---+
|   1   | foobar | 0 | octet  | 0 | timeout| 0 |   1   | 0 |
+-------+--------+---+--------+---+--------+---+-------+---+
```

is a Read Request, for the file named "foobar", in octet (binary)
transfer mode, with a timeout interval of 1 second.

If the server is willing to accept the timeout option, it sends an
Option Acknowledgment (OACK) to the client.  The specified timeout
value must match the value specified by the client.

Transfer Size Option Specification

The TFTP Read Request or Write Request packet is modified to include
the tsize option as follows:

```
+-------+---~----+---+---~----+---+---~----+---+---~----+---+
|  opc  |filename| 0 |  mode  | 0 | tsize  | 0 | size   | 0 |
+-------+---~----+---+---~----+---+---~----+---+---~----+---+
```

opc
    The opcode field contains either a 1, for Read Requests, or 2,
    for Write Requests, as defined in [1].

filename
    The name of the file to be read or written, as defined in [1].
    This is a NULL-terminated field.

mode
    The mode of the file transfer: "netascii", "octet", or "mail",
    as defined in [1].  This is a NULL-terminated field.

tsize
    The Transfer Size option, "tsize" (case in-sensitive).  This is
    a NULL-terminated field.

size
    The size of the file to be transfered.  This is a NULL-
    terminated field.

For example:

```
+-------+--------+---+--------+---+--------+---+--------+---+
|   2   | foobar | 0 | octet  | 0 | tsize  | 0 | 673312 | 0 |
+-------+--------+---+--------+---+--------+---+--------+---+
```

is a Write Request, with the 673312-octet file named "foobar", in
octet (binary) transfer mode.

In Read Request packets, a size of "0" is specified in the request
and the size of the file, in octets, is returned in the OACK.  If the
file is too large for the client to handle, it may abort the transfer
with an Error packet (error code 3).  In Write Request packets, the
size of the file, in octets, is specified in the request and echoed
back in the OACK.  If the file is too large for the server to handle,
it may abort the transfer with an Error packet (error code 3).

Security Considerations

    The basic TFTP protocol has no security mechanism.  This is why it
    has no rename, delete, or file overwrite capabilities.  This document
    does not add any security to TFTP; however, the specified extensions
    do not add any additional security risks.

References

    [1] Sollins, K., "The TFTP Protocol (Revision 2)", STD 33, RFC 1350,
        October 92.

    [2] Malkin, G., and A. Harkin, "TFTP Option Extension", RFC 2347,
        May 1998.

Authors' Addresses

    Gary Scott Malkin
    Bay Networks
    8 Federal Street
    Billerica, MA  01821

    Phone:  (978) 916-4237
    EMail:  gmalkin@baynetworks.com


    Art Harkin
    Internet Services Project
    Information Networks Division
    19420 Homestead Road MS 43LN
    Cupertino, CA  95014

    Phone: (408) 447-3755
    EMail: ash@cup.hp.com

Full Copyright Statement

Network Working Group                                    P. Hethmon
Request for Comments: 2389                        Hethmon Brothers
See Also: 959                                              R. Elz
Category: Standards Track                  University of Melbourne
                                                      August 1998

Feature negotiation mechanism for the File Transfer Protocol

Status of this Memo

   This document specifies an Internet standards track protocol for the
   Internet community, and requests discussion and suggestions for
   improvements.  Please refer to the current edition of the "Internet
   Official Protocol Standards" (STD 1) for the standardization state
   and status of this protocol.  Distribution of this memo is unlimited.

Abstract

   The File Transfer Protocol is, from time to time, extended with new
   commands, or facilities.  Implementations of the FTP protocol cannot
   be assumed to all immediately implement all newly defined mechanisms.
   This document provides a mechanism by which clients of the FTP
   protocol can discover which new features are supported by a
   particular FTP server.

RFC 2389

2

## Table of Contents

|  |  |  |
|---|---|---|
|   | Abstract ............................................... | 1 |
| 1 | Introduction .......................................... | 2 |
| 2 | Document Conventions .................................. | 2 |
| 2.1 | Basic Tokens ........................................ | 3 |
| 2.2 | Server Replies ...................................... | 3 |
| 3 | Knowledge of Extra Capabilities - the FEAT Command ...... | 3 |
| 3.1 | Feature (FEAT) Command Syntax ........................ | 4 |
| 3.2 | FEAT Command Responses .............................. | 4 |
| 3.3 | Rationale for FEAT .................................. | 6 |
| 4 | The OPTS Command .................................... | 6 |
| 5 | Security Considerations ............................. | 7 |
| 6 | References .......................................... | 8 |
|   | Acknowledgements .................................... | 8 |
|   | Editors' Addresses ................................. | 8 |
|   | Full Copyright Statement ............................ | 9 |

## 1. Introduction

This document amends the File Transfer Protocol (FTP) [1].  Two new
commands are added: "FEAT" and "OPTS".

These commands allow a client to discover which optional commands a
server supports, and how they are supported, and to select among
various options that any FTP command may support.

## 2. Document Conventions

This document makes use of the document conventions defined in BCP14
[2].  That provides the interpretation of some capitalized words like
MUST, SHOULD, etc.

Terms defined in [1] will be used here as defined there.  These
include ASCII, reply, server-FTP process, user-FTP process, server-
PI, user-PI, and user.

Syntax required is defined using the Augmented BNF defined in [3].
Some general ABNF definitions are required throughout the document,
those will be defined here.  At first reading, it may be wise to
simply recall that these definitions exist here, and skip to the next
section.

## 2.1. Basic Tokens

This document imports the definitions given in Appendix A of [3].
There definitions will be found for basic ABNF elements like ALPHA,
DIGIT, VCHAR, SP, etc.  To that, the following terms are added for
use in this document.

```
TCHAR            = VCHAR / SP / HTAB    ; visible plus white space
```

The TCHAR type, and VCHAR from [3], give basic character types from
varying sub-sets of the ASCII character set for use in various
commands and responses.

```
error-response = error-code SP *TCHAR CRLF
error-code     = ("4" / "5") 2DIGIT
```

Note that in ABNF, strings literals are case insensitive.  That
convention is preserved in this document.  However note that ALPHA,
in particular, is case sensitive, as are VCHAR and TCHAR.

## 2.2. Server Replies

Section 4.2 of [1] defines the format and meaning of replies by the
server-PI to FTP commands from the user-PI.  Those reply conventions
are used here without change.  Implementors should note that the ABNF
syntax (which was not used in [1]) in this document, and other FTP
related documents, sometimes shows replies using the one line format.
Unless otherwise explicitly stated, that is not intended to imply
that multi-line responses are not permitted.  Implementors should
assume that, unless stated to the contrary, any reply to any FTP
command (including QUIT) may be of the multiline format described in
[1].

Throughout this document, replies will be identified by the three
digit code that is their first element.  Thus the term "500 Reply"
means a reply from the server-PI using the three digit code "500".

## 3. Knowledge of Extra Capabilities - the FEAT Command

It is not to be expected that all servers will necessarily support
all of the new commands defined in all future amendments to the FTP
protocol.  In order to permit clients to determine which new commands
are supported by a particular server, without trying each possible
command, one new command is added to the FTP command repertoire.
This command requests the server to list all extension commands, or
extended mechanisms, that it supports.  That is, all defined and
specified commands and features not defined in [1], or this document,
must be included in the FEAT command output in the form specified in

the document that defines the extension.

User-FTP PIs must expect to see, in FEAT command responses, unknown features listed.  This is not an error, and simply indicates that the server-FTP implementor has seen, and implemented, the specification of a new feature that is unknown to the user-FTP.

3.1. Feature (FEAT) Command Syntax

            feat            = "Feat" CRLF

The FEAT command consists solely of the word "FEAT".  It has no parameters or arguments.

3.2. FEAT Command Responses

Where a server-FTP process does not support the FEAT command, it will respond to the FEAT command with a 500 or 502 reply.  This is simply the normal "unrecognized command" reply that any unknown command would elicit.  Errors in the command syntax, such as giving parameters, will result in a 501 reply.

Server-FTP processes that recognize the FEAT command, but implement no extended features, and therefore have nothing to report, SHOULD respond with the "no-features" 211 reply.  However, as this case is practically indistinguishable from a server-FTP that does not recognize the FEAT command, a 500 or 502 reply MAY also be used.  The "no-features" reply MUST NOT use the multi-line response format, exactly one response line is required and permitted.

Replies to the FEAT command MUST comply with the following syntax. Text on the first line of the reply is free form, and not interpreted, and has no practical use, as this text is not expected to be revealed to end users.  The syntax of other reply lines is precisely defined, and if present, MUST be exactly as specified.

            feat-response   = error-response / no-features / feature-listing
            no-features     = "211" SP *TCHAR CRLF
            feature-listing = "211-" *TCHAR CRLF
                              1*( SP feature CRLF )
                              "211 End" CRLF
            feature         = feature-label [ SP feature-parms ]
            feature-label   = 1*VCHAR
            feature-parms   = 1*TCHAR

Note that each feature line in the feature-listing begins with a single space.  That space is not optional, nor does it indicate general white space.  This space guarantees that the feature line can

never be misinterpreted as the end of the feature-listing, but is
required even where there is no possibility of ambiguity.

Each extension supported must be listed on a separate line to
facilitate the possible inclusion of parameters supported by each
extension command.  The feature-label to be used in the response to
the FEAT command will be specified as each new feature is added to
the FTP command set.  Often it will be the name of a new command
added, however this is not required.  In fact it is not required that
a new feature actually add a new command.  Any parameters included
are to be specified with the definition of the command concerned.
That specification shall also specify how any parameters present are
to be interpreted.

The feature-label and feature-parms are nominally case sensitive,
however the definitions of specific labels and parameters specify the
precise interpretation, and it is to be expected that those
definitions will usually specify the label and parameters in a case
independent manner.  Where this is done, implementations are
recommended to use upper case letters when transmitting the feature
response.

The FEAT command itself is not included in the list of features
supported, support for the FEAT command is indicated by return of a
reply other than a 500 or 502 reply.

A typical example reply to the FEAT command might be a multiline
reply of the form:

        C> feat
        S> 211-Extensions supported:
        S>  MLST size*;create;modify*;perm;media-type
        S>  SIZE
        S>  COMPRESSION
        S>  MDTM
        S> 211 END

The particular extensions shown here are simply examples of what may
be defined in other places, no particular meaning should be
attributed to them.  Recall also, that the feature names returned are
not command names, as such, but simply indications that the server
possesses some attribute or other.

The order in which the features are returned is of no importance,
server-FTP processes are not required to implement any particular
order, or even to consistently return the same order when the command
is repeated.

FTP implementations which support FEAT MUST include in the response
to the FEAT command all properly documented FTP extensions beyond
those commands and mechanisms described in RFC959 [1], including any
which existed before the existence of FEAT.  That is, when a client
receives a FEAT response from an FTP server, it can assume that the
only extensions the server supports are those that are listed in the
FEAT response.

User-FTP processes should, however, be aware that there have been
several FTP extensions developed, and in widespread use, prior to the
adoption of this document and the FEAT command.  The effect of this
is that an error response to the FEAT command does not necessarily
imply that those extensions are not supported by the server-FTP
process.  User-PIs should test for such extensions individually if an
error response has been received to the FEAT command.

3.3. Rationale for FEAT

While not absolutely necessary, a standard mechanism for the server-
PI to inform the user-PI of any features and extensions supported
will help reduce unnecessary traffic between the user-PI and server-
PI as more extensions may be introduced in the future.  If no
mechanism existed for this, a user-FTP process would have to try each
extension in turn resulting in a series of exchanges between the
user-PI and server-PI.  Apart from being possibly wasteful, this
procedure may not always be possible, as issuing of a command just to
determine if it is supported or not may have some effect that is not
desired.

4. The OPTS Command

The OPTS (options) command allows a user-PI to specify the desired
behavior of a server-FTP process when another FTP command (the target
command) is later issued.  The exact behavior, and syntax, will vary
with the target command indicated, and will be specified with the
definition of that command.  Where no OPTS behavior is defined for a
particular command there are no options available for that command.

Request Syntax:
     opts                    = opts-cmd SP command-name
                                 [ SP command-options ] CRLF
     opts-cmd                = "opts"
     command-name            = <any FTP command which allows option setting>
     command-options         = <format specified by individual FTP command>

Response Syntax:
```
    opts-response      = opts-good / opts-bad
    opts-good          = "200" SP response-message CRLF
    opts-bad           = "451" SP response-message CRLF /
                         "501" SP response-message CRLF
    response-message   = *TCHAR
```

An "opts-good" response (200 reply) MUST be sent when the command-
name specified in the OPTS command is recognized, and the command-
options, if any, are recognized, and appropriate.  An "opts-bad"
response is sent in other cases.  A 501 reply is appropriate for any
permanent error.  That is, for any case where simply repeating the
command at some later time, without other changes of state, will also
be an error.  A 451 reply should be sent where some temporary
condition at the server, not related to the state of communications
between user and server, prevents the command being accepted when
issued, but where if repeated at some later time, a changed
environment for the server-FTP process may permit the command to
succeed.  If the OPTS command itself is not recognized, a 500 or 502
reply will, of course, result.

The OPTS command MUST be implemented whenever the FEAT command is
implemented.  Because of that, there is no indication in the list of
features returned by FEAT to indicate that the OPTS command itself is
supported.  Neither the FEAT command, nor the OPTS command, have any
optional functionality, thus there are no "OPTS FEAT" or "OPTS OPTS"
commands.

5. Security Considerations

No significant new security issues, not already present in the FTP
protocol, are believed to have been created by this extension.
However, this extension does provide a mechanism by which users can
determine the capabilities of an FTP server, and from which
additional information may be able to be deduced.  While the same
basic information could be obtained by probing the server for the
various commands, if the FEAT command were not provided, that method
may reveal an attacker by logging the attempts to access various
extension commands.  This possibility is not considered a serious
enough threat to be worthy of any remedial action.

The security of any additional features that might be reported by the
FEAT command, and manipulated by the OPTS command, should be
addressed where those features are defined.

6. References

    [1]   Postel, J. and J. Reynolds, "File Transfer Protocol (FTP)",
          STD 9, RFC 959, October 1985.

    [2]   Bradner, S., "Key words for use in RFCs to Indicate
          Requirement Levels", BCP 14, RFC 2119, March 1997.

    [3]   Crocker, D. and P. Overell, "Augmented BNF for Syntax
          Specifications: ABNF", RFC 2234, November 1997.

Acknowledgements

    This protocol extension was developed in the FTPEXT Working Group of
    the IETF, and the members of that group are all acknowledged as its
    creators.

Editors' Addresses

    Paul Hethmon
    Hethmon Brothers
    2305 Chukar Road
    Knoxville, TN 37923 USA

    Phone: +1 423 690 8990
    Email: phethmon@hethmon.com


    Robert Elz
    University of Melbourne
    Department of Computer Science
    Parkville, Vic   3052
    Australia

    Email: kre@munnari.OZ.AU

Full Copyright Statement

Network Working Group                                    M. Allman
Request for Comments: 2428                  NASA Lewis/Sterling Software
Category: Standards Track                              S. Ostermann
                                                    Ohio University
                                                           C. Metz
                                                     The Inner Net
                                                    September 1998

                    FTP Extensions for IPv6 and NATs

Status of this Memo

   This document specifies an Internet standards track protocol for the
   Internet community, and requests discussion and suggestions for
   improvements.  Please refer to the current edition of the "Internet
   Official Protocol Standards" (STD 1) for the standardization state
   and status of this protocol.  Distribution of this memo is unlimited.

Copyright Notice

Abstract

   The specification for the File Transfer Protocol assumes that the
   underlying network protocol uses a 32-bit network address
   (specifically IP version 4).  With the deployment of version 6 of the
   Internet Protocol, network addresses will no longer be 32-bits.  This
   paper specifies extensions to FTP that will allow the protocol to
   work over IPv4 and IPv6.  In addition, the framework defined can
   support additional network protocols in the future.

1.  Introduction

   The keywords, such as MUST and SHOULD, found in this document are
   used as defined in RFC 2119 [Bra97].

   The File Transfer Protocol [PR85] only provides the ability to
   communicate information about IPv4 data connections.  FTP assumes
   network addresses will be 32 bits in length.  However, with the
   deployment of version 6 of the Internet Protocol [DH96] addresses
   will no longer be 32 bits long.  RFC 1639 [Pis94] specifies
   extensions to FTP to enable its use over various network protocols.
   Unfortunately, the mechanism can fail in a multi-protocol
   environment.  During the transition between IPv4 and IPv6, FTP needs
   the ability to negotiate the network protocol that will be used for
   data transfer.

This document provides a specification for a way that FTP can
communicate data connection endpoint information for network
protocols other than IPv4.  In this specification, the FTP commands
PORT and PASV are replaced with EPRT and EPSV, respectively.  This
document is organized as follows.  Section 2 outlines the EPRT
command and Section 3 outlines the EPSV command.  Section 4 defines
the utilization of these two new FTP commands.  Section 5 briefly
presents security considerations.  Finally, Section 6 provides
conclusions.

2.  The EPRT Command

The EPRT command allows for the specification of an extended address
for the data connection.  The extended address MUST consist of the
network protocol as well as the network and transport addresses.  The
format of EPRT is:

        EPRT<space><d><net-prt><d><net-addr><d><tcp-port><d>

The EPRT command keyword MUST be followed by a single space (ASCII
32).  Following the space, a delimiter character (<d>) MUST be
specified.  The delimiter character MUST be one of the ASCII
characters in range 33-126 inclusive.  The character "|" (ASCII 124)
is recommended unless it coincides with a character needed to encode
the network address.

The <net-prt> argument MUST be an address family number defined by
IANA in the latest Assigned Numbers RFC (RFC 1700 [RP94] as of the
writing of this document).  This number indicates the protocol to be
used (and, implicitly, the address length).  This document will use
two of address family numbers from [RP94] as examples, according to
the following table:

| AF Number | Protocol |
| --------- | -------- |
| 1 | Internet Protocol, Version 4 [Pos81a] |
| 2 | Internet Protocol, Version 6 [DH96] |

The <net-addr> is a protocol specific string representation of the
network address.  For the two address families specified above (AF
Number 1 and 2), addresses MUST be in the following format:

| AF Number | Address Format | Example |
| --------- | -------------- | ------- |
| 1 | dotted decimal | 132.235.1.2 |
| 2 | IPv6 string representations defined in [HD96] | 1080::8:800:200C:417A |

The <tcp-port> argument must be the string representation of the
number of the TCP port on which the host is listening for the data
connection.

The following are sample EPRT commands:

     EPRT |1|132.235.1.2|6275|

     EPRT |2|1080::8:800:200C:417A|5282|

The first command specifies that the server should use IPv4 to open a
data connection to the host "132.235.1.2" on TCP port 6275.   The
second command specifies that the server should use the IPv6 network
protocol and the network address "1080::8:800:200C:417A" to open a
TCP data connection on port 5282.

Upon receipt of a valid EPRT command, the server MUST return a code
of 200 (Command OK).  The standard negative error code 500 and 501
[PR85] are sufficient to handle most errors (e.g., syntax errors)
involving the EPRT command.  However, an additional error code is
needed.  The response code 522 indicates that the server does not
support the requested network protocol.  The interpretation of this
new error code is:

     5yz Negative Completion
     x2z Connections
     xy2 Extended Port Failure - unknown network protocol

The text portion of the response MUST indicate which network
protocols the server does support.  If the network protocol is
unsupported, the format of the response string MUST be:

     <text stating that the network protocol is unsupported> \
         (prot1,prot2,...,protn)

Both the numeric code specified above and the protocol information
between the characters '(' and ')' are intended for the software
automata receiving the response; the textual message between the
numeric code and the '(' is intended for the human user and can be
any arbitrary text, but MUST NOT include the characters '(' and ')'.
In the above case, the text SHOULD indicate that the network protocol
in the EPRT command is not supported by the server.  The list of
protocols inside the parenthesis MUST be a comma separated list of
address family numbers.  Two example response strings follow:

     Network protocol not supported, use (1)

     Network protocol not supported, use (1,2)

3.  The EPSV Command

The EPSV command requests that a server listen on a data port and
wait for a connection.  The EPSV command takes an optional argument.
The response to this command includes only the TCP port number of the
listening connection.  The format of the response, however, is
similar to the argument of the EPRT command.  This allows the same
parsing routines to be used for both commands.  In addition, the
format leaves a place holder for the network protocol and/or network
address, which may be needed in the EPSV response in the future.  The
response code for entering passive mode using an extended address
MUST be 229.  The interpretation of this code, according to [PR85]
is:

    2yz Positive Completion
    x2z Connections
    xy9 Extended Passive Mode Entered

The text returned in response to the EPSV command MUST be:

    <text indicating server is entering extended passive mode> \
        (<d><d><d><tcp-port><d>)

The portion of the string enclosed in parentheses MUST be the exact
string needed by the EPRT command to open the data connection, as
specified above.

The first two fields contained in the parenthesis MUST be blank.  The
third field MUST be the string representation of the TCP port number
on which the server is listening for a data connection.  The network
protocol used by the data connection will be the same network
protocol used by the control connection.  In addition, the network
address used to establish the data connection will be the same
network address used for the control connection.  An example response
string follows:

    Entering Extended Passive Mode (|||6446|)

The standard negative error codes 500 and 501 are sufficient to
handle all errors involving the EPSV command (e.g., syntax errors).

When the EPSV command is issued with no argument, the server will
choose the network protocol for the data connection based on the
protocol used for the control connection.  However, in the case of
proxy FTP, this protocol might not be appropriate for communication
between the two servers.  Therefore, the client needs to be able to
request a specific protocol.  If the server returns a protocol that
is not supported by the host that will be connecting to the port, the

client MUST issue an ABOR (abort) command to allow the server to
close down the listening connection.  The client can then send an
EPSV command requesting the use of a specific network protocol, as
follows:

  EPSV<space><net-prt>

If the requested protocol is supported by the server, it SHOULD use
the protocol.  If not, the server MUST return the 522 error messages
as outlined in section 2.

Finally, the EPSV command can be used with the argument "ALL" to
inform Network Address Translators that the EPRT command (as well as
other data commands) will no longer be used.  An example of this
command follows:

  EPSV<space>ALL

Upon receipt of an EPSV ALL command, the server MUST reject all data
connection setup commands other than EPSV (i.e., EPRT, PORT, PASV, et
al.).  This use of the EPSV command is further explained in section
4.

4.  Command Usage

For all FTP transfers where the control and data connection(s) are
being established between the same two machines, the EPSV command
MUST be used.  Using the EPSV command benefits performance of
transfers that traverse firewalls or Network Address Translators
(NATs).  RFC 1579 [Bel94] recommends using the passive command when
behind firewalls since firewalls do not generally allow incoming
connections (which are required when using the PORT (EPRT) command).
In addition, using EPSV as defined in this document does not require
NATs to change the network address in the traffic as it is forwarded.
The NAT would have to change the address if the EPRT command was
used.  Finally, if the client issues an "EPSV ALL" command, NATs may
be able to put the connection on a "fast path" through the
translator, as the EPRT command will never be used and therefore,
translation of the data portion of the segments will never be needed.
When a client only expects to do two-way FTP transfers, it SHOULD
issue this command as soon as possible.  If a client later finds that
it must do a three-way FTP transfer after issuing an EPSV ALL
command, a new FTP session MUST be started.

5.  Security Issues

   The authors do not believe that these changes to FTP introduce new
   security problems.  A companion Work in Progress [AO98] is a more
   general discussion of FTP security issues and techniques to reduce
   these security problems.

6.  Conclusions

   The extensions specified in this paper will enable FTP to operate
   over a variety of network protocols.

References

   [AO98]   Allman, M., and S. Ostermann, "FTP Security
            Considerations", Work in Progress.

   [Bel94]  Bellovin, S., "Firewall-Friendly FTP", RFC 1579, February
            1994.

   [Bra97]  Bradner, S., "Key words for use in RFCs to Indicate
            Requirement Levels", BCP 14, RFC 2119, March 1997.

   [DH96]   Deering, S., and R. Hinden, "Internet Protocol, Version 6
            (IPv6) Specification", RFC 1883, December 1995.

   [HD96]   Hinden, R., and S. Deering, "IP Version 6 Addressing
            Architecture", RFC 2373, July 1998.

   [Pis94]  Piscitello, D., "FTP Operation Over Big Address Records
            (FOOBAR)", RFC 1639, June 1994.

   [Pos81a] Postel, J., "Internet Protocol", STD 5, RFC 791, September
            1981.

   [Pos81b] Postel, J., "Transmission Control Protocol", STD 7, RFC 793,
            September 1981.

   [PR85]   Postel, J., and J. Reynolds, "File Transfer Protocol (FTP)",
            STD 9, RFC 959, October 1985.

   [RP94]   Reynolds, J., and J. Postel, "Assigned Numbers", STD 2, RFC
            1700, October 1994.  See also:
            http://www.iana.org/numbers.html

Authors' Addresses

   Mark Allman
   NASA Lewis Research Center/Sterling Software
   21000 Brookpark Rd.   MS 54-2
   Cleveland, OH   44135

   Phone: (216) 433-6586
   EMail: mallman@lerc.nasa.gov
   http://gigahertz.lerc.nasa.gov/~mallman/


   Shawn Ostermann
   School of Electrical Engineering and Computer Science
   Ohio University
   416 Morton Hall
   Athens, OH   45701

   Phone: (740) 593-1234
   EMail: ostermann@cs.ohiou.edu


   Craig Metz
   The Inner Net
   Box 10314-1954
   Blacksburg, VA   24062-0314

   Phone:  (DSN) 754-8590
   EMail: cmetz@inner.net

Full Copyright Statement

Network Working Group                                    M. Allman
Request for Comments: 2577                  NASA Glenn/Sterling Software
Category: Informational                                  S. Ostermann
                                                     Ohio University
                                                          May 1999


                    FTP Security Considerations

Status of this Memo

Copyright Notice

Abstract

   The specification for the File Transfer Protocol (FTP) contains a
   number of mechanisms that can be used to compromise network security.
   The FTP specification allows a client to instruct a server to
   transfer files to a third machine.  This third-party mechanism, known
   as proxy FTP, causes a well known security problem.  The FTP
   specification also allows an unlimited number of attempts at entering
   a user's password.  This allows brute force "password guessing"
   attacks.  This document provides suggestions for system
   administrators and those implementing FTP servers that will decrease
   the security problems associated with FTP.

1   Introduction

   The File Transfer Protocol specification (FTP) [PR85] provides a
   mechanism that allows a client to establish an FTP control connection
   and transfer a file between two FTP servers.  This "proxy FTP"
   mechanism can be used to decrease the amount of traffic on the
   network; the client instructs one server to transfer a file to
   another server, rather than transferring the file from the first
   server to the client and then from the client to the second server.
   This is particularly useful when the client connects to the network
   using a slow link (e.g., a modem).  While useful, proxy FTP provides
   a security problem known as a "bounce attack" [CERT97:27].  In
   addition to the bounce attack, FTP servers can be used by attackers
   to guess passwords using brute force.

This document does not contain a discussion of FTP when used in conjunction with strong security protocols, such as IP Security. These security concerns should be documented, however they are out of the scope of this document.

This paper provides information for FTP server implementers and system administrators, as follows.  Section 2 describes the FTP "bounce attack".  Section 3 provides suggestions for minimizing the bounce attack.  Section 4 provides suggestions for servers which limit access based on network address.  Section 5 provides recommendations for limiting brute force "password guessing" by clients.  Next, section 6 provides a brief discussion of mechanisms to improve privacy.  Section 7 provides a mechanism to prevent user identity guessing.  Section 8 discusses the practice of port stealing.  Finally, section 9 provides an overview of other FTP security issues related to software bugs rather than protocol issues.

2    The Bounce Attack

The version of FTP specified in the standard [PR85] provides a method for attacking well known network servers, while making the perpetrators difficult to track down.  The attack involves sending an FTP "PORT" command to an FTP server containing the network address and the port number of the machine and service being attacked.  At this point, the original client can instruct the FTP server to send a file to the service being attacked.  Such a file would contain commands relevant to the service being attacked (SMTP, NNTP, etc.). Instructing a third party to connect to the service, rather than connecting directly, makes tracking down the perpetrator difficult and can circumvent network-address-based access restrictions.

As an example, a client uploads a file containing SMTP commands to an FTP server.  Then, using an appropriate PORT command, the client instructs the server to open a connection to a third machine's SMTP port.  Finally, the client instructs the server to transfer the uploaded file containing SMTP commands to the third machine.  This may allow the client to forge mail on the third machine without making a direct connection.  This makes it difficult to track attackers.

3    Protecting Against the Bounce Attack

The original FTP specification [PR85] assumes that data connections will be made using the Transmission Control Protocol (TCP) [Pos81]. TCP port numbers in the range 0 - 1023 are reserved for well known services such as mail, network news and FTP control connections [RP94].  The FTP specification makes no restrictions on the TCP port number used for the data connection.  Therefore, using proxy FTP,

clients have the ability to tell the server to attack a well known
service on any machine.

To avoid such bounce attacks, it is suggested that servers not open
data connections to TCP ports less than 1024.  If a server receives a
PORT command containing a TCP port number less than 1024, the
suggested response is 504 (defined as "Command not implemented for
that parameter" by [PR85]).  Note that this still leaves non-well
known servers (those running on ports greater than 1023) vulnerable
to bounce attacks.

Several proposals (e.g., [AOM98] and [Pis94]) provide a mechanism
that would allow data connections to be made using a transport
protocol other than TCP.  Similar precautions should be taken to
protect well known services when using these protocols.

Also note that the bounce attack generally requires that a
perpetrator be able to upload a file to an FTP server and later
download it to the service being attacked.  Using proper file
protections will prevent this behavior.  However, attackers can also
attack services by sending random data from a remote FTP server which
may cause problems for some services.

Disabling the PORT command is also an option for protecting against
the bounce attack.  Most file transfers can be made using only the
PASV command [Bel94].  The disadvantage of disabling the PORT command
is that one loses the ability to use proxy FTP, but proxy FTP may not
be necessary in a particular environment.

4   Restricted Access

For some FTP servers, it is desirable to restrict access based on
network address.  For example, a server might want to restrict access
to certain files from certain places (e.g., a certain file should not
be transferred out of an organization).  In such a situation, the
server should confirm that the network address of the remote hosts on
both the control connection and the data connection are within the
organization before sending a restricted file.  By checking both
connections, a server is protected against the case when the control
connection is established with a trusted host and the data connection
is not.  Likewise, the client should verify the IP address of the
remote host after accepting a connection on a port opened in listen
mode to verify that the connection was made by the expected server.

Note that restricting access based on network address leaves the FTP
server vulnerable to "spoof" attacks.  In a spoof attack, for
example, an attacking machine could assume the host address of
another machine inside an organization and download files that are

not accessible from outside the organization.  Whenever possible,
secure authentication mechanisms should be used, such as those
outlined in [HL97].

5   Protecting Passwords

To minimize the risk of brute force password guessing through the FTP
server, it is suggested that servers limit the number of attempts
that can be made at sending a correct password.  After a small number
of attempts (3-5), the server should close the control connection
with the client.  Before closing the control connection the server
must send a return code of 421 ("Service not available, closing
control connection." [PR85]) to the client.  In addition, it is
suggested that the server impose a 5 second delay before replying to
an invalid "PASS" command to diminish the efficiency of a brute force
attack.  If available, mechanisms already provided by the target
operating system should be used to implement the above suggestions.

An intruder can subvert the above mechanisms by establishing
multiple, parallel control connections to a server.  To combat the
use of multiple concurrent connections, the server could either limit
the total number of control connections possible or attempt to detect
suspicious activity across sessions and refuse further connections
from the site.  However, both of these mechanisms open the door to
"denial of service" attacks, in which an attacker purposely initiates
the attack to disable access by a valid user.

Standard FTP [PR85] sends passwords in clear text using the "PASS"
command.  It is suggested that FTP clients and servers use alternate
authentication mechanisms that are not subject to eavesdropping (such
as the mechanisms being developed by the IETF Common Authentication
Technology Working Group [HL97]).

6   Privacy

All data and control information (including passwords) is sent across
the network in unencrypted form by standard FTP [PR85].  To guarantee
the privacy of the information FTP transmits, a strong encryption
scheme should be used whenever possible.  One such mechanism is
defined in [HL97].

7   Protecting Usernames

Standard FTP [PR85] specifies a 530 response to the USER command when
the username is rejected.  If the username is valid and a password is
required FTP returns a 331 response instead.  In order to prevent a
malicious client from determining valid usernames on a server, it is
suggested that a server always return 331 to the USER command and

then reject the combination of username and password for an invalid
username.

8   Port Stealing

Many operating systems assign dynamic port numbers in increasing
order.  By making a legitimate transfer, an attacker can observe the
current port number allocated by the server and "guess" the next one
that will be used.  The attacker can make a connection to this port,
thus denying another legitimate client the ability to make a
transfer.  Alternatively, the attacker can steal a file meant for a
legitimate user.  In addition, an attacker can insert a forged file
into a data stream thought to come from an authenticated client.
This problem can be mitigated by making FTP clients and servers use
random local port numbers for data connections, either by requesting
random ports from the operating system or using system dependent
mechanisms.

9   Software-Base Security Problems

The emphasis in this document is on protocol-related security issues.
There are a number of documented FTP security-related problems that
are due to poor implementation as well.  Although the details of
these types of problems are beyond the scope of this document, it
should be pointed out that the following FTP features has been abused
in the past and should be treated with great care by future
implementers:

Anonymous FTP

    Anonymous FTP refers to the ability of a client to connect to an
    FTP server with minimal authentication and gain access to public
    files.  Security problems arise when such a user can read all
    files on the system or can create files. [CERT92:09] [CERT93:06]

Remote Command Execution

    An optional FTP extension, "SITE EXEC", allows clients to execute
    arbitrary commands on the server.  This feature should obviously
    be implemented with great care.  There are several documented
    cases of the FTP "SITE EXEC" command being used to subvert server
    security [CERT94:08] [CERT95:16]

Debug Code

    Several previous security compromises related to FTP can be
    attributed to software that was installed with debugging features
    enabled [CERT88:01].

This document recommends that implementors of FTP servers with these capabilities review all of the CERT advisories for attacks on these or similar mechanisms before releasing their software.

10  Conclusion

Using the above suggestions can decrease the security problems associated with FTP servers without eliminating functionality.

11  Security Considerations

Security issues are discussed throughout this memo.

Acknowledgments

We would like to thank Alex Belits, Jim Bound, William Curtin, Robert Elz, Paul Hethmon, Alun Jones and Stephen Tihor for their helpful comments on this paper.  Also, we thank the FTPEXT WG members who gave many useful suggestions at the Memphis IETF meeting.

References

[AOM98]      Allman, M., Ostermann, S. and C. Metz, "FTP Extensions
             for IPv6 and NATs", RFC 2428, September 1998.

[Bel94]      Bellovin. S., "Firewall-Friendly FTP", RFC 1579, February
             1994.

[CERT88:01] CERT Advisory CA-88:01. ftpd Vulnerability. December,
             1988 ftp://info.cert.org/pub/cert_advisories/

[CERT92:09] CERT Advisory CA-92:09. AIX Anonymous FTP Vulnerability.
             April 27, 1992. ftp://info.cert.org/pub/cert_advisories/

[CERT93:06] CERT Advisory CA-93:06. Wuarchive ftpd Vulnerability.
             September 19,1997
             ftp://info.cert.org/pub/cert_advisories/

[CERT94:08] CERT Advisory CA-94:08. ftpd Vulnerabilities. September
             23, 1997.  ftp://info.cert.org/pub/cert_advisories/

[CERT95:16] CERT Advisory CA-95:16. wu-ftpd Misconfiguration
             Vulnerability.  September 23, 1997
             ftp://info.cert.org/pub/cert_advisories/

[CERT97:27] CERT Advisory CA-97.27. FTP Bounce.  January 8, 1998.
             ftp://info.cert.org/pub/cert_advisories/

   [HL97]        Horowitz, M. and S. Lunt, "FTP Security Extensions", RFC
                 2228, October 1997.

   [Pis94]       Piscitello, D., "FTP Operation Over Big Address Records
                 (FOOBAR), RFC 1639, June 1994.

   [Pos81]       Postel, J., "Transmission Control Protocol", STD 7, RFC
                 793, September 1981.

   [PR85]        Postel, J. and J. Reynolds, "File Transfer Protocol
                 (FTP)", STD 9, RFC 959, October 1985.

   [RP94]        Reynolds, J. and J. Postel, "Assigned Numbers", STD 2,
                 RFC 1700, October 1994.  See also:
                 http://www.iana.org/numbers.html

Authors' Addresses

   Mark Allman
   NASA Glenn Research Center/Sterling Software
   21000 Brookpark Rd.  MS 54-2
   Cleveland, OH  44135

   EMail: mallman@grc.nasa.gov


   Shawn Ostermann
   School of Electrical Engineering and Computer Science
   Ohio University
   416 Morton Hall
   Athens, OH  45701

   EMail: ostermann@cs.ohiou.edu

Acknowledgement

   Funding for the RFC Editor function is currently provided by the
   Internet Society.

Network Working Group                                          R. Housley
Request for Comments: 2585                                          SPYRUS
Category: Standards Track                                      P. Hoffman
                                                                      IMC
                                                                 May 1999

Internet X.509 Public Key Infrastructure
Operational Protocols: FTP and HTTP

Status of this Memo

   This document specifies an Internet standards track protocol for the
   Internet community, and requests discussion and suggestions for
   improvements.  Please refer to the current edition of the "Internet
   Official Protocol Standards" (STD 1) for the standardization state
   and status of this protocol.  Distribution of this memo is unlimited.

Copyright Notice

Abstract

   The protocol conventions described in this document satisfy some of
   the operational requirements of the Internet Public Key
   Infrastructure (PKI).  This document specifies the conventions for
   using the File Transfer Protocol (FTP) and the Hypertext Transfer
   Protocol (HTTP) to obtain certificates and certificate revocation
   lists (CRLs) from PKI repositories.  Additional mechanisms addressing
   PKIX operational requirements are specified in separate documents.

1   Introduction

   This specification is part of a multi-part standard for the Internet
   Public Key Infrastructure (PKI) using X.509 certificates and
   certificate revocation lists (CRLs).  This document specifies the
   conventions for using the File Transfer Protocol (FTP) and the
   Hypertext Transfer Protocol (HTTP) to obtain certificates and CRLs
   from PKI repositories.  Additional mechanisms addressing PKI
   repository access are specified in separate documents.

RFC 2585

1.1. Model

   The following is a simplified view of the architectural model assumed
   by the Internet PKI specifications.

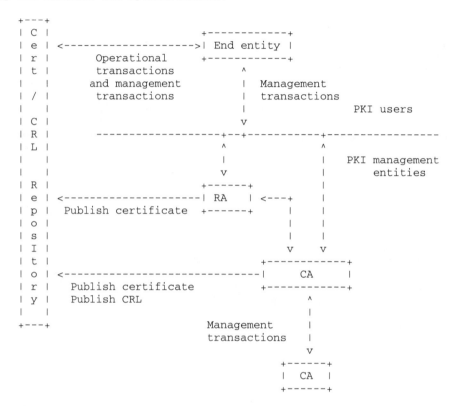

   The components in this model are:

   End Entity:  user of PKI certificates and/or end user system that is
                the subject of a certificate;

   CA:          certification authority;

   RA:          registration authority, i.e., an optional system to
                which a CA delegates certain management functions;

Repository:  a system or collection of distributed systems that store
             certificates and CRLs and serves as a means of
             distributing these certificates and CRLs to end
             entities.

## 1.2.  Certificate and CRL Repository

Some CAs mandate the use of on-line validation services, while others
distribute CRLs to allow certificate users to perform certificate
validation themselves.  In general, CAs make CRLs available to
certificate users by publishing them in the Directory.  The Directory
is also the normal distribution mechanism for certificates.  However,
Directory Services are not available in many parts of the Internet
today. The File Transfer Protocol (FTP) defined in RFC 959 and the
Hypertext Transfer Protocol (HTTP) defined in RFC 2068 offer
alternate methods for certificate and CRL distribution.

End entities and CAs may retrieve certificates and CRLs from the
repository using FTP or HTTP.  End entities may publish their own
certificate in the repository using FTP or HTTP, and RAs and CAs may
publish certificates and CRLs in the repository using FTP or HTTP.

## 2   FTP Conventions

Within certificate extensions and CRL extensions, the URI form of
GeneralName is used to specify the location where issuer certificates
and CRLs may be obtained.  For instance, a URI identifying the
subject of a certificate may be carried in subjectAltName certificate
extension. An IA5String describes the use of anonymous FTP to fetch
certificate or CRL information.  For example:

    ftp://ftp.netcom.com/sp/spyrus/housley.cer
    ftp://ftp.your.org/pki/id48.cer
    ftp://ftp.your.org/pki/id48.no42.crl

Internet users may publish the URI reference to a file that contains
their certificate on their business card.  This practice is useful
when there is no Directory entry for that user.  FTP is widely
deployed, and anonymous FTP are accommodated by many firewalls.
Thus, FTP is an attractive alternative to Directory access protocols
for certificate and CRL distribution.  While this service satisfies
the requirement to retrieve information related to a certificate
which is already identified by a URI, it is not intended to satisfy
the more general problem of finding a certificate for a user about
whom some other information, such as their electronic mail address or
corporate affiliation, is known.

For convenience, the names of files that contain certificates should
have a suffix of ".cer".  Each ".cer" file contains exactly one
certificate, encoded in DER format.  Likewise, the names of files
that contain CRLs should have a suffix of ".crl".  Each ".crl" file
contains exactly one CRL, encoded in DER format.

3   HTTP Conventions

Within certificate extensions and CRL extensions, the URI form of
GeneralName is used to specify the location where issuer certificates
and CRLs may be obtained.  For instance, a URI identifying the
subject of a certificate may be carried in subjectAltName certificate
extension. An IA5String describes the use of HTTP to fetch
certificate or CRL information.  For example:

    http://www.netcom.com/sp/spyrus/housley.cer
    http://www.your.org/pki/id48.cer
    http://www.your.org/pki/id48.no42.crl

Internet users may publish the URI reference to a file that contains
their certificate on their business card.  This practice is useful
when there is no Directory entry for that user.  HTTP is widely
deployed, and HTTP is accommodated by many firewalls.  Thus, HTTP is
an attractive alternative to Directory access protocols for
certificate and CRL distribution.  While this service satisfies the
requirement to retrieve information related to a certificate which is
already identified by a URI, it is not intended to satisfy the more
general problem of finding a certificate for a user about whom some
other information, such as their electronic mail address or corporate
affiliation, is known.

For convenience, the names of files that contain certificates should
have a suffix of ".cer".  Each ".cer" file contains exactly one
certificate, encoded in DER format.  Likewise, the names of files
that contain CRLs should have a suffix of ".crl".  Each ".crl" file
contains exactly one CRL, encoded in DER format.

4   MIME registrations

Two MIME types are defined to support the transfer of certificates
and CRLs.  They are:

    application/pkix-cert
    application/pkix-crl

4.1. application/pkix-cert

   To: ietf-types@iana.org
   Subject: Registration of MIME media type application/pkix-cert

   MIME media type name: application

   MIME subtype name: pkix-cert

   Required parameters: None

   Optional parameters: version (default value is "1")

   Encoding considerations: will be none for 8-bit transports and most
   likely Base64 for SMTP or other 7-bit transports

   Security considerations: Carries a cryptographic certificate

   Interoperability considerations: None

   Published specification: draft-ietf-pkix-ipki-part1

   Applications which use this media type: Any MIME-complaint transport

   Additional information:
     Magic number(s): None
     File extension(s): .CER
     Macintosh File Type Code(s): none

   Person & email address to contact for further information:
   Russ Housley <housley@spyrus.com>

   Intended usage: COMMON

   Author/Change controller:
   Russ Housley <housley@spyrus.com>

4.2. application/pkix-crl

   To: ietf-types@iana.org
   Subject: Registration of MIME media type application/pkix-crl

   MIME media type name: application

   MIME subtype name: pkix-crl

   Required parameters: None

Optional parameters: version (default value is "1")

Encoding considerations: will be none for 8-bit transports and most
likely Base64 for SMTP or other 7-bit transports

Security considerations: Carries a cryptographic certificate
revocation list

Interoperability considerations: None

Published specification: draft-ietf-pkix-ipki-part1

Applications which use this media type: Any MIME-complaint transport

Additional information:
  Magic number(s): None
  File extension(s): .CRL
  Macintosh File Type Code(s): none

Person & email address to contact for further information:
Russ Housley <housley@spyrus.com>

Intended usage: COMMON

Author/Change controller:
Russ Housley <housley@spyrus.com>

References

  [RFC 959]    Postel, J. and J. Reynolds, "File Transfer Protocol (FTP)",
               STD 5, RFC 959, October 1985.

  [RFC 1738]   Berners-Lee, T., Masinter, L. and M. McCahill, "Uniform
               Resource Locators (URL)", RFC 1738, December 1994.

  [RFC 2068]   Fielding, R., Gettys, J., Mogul, J., Frystyk, H. and
               T. Berners-Lee; "Hypertext Transfer Protocol -- HTTP/1.1",
               RFC 2068, January 1997.

Security Considerations

Since certificates and CRLs are digitally signed, no additional
integrity service is necessary.  Neither certificates nor CRLs need
be kept secret, and anonymous access to certificates and CRLs is
generally acceptable.  Thus, no privacy service is necessary.

HTTP caching proxies are common on the Internet, and some proxies do not check for the latest version of an object correctly. If an HTTP request for a certificate or CRL goes through a misconfigured or otherwise broken proxy, the proxy may return an out-of-date response.

Operators of FTP sites and World Wide Web servers should authenticate end entities who publish certificates as well as CAs and RAs who publish certificates and CRLs.  However, authentication is not necessary to retrieve certificates and CRLs.

Authors' Addresses

Russell Housley
SPYRUS
381 Elden Street, Suite 1120
Herndon, VA 20170 USA

EMail: housley@spyrus.com


Paul Hoffman
Internet Mail Consortium
127 Segre Place
Santa Cruz, CA 95060 USA

EMail: phoffman@imc.org

Full Copyright Statement

   Copyright (C) The Internet Society (1999).  All Rights Reserved.

   This document and translations of it may be copied and furnished to
   others, and derivative works that comment on or otherwise explain it
   or assist in its implementation may be prepared, copied, published
   and distributed, in whole or in part, without restriction of any
   kind, provided that the above copyright notice and this paragraph are
   included on all such copies and derivative works.  However, this
   document itself may not be modified in any way, such as by removing
   the copyright notice or references to the Internet Society or other
   Internet organizations, except as needed for the purpose of
   developing Internet standards in which case the procedures for
   copyrights defined in the Internet Standards process must be
   followed, or as required to translate it into languages other than
   English.

   The limited permissions granted above are perpetual and will not be
   revoked by the Internet Society or its successors or assigns.

   This document and the information contained herein is provided on an
   "AS IS" basis and THE INTERNET SOCIETY AND THE INTERNET ENGINEERING
   TASK FORCE DISCLAIMS ALL WARRANTIES, EXPRESS OR IMPLIED, INCLUDING
   BUT NOT LIMITED TO ANY WARRANTY THAT THE USE OF THE INFORMATION
   HEREIN WILL NOT INFRINGE ANY RIGHTS OR ANY IMPLIED WARRANTIES OF
   MERCHANTABILITY OR FITNESS FOR A PARTICULAR PURPOSE.

Acknowledgement

   Funding for the RFC Editor function is currently provided by the
   Internet Society.

Network Working Group                              B. Curtin
Request for Comments: 2640         Defense Information Systems Agency
Updates: 959                                       July 1999
Category: Proposed Standard

Internationalization of the File Transfer Protocol

Status of this Memo

This document specifies an Internet standards track protocol for the
Internet community, and requests discussion and suggestions for
improvements.  Please refer to the current edition of the "Internet
Official Protocol Standards" (STD 1) for the standardization state
and status of this protocol.  Distribution of this memo is unlimited.

Copyright Notice

Abstract

The File Transfer Protocol, as defined in RFC 959 [RFC959] and RFC
1123 Section 4 [RFC1123], is one of the oldest and widely used
protocols on the Internet. The protocol's primary character set, 7
bit ASCII, has served the protocol well through the early growth
years of the Internet. However, as the Internet becomes more global,
there is a need to support character sets beyond 7 bit ASCII.

This document addresses the internationalization (I18n) of FTP, which
includes supporting the multiple character sets and languages found
throughout the Internet community.  This is achieved by extending the
FTP specification and giving recommendations for proper
internationalization support.

Table of Contents

ABSTRACT......................................................1
1 INTRODUCTION................................................2
  1.1 Requirements Terminology................................2
2 INTERNATIONALIZATION........................................3
  2.1 International Character Set..............................3
  2.2 Transfer Encoding Set...................................4
3 PATHNAMES...................................................5
  3.1 General compliance......................................5
  3.2 Servers compliance......................................6
  3.3 Clients compliance......................................7
4 LANGUAGE SUPPORT............................................7

     4.1 The LANG command.........................................8
     4.2 Syntax of the LANG command..............................9
     4.3 Feat response for LANG command.........................11
        4.3.1 Feat examples.....................................11
     5 SECURITY CONSIDERATIONS..................................12
     6 ACKNOWLEDGMENTS..........................................12
     7 GLOSSARY.................................................13
     8 BIBLIOGRAPHY.............................................13
     9 AUTHOR'S ADDRESS.........................................15
     ANNEX A - IMPLEMENTATION CONSIDERATIONS....................16
     A.1 General Considerations.................................16
     A.2 Transition Considerations..............................18
     ANNEX B - SAMPLE CODE AND EXAMPLES.........................19
     B.1 Valid UTF-8 check......................................19
     B.2 Conversions............................................20
        B.2.1 Conversion from Local Character Set to UTF-8......20
        B.2.2 Conversion from UTF-8 to Local Character Set......23
        B.2.3 ISO/IEC 8859-8 Example............................25
        B.2.4 Vendor Codepage Example...........................25
     B.3 Pseudo Code for Translating Servers....................26
     Full Copyright Statement...................................27

1 Introduction

     As the Internet grows throughout the world the requirement to support
     character sets outside of the ASCII [ASCII] / Latin-1 [ISO-8859]
     character set becomes ever more urgent. For FTP, because of the
     large installed base, it is paramount that this is done without
     breaking existing clients and servers. This document addresses this
     need. In doing so it defines a solution which will still allow the
     installed base to interoperate with new clients and servers.

     This document enhances the capabilities of the File Transfer Protocol
     by removing the 7-bit restrictions on pathnames used in client
     commands and server responses, RECOMMENDs the use of a Universal
     Character Set (UCS) ISO/IEC 10646 [ISO-10646], RECOMMENDs a UCS
     transformation format (UTF) UTF-8 [UTF-8], and defines a new command
     for language negotiation.

     The recommendations made in this document are consistent with the
     recommendations expressed by the IETF policy related to character
     sets and languages as defined in RFC 2277 [RFC2277].

1.1.  Requirements Terminology

     The key words "MUST", "MUST NOT", "REQUIRED", "SHALL", "SHALL NOT",
     "SHOULD", "SHOULD NOT", "RECOMMENDED",  "MAY", and "OPTIONAL" in this
     document are to be interpreted as described in BCP 14 [BCP14].

## 2 Internationalization

The File Transfer Protocol was developed when the predominate
character sets were 7 bit ASCII and 8 bit EBCDIC. Today these
character sets cannot support the wide range of characters needed by
multinational systems. Given that there are a number of character
sets in current use that provide more characters than 7-bit ASCII, it
makes sense to decide on a convenient way to represent the union of
those possibilities. To work globally either requires support of a
number of character sets and to be able to convert between them, or
the use of a single preferred character set. To assure global
interoperability this document RECOMMENDS the latter approach and
defines a single character set, in addition to NVT ASCII and EBCDIC,
which is understandable by all systems. For FTP this character set
SHALL be ISO/IEC 10646:1993. For support of global compatibility it
is STRONGLY RECOMMENDED that clients and servers use UTF-8 encoding
when exchanging pathnames. Clients and servers are, however, under
no obligation to perform any conversion on the contents of a file for
operations such as STOR or RETR.

The character set used to store files SHALL remain a local decision
and MAY depend on the capability of local operating systems. Prior to
the exchange of pathnames they SHOULD be converted into a ISO/IEC
10646 format and UTF-8 encoded. This approach, while allowing
international exchange of pathnames, will still allow backward
compatibility with older systems because the code set positions for
ASCII characters are identical to the one byte sequence in UTF-8.

Sections 2.1 and 2.2 give a brief description of the international
character set and transfer encoding RECOMMENDED by this document. A
more thorough description of UTF-8, ISO/IEC 10646, and UNICODE
[UNICODE], beyond that given in this document, can be found in RFC
2279 [RFC2279].

### 2.1 International Character Set

The character set defined for international support of FTP SHALL be
the Universal Character Set as defined in ISO 10646:1993 as amended.
This standard incorporates the character sets of many existing
international, national, and corporate standards. ISO/IEC 10646
defines two alternate forms of encoding, UCS-4 and UCS-2. UCS-4 is a
four byte (31 bit) encoding containing $2**31$ code positions divided
into 128 groups of 256 planes. Each plane consists of 256 rows of 256
cells. UCS-2 is a 2 byte (16 bit) character set consisting of plane
zero or the Basic Multilingual Plane (BMP). Currently, no codesets
have been defined outside of the 2 byte BMP.

The Unicode standard version 2.0 [UNICODE] is consistent with the
UCS-2 subset of ISO/IEC 10646. The Unicode standard version 2.0
includes the repertoire of IS 10646 characters, amendments 1-7 of IS
10646, and editorial and technical corrigenda.

2.2 Transfer Encoding

UCS Transformation Format 8 (UTF-8), in the past referred to as UTF-2
or UTF-FSS, SHALL be used as a transfer encoding to transmit the
international character set. UTF-8 is a file safe encoding which
avoids the use of byte values that have special significance during
the parsing of pathname character strings. UTF-8 is an 8 bit encoding
of the characters in the UCS. Some of UTF-8's benefits are that it is
compatible with 7 bit ASCII, so it doesn't affect programs that give
special meanings to various ASCII characters; it is immune to
synchronization errors; its encoding rules allow for easy
identification; and it has enough space to support a large number of
character sets.

UTF-8 encoding represents each UCS character as a sequence of 1 to 6
bytes in length. For all sequences of one byte the most significant
bit is ZERO. For all sequences of more than one byte the number of
ONE bits in the first byte, starting from the most significant bit
position, indicates the number of bytes in the UTF-8 sequence
followed by a ZERO bit. For example, the first byte of a 3 byte UTF-8
sequence would have 1110 as its most significant bits. Each
additional bytes (continuing bytes) in the UTF-8 sequence, contain a
ONE bit followed by a ZERO bit as their most significant bits. The
remaining free bit positions in the continuing bytes are used to
identify characters in the UCS. The relationship between UCS and
UTF-8 is demonstrated in the following table:

```
UCS-4 range(hex)           UTF-8 byte sequence(binary)
00000000 - 0000007F        0xxxxxxx
00000080 - 000007FF        110xxxxx 10xxxxxx
00000800 - 0000FFFF        1110xxxx 10xxxxxx 10xxxxxx
00010000 - 001FFFFF        11110xxx 10xxxxxx 10xxxxxx 10xxxxxx
00200000 - 03FFFFFF        111110xx 10xxxxxx 10xxxxxx 10xxxxxx
                           10xxxxxx
04000000 - 7FFFFFFF        1111110x 10xxxxxx 10xxxxxx 10xxxxxx
                           10xxxxxx 10xxxxxx
```

A beneficial property of UTF-8 is that its single byte sequence is
consistent with the ASCII character set. This feature will allow a
transition where old ASCII-only clients can still interoperate with
new servers that support the UTF-8 encoding.

Another feature is that the encoding rules make it very unlikely that
a character sequence from a different character set will be mistaken
for a UTF-8 encoded character sequence. Clients and servers can use a
simple routine to determine if the character set being exchanged is
valid UTF-8. Section B.1 shows a code example of this check.

3 Pathnames

3.1 General compliance

- The 7-bit restriction for pathnames exchanged is dropped.

- Many operating system allow the use of spaces <SP>, carriage return
  <CR>, and line feed <LF> characters as part of the pathname. The
  exchange of pathnames with these special command characters will
  cause the pathnames to be parsed improperly. This is because ftp
  commands associated with pathnames have the form:

    COMMAND <SP> <pathname> <CRLF>.

To allow the exchange of pathnames containing these characters, the
definition of pathname is changed from

    <pathname> ::= <string>    ; in BNF format
to
    pathname = 1*(%x01..%xFF) ; in ABNF format [ABNF].

To avoid mistaking these characters within pathnames as special
command characters the following rules will apply:

There MUST be only one <SP> between a ftp command and the pathname.
Implementations MUST assume <SP> characters following the initial
<SP> as part of the pathname. For example the pathname in STOR
<SP><SP><SP>foo.bar<CRLF> is <SP><SP>foo.bar.

Current implementations, which may allow multiple <SP> characters as
separators between the command and pathname, MUST assure that they
comply with this single <SP> convention. Note: Implementations which
treat 3 character commands (e.g. CWD, MKD, etc.) as a fixed 4
character command by padding the command with a trailing <SP> are in
non-compliance to this specification.

When a <CR> character is encountered as part of a pathname it MUST be
padded with a <NUL> character prior to sending the command. On
receipt of a pathname containing a <CR><NUL> sequence the <NUL>
character MUST be stripped away. This approach is described in the
Telnet protocol [RFC854] on pages 11 and 12. For example, to store a
pathname foo<CR><LF>boo.bar the pathname would become

foo<CR><NUL><LF>boo.bar prior to sending the command STOR
<SP>foo<CR><NUL><LF>boo.bar<CRLF>. Upon receipt of the altered
pathname the <NUL> character following the <CR> would be stripped
away to form the original pathname.

- Conforming clients and servers MUST support UTF-8 for the transfer
  and receipt of pathnames. Clients and servers MAY in addition give
  users a choice of specifying interpretation of pathnames in another
  encoding. Note that configuring clients and servers to use
  character sets / encoding other than UTF-8 is outside of the scope
  of this document. While it is recognized that in certain
  operational scenarios this may be desirable, this is left as a
  quality of implementation and operational issue.

- Pathnames are sequences of bytes.  The encoding of names that are
  valid UTF-8 sequences is assumed to be UTF-8.  The character set of
  other names is undefined. Clients and servers, unless otherwise
  configured to support a specific native character set, MUST check
  for a valid UTF-8 byte sequence to determine if the pathname being
  presented is UTF-8.

- To avoid data loss, clients and servers SHOULD use the UTF-8
  encoded pathnames when unable to convert them to a usable code set.

- There may be cases when the code set / encoding presented to the
  server or client cannot be determined. In such cases the raw bytes
  SHOULD be used.

3.2 Servers compliance

- Servers MUST support the UTF-8 feature in response to the FEAT
  command [RFC2389]. The UTF-8 feature is a line containing the exact
  string "UTF8". This string is not case sensitive, but SHOULD be
  transmitted in upper case. The response to a FEAT command SHOULD
  be:

      C> feat
      S> 211- <any descriptive text>
      S>  ...
      S>  UTF8
      S>  ...
      S> 211 end

The ellipses indicate placeholders where other features may be
included, but are NOT REQUIRED. The one space indentation of the
feature lines is mandatory [RFC2389].

- Mirror servers may want to exactly reflect the site that they are
  mirroring. In such cases servers MAY store and present the exact
  pathname bytes that it received from the main server.

3.3 Clients compliance

- Clients which do not require display of pathnames are under no
  obligation to do so. Non-display clients do not need to conform to
  requirements associated with display.

- Clients, which are presented UTF-8 pathnames by the server, SHOULD
  parse UTF-8 correctly and attempt to display the pathname within
  the limitation of the resources available.

- Clients MUST support the FEAT command and recognize the "UTF8"
  feature (defined in 3.2 above) to determine if a server supports
  UTF-8 encoding.

- Character semantics of other names shall remain undefined. If a
  client detects that a server is non UTF-8, it SHOULD change its
  display appropriately. How a client implementation handles non
  UTF-8 is a quality of implementation issue. It MAY try to assume
  some other encoding, give the user a chance to try to assume
  something, or save encoding assumptions for a server from one FTP
  session to another.

- Glyph rendering is outside the scope of this document. How a client
  presents characters it cannot display is a quality of
  implementation issue. This document RECOMMENDS that octets
  corresponding to non-displayable characters SHOULD be presented in
  URL %HH format defined in RFC 1738 [RFC1738]. They MAY, however,
  display them as question marks, with their UCS hexadecimal value,
  or in any other suitable fashion.

- Many existing clients interpret 8-bit pathnames as being in the
  local character set. They MAY continue to do so for pathnames that
  are not valid UTF-8.

4. Language Support

The Character Set Workshop Report [RFC2130] suggests that clients and
servers SHOULD negotiate a language for "greetings" and "error
messages". This specification interprets the use of the term  "error
message", by RFC 2130, to mean any explanatory text string returned
by server-PI in response to a user-PI command.

Implementers SHOULD note that FTP commands and numeric responses are protocol elements. As such, their use is not affected by any guidance expressed by this specification.

Language support of greetings and command responses shall be the default language supported by the server or the language supported by the server and selected by the client.

It may be possible to achieve language support through a virtual host as described in [MLST]. However, an FTP server might not support virtual servers, or virtual servers might be configured to support an environment without regard for language. To allow language negotiation this specification defines a new LANG command. Clients and servers that comply with this specification MUST support the LANG command.

4.1 The LANG command

A new command "LANG" is added to the FTP command set to allow server-FTP process to determine in which language to present server greetings and the textual part of command responses. The parameter associated with the LANG command SHALL be one of the language tags defined in RFC 1766 [RFC1766]. If a LANG command without a parameter is issued the server's default language will be used.

Greetings and responses issued prior to language negotiation SHALL be in the server's default language. Paragraph 4.5 of [RFC2277] state that this "default language MUST be understandable by an English-speaking person". This specification RECOMMENDS that the server default language be English encoded using ASCII. This text may be augmented by text from other languages. Once negotiated, server-PI MUST return server messages and textual part of command responses in the negotiated language and encoded in UTF-8. Server-PI MAY wish to re-send previously issued server messages in the newly negotiated language.

The LANG command only affects presentation of greeting messages and explanatory text associated with command responses. No attempt should be made by the server to translate protocol elements (FTP commands and numeric responses) or data transmitted over the data connection.

User-PI MAY issue the LANG command at any time during an FTP session. In order to gain the full benefit of this command, it SHOULD be presented prior to authentication. In general, it will be issued after the HOST command [MLST]. Note that the issuance of a HOST or

REIN command [RFC959] will negate the affect of the LANG command. User-PI SHOULD be capable of supporting UTF-8 encoding for the language negotiated. Guidance on interpretation and rendering of UTF-8, defined in section 3, SHALL apply.

Although NOT REQUIRED by this specification, a user-PI SHOULD issue a FEAT command [RFC2389] prior to a LANG command. This will allow the user-PI to determine if the server supports the LANG command and which language options.

In order to aid the server in identifying whether a connection has been established with a client which conforms to this specification or an older client, user-PI MUST send a HOST [MLST] and/or LANG command prior to issuing any other command (other than FEAT [RFC2389]). If user-PI issues a HOST command, and the server's default language is acceptable, it need not issue a LANG command. However, if the implementation does not support the HOST command, a LANG command MUST be issued. Until server-PI is presented with either a HOST or LANG command it SHOULD assume that the user-PI does not comply with this specification.

4.2 Syntax of the LANG command

The LANG command is defined as follows:

```
lang-command        = "Lang" [(SP lang-tag)] CRLF
lang-tag            = Primary-tag *( "-" Sub-tag)
Primary-tag         = 1*8ALPHA
Sub-tag             = 1*8ALPHA

lang-response       = lang-ok / error-response
lang-ok             = "200" [SP *(%x00..%xFF) ] CRLF
error-response      = command-unrecognized / bad-argument /
                      not-implemented / unsupported-parameter
command-unrecognized = "500" [SP *(%x01..%xFF) ] CRLF
bad-argument        = "501" [SP *(%x01..%xFF) ] CRLF
not-implemented     = "502" [SP *(%x01..%xFF) ] CRLF
unsupported-parameter = "504" [SP *(%x01..%xFF) ] CRLF
```

The "lang" command word is case independent and may be specified in any character case desired. Therefore "LANG", "lang", "Lang", and "lAnG" are equivalent commands.

The OPTIONAL "Lang-tag" given as a parameter specifies the primary language tags and zero or more sub-tags as defined in [RFC1766]. As described in [RFC1766] language tags are treated as case insensitive. If omitted server-PI MUST use the server's default language.

Server-FTP responds to the "Lang" command with either "lang-ok" or "error-response". "lang-ok" MUST be sent if Server-FTP supports the "Lang" command and can support some form of the "lang-tag". Support SHOULD be as follows:

- If server-FTP receives "Lang" with no parameters it SHOULD return messages and command responses in the server default language.

- If server-FTP receives "Lang" with only a primary tag argument (e.g. en, fr, de, ja, zh, etc.), which it can support, it SHOULD return messages and command responses in the language associated with that primary tag. It is possible that server-FTP will only support the primary tag when combined with a sub-tag (e.g. en-US, en-UK, etc.). In such cases, server-FTP MAY determine the appropriate variant to use during the session. How server-FTP makes that determination is outside the scope of this specification. If server-FTP cannot determine if a sub-tag variant is appropriate it SHOULD return an "unsupported-parameter" (504) response.

- If server-FTP receives "Lang" with a primary tag and sub-tag(s) argument, which is implemented, it SHOULD return messages and command responses in support of the language argument. It is possible that server-FTP can support the primary tag of the "Lang" argument but not the sub-tag(s). In such cases server-FTP MAY return messages and command responses in the most appropriate variant of the primary tag that has been implemented. How server-FTP makes that determination is outside the scope of this specification. If server-FTP cannot determine if a sub-tag variant is appropriate it SHOULD return an "unsupported-parameter" (504) response.

For example if client-FTP sends a "LANG en-AU" command and server-FTP has implemented language tags en-US and en-UK it may decide that the most appropriate language tag is en-UK and return "200 en-AU not supported. Language set to en-UK". The numeric response is a protocol element and can not be changed. The associated string is for illustrative purposes only.

Clients and servers that conform to this specification MUST support the LANG command. Clients SHOULD, however, anticipate receiving a 500 or 502 command response, in cases where older or non-compliant servers do not recognize or have not implemented the "Lang". A 501 response SHOULD be sent if the argument to the "Lang" command is not syntactically correct. A 504 response SHOULD be sent if the "Lang" argument, while syntactically correct, is not implemented. As noted above, an argument may be considered a lexicon match even though it is not an exact syntax match.

4.3 Feat response for LANG command

   A server-FTP process that supports the LANG command, and language
   support for messages and command responses, MUST include in the
   response to the FEAT command [RFC2389], a feature line indicating
   that the LANG command is supported and a fact list of the supported
   language tags. A response to a FEAT command SHALL be in the following
   format:

        Lang-feat    = SP "LANG" SP lang-fact CRLF
        lang-fact    = lang-tag ["*"] *(";" lang-tag ["*"])

        lang-tag     = Primary-tag *( "-" Sub-tag)
        Primary-tag= 1*8ALPHA
        Sub-tag      = 1*8ALPHA

   The lang-feat response contains the string "LANG" followed by a
   language fact. This string is not case sensitive, but SHOULD be
   transmitted in upper case, as recommended in [RFC2389]. The initial
   space shown in the Lang-feat response is REQUIRED by the FEAT
   command. It MUST be a single space character. More or less space
   characters are not permitted. The lang-fact SHALL include the lang-
   tags which server-FTP can support. At least one lang-tag MUST be
   included with the FEAT response. The lang-tag SHALL be in the form
   described earlier in this document. The OPTIONAL asterisk, when
   present, SHALL indicate the current lang-tag being used by server-FTP
   for messages and responses.

4.3.1 Feat examples

        C> feat
        S> 211- <any descriptive text>
        S>  ...
        S>  LANG EN*
        S>  ...
        S> 211 end

   In this example server-FTP can only support English, which is the
   current language (as shown by the asterisk) being used by the server
   for messages and command responses.

        C> feat
        S> 211- <any descriptive text>
        S>  ...
        S>  LANG EN*;FR
        S>  ...
        S> 211 end

```
C> LANG fr
S> 200 Le response sera changez au francais

C> feat
S> 211- <quelconque descriptif texte>
S>  ...
S>   LANG EN;FR*
S>  ...
S> 211 end
```

In this example server-FTP supports both English and French as shown
by the initial response to the FEAT command. The asterisk indicates
that English is the current language in use by server-FTP. After a
LANG command is issued to change the language to French, the FEAT
response shows French as the current language in use.

In the above examples ellipses indicate placeholders where other
features may be included, but are NOT REQUIRED.

5 Security Considerations

This document addresses the support of character sets beyond 1 byte
and a new language negotiation command. Conformance to this document
should not induce a security risk.

6 Acknowledgments

The following people have contributed to this document:

D. J. Bernstein
Martin J. Duerst
Mark Harris
Paul Hethmon
Alun Jones
Gregory Lundberg
James Matthews
Keith Moore
Sandra O'Donnell
Benjamin Riefenstahl
Stephen Tihor

(and others from the FTPEXT working group)

## 7 Glossary

BIDI - abbreviation for Bi-directional, a reference to mixed right-to-left and left-to-right text.

Character Set - a collection of characters used to represent textual information in which each character has a numeric value

Code Set - (see character set).

Glyph - a character image represented on a display device.

I18N - "I eighteen N", the first and last letters of the word "internationalization" and the eighteen letters in between.

UCS-2 - the ISO/IEC 10646 two octet Universal Character Set form.

UCS-4 - the ISO/IEC 10646 four octet Universal Character Set form.

UTF-8 - the UCS Transformation Format represented in 8 bits.

TF-16 - A 16-bit format including the BMP (directly encoded) and surrogate pairs to represent characters in planes 01-16; equivalent to Unicode.

## 8 Bibliography

[ABNF]          Crocker, D. and P. Overell, "Augmented BNF for Syntax Specifications: ABNF", RFC 2234, November 1997.

[ASCII]         ANSI X3.4:1986 Coded Character Sets - 7 Bit American National Standard Code for Information Interchange (7-bit ASCII)

[ISO-8859]      ISO 8859. International standard -- Information processing -- 8-bit single-byte coded graphic character sets -- Part 1:Latin alphabet No. 1 (1987) -- Part 2: Latin alphabet No. 2 (1987) -- Part 3: Latin alphabet No. 3 (1988) -- Part 4: Latin alphabet No. 4 (1988) -- Part 5: Latin/Cyrillic alphabet (1988) -- Part 6: Latin/Arabic alphabet (1987) -- Part : Latin/Greek alphabet (1987) -- Part 8: Latin/Hebrew alphabet (1988) -- Part 9: Latin alphabet No. 5 (1989) -- Part10: Latin alphabet No. 6 (1992)

[BCP14]         Bradner, S., "Key words for use in RFCs to Indicate Requirement Levels", BCP 14, RFC 2119, March 1997.

[ISO-10646]   ISO/IEC 10646-1:1993. International standard --
              Information technology -- Universal multiple-octet coded
              character set (UCS) -- Part 1: Architecture and basic
              multilingual plane.

[MLST]        Elz, R. and P. Hethmon, "Extensions to FTP", Work in
              Progress.

[RFC854]      Postel, J. and J. Reynolds, "Telnet Protocol
              Specification", STD 8, RFC 854, May 1983.

[RFC959]      Postel, J. and J. Reynolds, "File Transfer Protocol
              (FTP)", STD 9, RFC 959, October 1985.

[RFC1123]     Braden, R., "Requirements for Internet Hosts --
              Application and Support", STD 3, RFC 1123, October 1989.

[RFC1738]     Berners-Lee, T., Masinter, L. and M. McCahill, "Uniform
              Resource Locators (URL)", RFC 1738, December 1994.

[RFC1766]     Alvestrand, H., "Tags for the Identification of
              Languages", RFC 1766, March 1995.

[RFC2130]     Weider, C., Preston, C., Simonsen, K., Alvestrand, H.,
              Atkinson, R., Crispin, M. and P. Svanberg, "Character
              Set Workshop Report", RFC 2130, April 1997.

[RFC2277]     Alvestrand, H., " IETF Policy on Character Sets and
              Languages", RFC 2277, January 1998.

[RFC2279]     Yergeau, F., "UTF-8, a transformation format of ISO
              10646", RFC 2279, January 1998.

[RFC2389]     Elz, R. and P. Hethmon, "Feature Negotiation Mechanism
              for the File Transfer Protocol", RFC 2389, August 1998.

[UNICODE]     The Unicode Consortium, "The Unicode Standard - Version
              2.0", Addison Westley Developers Press, July 1996.

[UTF-8]       ISO/IEC 10646-1:1993 AMENDMENT 2 (1996). UCS
              Transformation Format 8 (UTF-8).

9 Author's Address

    Bill Curtin
    JIEO
    Attn: JEBBD
    Ft. Monmouth, N.J. 07703-5613

    EMail: curtinw@ftm.disa.mil

Annex A - Implementation Considerations

A.1 General Considerations

- Implementers should ensure that their code accounts for potential problems, such as using a NULL character to terminate a string or no longer being able to steal the high order bit for internal use, when supporting the extended character set.

- Implementers should be aware that there is a chance that pathnames that are non UTF-8 may be parsed as valid UTF-8. The probabilities are low for some encoding or statistically zero to zero for others. A recent non-scientific analysis found that EUC encoded Japanese words had a 2.7% false reading; SJIS had a 0.0005% false reading; other encoding such as ASCII or KOI-8 have a 0% false reading. This probability is highest for short pathnames and decreases as pathname size increases. Implementers may want to look for signs that pathnames which parse as UTF-8 are not valid UTF-8, such as the existence of multiple local character sets in short pathnames. Hopefully, as more implementations conform to UTF-8 transfer encoding there will be a smaller need to guess at the encoding.

- Client developers should be aware that it will be possible for pathnames to contain mixed characters (e.g. //Latin1DirectoryName/HebrewFileName). They should be prepared to handle the Bi-directional (BIDI) display of these character sets (i.e. right to left display for the directory and left to right display for the filename). While bi-directional display is outside the scope of this document and more complicated than the above example, an algorithm for bi-directional display can be found in the UNICODE 2.0 [UNICODE] standard. Also note that pathnames can have different byte ordering yet be logically and display-wise equivalent due to the insertion of BIDI control characters at different points during composition. Also note that mixed character sets may also present problems with font swapping.

- A server that copies pathnames transparently from a local filesystem may continue to do so. It is then up to the local file creators to use UTF-8 pathnames.

- Servers can supports charset labeling of files and/or directories, such that different pathnames may have different charsets. The server should attempt to convert all pathnames to UTF-8, but if it can't then it should leave that name in its raw form.

- Some server's OS do not mandate character sets, but allow administrators to configure it in the FTP server. These servers should be configured to use a particular mapping table (either

external or built-in). This will allow the flexibility of defining
different charsets for different directories.

- If the server's OS does not mandate the character set and the FTP
  server cannot be configured, the server should simply use the raw
  bytes in the file name.  They might be ASCII or UTF-8.

- If the server is a mirror, and wants to look just like the site it
  is mirroring, it should store the exact file name bytes that it
  received from the main server.

A.2 Transition Considerations

- Servers which support this specification, when presented a pathname
  from an old client (one which does not support this specification),
  can nearly always tell whether the pathname is in UTF-8 (see B.1)
  or in some other code set. In order to support these older clients,
  servers may wish to default to a non UTF-8 code set. However, how a
  server supports non UTF-8 is outside the scope of this
  specification.

- Clients which support this specification will be able to determine
  if the server can support UTF-8 (i.e. supports this specification)
  by the ability of the server to support the FEAT command and the
  UTF8 feature (defined in 3.2). If the newer clients determine that
  the server does not support UTF-8 it may wish to default to a
  different code set. Client developers should take into
  consideration that pathnames, associated with older servers, might
  be stored in UTF-8. However, how a client supports non UTF-8 is
  outside the scope of this specification.

- Clients and servers can transition to UTF-8 by either converting
  to/from the local encoding, or the users can store UTF-8 filenames.
  The former approach is easier on tightly controlled file systems
  (e.g. PCs and MACs). The latter approach is easier on more free
  form file systems (e.g. Unix).

- For interactive use attention should be focused on user interface
  and ease of use. Non-interactive use requires a consistent and
  controlled behavior.

- There may be many applications which reference files under their
  old raw pathname (e.g. linked URLs). Changing the pathname to UTF-8
  will cause access to the old URL to fail. A solution may be for the
  server to act as if there was 2 different pathnames associated with
  the file. This might be done internal to the server on controlled
  file systems or by using symbolic links on free form systems. While
  this approach may work for single file transfer non-interactive
  use, a non-interactive transfer of all of the files in a directory
  will produce duplicates. Interactive users may be presented with
  lists of files which are double the actual number files.

Annex B - Sample Code and Examples

B.1 Valid UTF-8 check

   The following routine checks if a byte sequence is valid UTF-8. This
   is done by checking for the proper tagging of the first and following
   bytes to make sure they conform to the UTF-8 format. It then checks
   to assure that the data part of the UTF-8 sequence conforms to the
   proper range allowed by the encoding. Note: This routine will not
   detect characters that have not been assigned and therefore do not
   exist.

```
int utf8_valid(const unsigned char *buf, unsigned int len)
{
 const unsigned char *endbuf = buf + len;
 unsigned char byte2mask=0x00, c;
 int trailing = 0;   // trailing (continuation) bytes to follow

 while (buf != endbuf)
 {
   c = *buf++;
   if (trailing)
    if ((c&0xC0) == 0x80)    // Does trailing byte follow UTF-8 format?
    {if (byte2mask)          // Need to check 2nd byte for proper range?
      if (c&byte2mask)       // Are appropriate bits set?
       byte2mask=0x00;
      else
       return 0;
     trailing--; }
    else
     return 0;
   else
    if ((c&0x80) == 0x00)  continue;       // valid 1 byte UTF-8
    else if ((c&0xE0) == 0xC0)             // valid 2 byte UTF-8
         if (c&0x1E)                       // Is UTF-8 byte in
                                           // proper range?

           trailing =1;
          else
           return 0;
    else if ((c&0xF0) == 0xE0)             // valid 3 byte UTF-8
         {if (!(c&0x0F))                   // Is UTF-8 byte in
                                           // proper range?

           byte2mask=0x20;                 // If not set mask
                                           // to check next byte

          trailing = 2;}
    else if ((c&0xF8) == 0xF0)             // valid 4 byte UTF-8
         {if (!(c&0x07))                   // Is UTF-8 byte in
                                           // proper range?
```

```
            byte2mask=0x30;              // If not set mask
                                         // to check next byte
            trailing = 3;}
    else if ((c&0xFC) == 0xF8)          // valid 5 byte UTF-8
          {if (!(c&0x03))               // Is UTF-8 byte in
                                         // proper range?
            byte2mask=0x38;              // If not set mask
                                         // to check next byte
            trailing = 4;}
    else if ((c&0xFE) == 0xFC)          // valid 6 byte UTF-8
          {if (!(c&0x01))               // Is UTF-8 byte in
                                         // proper range?
            byte2mask=0x3C;              // If not set mask
                                         // to check next byte
            trailing = 5;}
    else   return 0;
  }
  return trailing == 0;
}
```

## B.2 Conversions

The code examples in this section closely reflect the algorithm in
ISO 10646 and may not present the most efficient solution for
converting to / from UTF-8 encoding. If efficiency is an issue,
implementers should use the appropriate bitwise operators.

Additional code examples and numerous mapping tables can be found at
the Unicode site, HTTP://www.unicode.org or FTP://unicode.org.

Note that the conversion examples below assume that the local
character set supported in the operating system is something other
than UCS2/UTF-16. There are some operating systems that already
support UCS2/UTF-16 (notably Plan 9 and Windows NT). In this case no
conversion will be necessary from the local character set to the UCS.

## B.2.1 Conversion from Local Character Set to UTF-8

Conversion from the local filesystem character set to UTF-8 will
normally involve a two step process. First convert the local
character set to the UCS; then convert the UCS to UTF-8.

The first step in the process can be performed by maintaining a
mapping table that includes the local character set code and the
corresponding UCS code. For instance the ISO/IEC 8859-8 [ISO-8859]
code for the Hebrew letter "VAV" is 0xE4. The corresponding 4 byte
ISO/IEC 10646 code is 0x000005D5.

The next step is to convert the UCS character code to the UTF-8 encoding. The following routine can be used to determine and encode the correct number of bytes based on the UCS-4 character code:

```
unsigned int ucs4_to_utf8 (unsigned long *ucs4_buf, unsigned int
                           ucs4_len, unsigned char *utf8_buf)


{
 const unsigned long *ucs4_endbuf = ucs4_buf + ucs4_len;
 unsigned int utf8_len = 0;          // return value for UTF8 size
 unsigned char *t_utf8_buf = utf8_buf; // Temporary pointer
                                       // to load UTF8 values


 while (ucs4_buf != ucs4_endbuf)
 {
  if ( *ucs4_buf <= 0x7F)     // ASCII chars no conversion needed
  {
   *t_utf8_buf++ = (unsigned char) *ucs4_buf;
   utf8_len++;
   ucs4_buf++;
  }
  else
   if ( *ucs4_buf <= 0x07FF ) // In the 2 byte utf-8 range
   {
     *t_utf8_buf++= (unsigned char) (0xC0 + (*ucs4_buf/0x40));
     *t_utf8_buf++= (unsigned char) (0x80 + (*ucs4_buf%0x40));
     utf8_len+=2;
     ucs4_buf++;
   }
   else
    if ( *ucs4_buf <= 0xFFFF ) /* In the 3 byte utf-8 range. The
                                 values 0x0000FFFE, 0x0000FFFF
                                 and 0x0000D800 - 0x0000DFFF do
                                 not occur in UCS-4 */
    {
     *t_utf8_buf++= (unsigned char) (0xE0 +
                    (*ucs4_buf/0x1000));
     *t_utf8_buf++= (unsigned char) (0x80 +
                    ((*ucs4_buf/0x40)%0x40));
     *t_utf8_buf++= (unsigned char) (0x80 + (*ucs4_buf%0x40));
     utf8_len+=3;
     ucs4_buf++;
    }
    else
     if ( *ucs4_buf <= 0x1FFFFF ) //In the 4 byte utf-8 range
     {
      *t_utf8_buf++= (unsigned char) (0xF0 +
                     (*ucs4_buf/0x040000));
```

```
       *t_utf8_buf++= (unsigned char) (0x80 +
                      ((*ucs4_buf/0x10000)%0x40));
       *t_utf8_buf++= (unsigned char) (0x80 +
                      ((*ucs4_buf/0x40)%0x40));
       *t_utf8_buf++= (unsigned char) (0x80 + (*ucs4_buf%0x40));
       utf8_len+=4;
       ucs4_buf++;

    }
    else
    if ( *ucs4_buf <= 0x03FFFFFF )//In the 5 byte utf-8 range
    {
     *t_utf8_buf++= (unsigned char) (0xF8 +
                    (*ucs4_buf/0x01000000));
     *t_utf8_buf++= (unsigned char) (0x80 +
                    ((*ucs4_buf/0x040000)%0x40));
     *t_utf8_buf++= (unsigned char) (0x80 +
                    ((*ucs4_buf/0x1000)%0x40));
     *t_utf8_buf++= (unsigned char) (0x80 +
                    ((*ucs4_buf/0x40)%0x40));
     *t_utf8_buf++= (unsigned char) (0x80 +
                    (*ucs4_buf%0x40));
     utf8_len+=5;
     ucs4_buf++;
    }
    else
    if ( *ucs4_buf <= 0x7FFFFFFF )//In the 6 byte utf-8 range
    {
       *t_utf8_buf++= (unsigned char)
                      (0xF8 +(*ucs4_buf/0x40000000));
       *t_utf8_buf++= (unsigned char) (0x80 +
                      ((*ucs4_buf/0x01000000)%0x40));
       *t_utf8_buf++= (unsigned char) (0x80 +
                      ((*ucs4_buf/0x040000)%0x40));
       *t_utf8_buf++= (unsigned char) (0x80 +
                      ((*ucs4_buf/0x1000)%0x40));
       *t_utf8_buf++= (unsigned char) (0x80 +
                      ((*ucs4_buf/0x40)%0x40));
       *t_utf8_buf++= (unsigned char) (0x80 +
                      (*ucs4_buf%0x40));
       utf8_len+=6;
       ucs4_buf++;

    }
  }
  return (utf8_len);
  }
```

B.2.2 Conversion from UTF-8 to Local Character Set

When moving from UTF-8 encoding to the local character set the
reverse procedure is used. First the UTF-8 encoding is transformed
into the UCS-4 character set. The UCS-4 is then converted to the
local character set from a mapping table (i.e. the opposite of the
table used to form the UCS-4 character code).

To convert from UTF-8 to UCS-4 the free bits (those that do not
define UTF-8 sequence size or signify continuation bytes) in a UTF-8
sequence are concatenated as a bit string. The bits are then
distributed into a four-byte sequence starting from the least
significant bits. Those bits not assigned a bit in the four-byte
sequence are padded with ZERO bits. The following routine converts
the UTF-8 encoding to UCS-4 character codes:

```
int utf8_to_ucs4 (unsigned long *ucs4_buf, unsigned int utf8_len,
                  unsigned char *utf8_buf)
{

const unsigned char *utf8_endbuf = utf8_buf + utf8_len;
unsigned int ucs_len=0;

 while (utf8_buf != utf8_endbuf)
 {

  if ((*utf8_buf & 0x80) == 0x00)   /*ASCII chars no conversion
                                      needed */
  {
   *ucs4_buf++ = (unsigned long) *utf8_buf;
   utf8_buf++;
   ucs_len++;
  }
  else
   if ((*utf8_buf & 0xE0)== 0xC0) //In the 2 byte utf-8 range
   {
     *ucs4_buf++ = (unsigned long) (((*utf8_buf - 0xC0) * 0x40)
                   + ( *(utf8_buf+1) - 0x80));
     utf8_buf += 2;
     ucs_len++;
   }
   else
    if ( (*utf8_buf & 0xF0) == 0xE0 ) /*In the 3 byte utf-8
                                        range */
    {
     *ucs4_buf++ = (unsigned long) (((*utf8_buf - 0xE0) * 0x1000)
                   + (( *(utf8_buf+1) - 0x80) * 0x40)
                   + ( *(utf8_buf+2) - 0x80));
```

```
      utf8_buf+=3;
      ucs_len++;
    }
    else
     if ((*utf8_buf & 0xF8) == 0xF0) /* In the 4 byte utf-8
                                        range */
      {
       *ucs4_buf++ = (unsigned long)
                        (((*utf8_buf - 0xF0) * 0x040000)
                        + (( *(utf8_buf+1) -  0x80) * 0x1000)
                        + (( *(utf8_buf+2) -  0x80) * 0x40)
                        + ( *(utf8_buf+3) - 0x80));
      utf8_buf+=4;
      ucs_len++;
     }
     else
      if ((*utf8_buf & 0xFC) == 0xF8) /* In the 5 byte utf-8
                                         range */
       {
        *ucs4_buf++ = (unsigned long)
                         (((*utf8_buf - 0xF8) * 0x01000000)
                         + ((*(utf8_buf+1) - 0x80) * 0x040000)
                         + (( *(utf8_buf+2) -  0x80) * 0x1000)
                         + (( *(utf8_buf+3) -  0x80) * 0x40)
                         + ( *(utf8_buf+4) - 0x80));
       utf8_buf+=5;
       ucs_len++;
      }
      else
       if ((*utf8_buf & 0xFE) == 0xFC) /* In the 6 byte utf-8
                                          range */
        {
         *ucs4_buf++ = (unsigned long)
                          (((*utf8_buf - 0xFC) * 0x40000000)
                          + ((*(utf8_buf+1) - 0x80) * 0x010000000)
                          + ((*(utf8_buf+2) - 0x80) * 0x040000)
                          + (( *(utf8_buf+3) -  0x80) * 0x1000)
                          + (( *(utf8_buf+4) -  0x80) * 0x40)
                          + ( *(utf8_buf+5) - 0x80));
        utf8_buf+=6;
        ucs_len++;
       }

   }
  return (ucs_len);
  }
```

B.2.3 ISO/IEC 8859-8 Example

   This example demonstrates mapping ISO/IEC 8859-8 character set to
   UTF-8 and back to ISO/IEC 8859-8. As noted earlier, the Hebrew letter
   "VAV" is convertd from the ISO/IEC 8859-8 character code 0xE4 to the
   corresponding 4 byte ISO/IEC 10646 code of 0x000005D5 by a simple
   lookup of a conversion/mapping file.

   The UCS-4 character code is transformed into UTF-8 using the
   ucs4_to_utf8 routine described earlier by:

   1. Because the UCS-4 character is between 0x80 and 0x07FF it will map
      to a 2 byte UTF-8 sequence.
   2. The first byte is defined by (0xC0 + (0x000005D5 / 0x40)) = 0xD7.

   3. The second byte is defined by (0x80 + (0x000005D5 % 0x40)) = 0x95.

   The UTF-8 encoding is transferred back to UCS-4 by using the
   utf8_to_ucs4 routine described earlier by:

   1. Because the first byte of the sequence, when the '&' operator with
      a value of 0xE0 is applied, will produce 0xC0 (0xD7 & 0xE0 = 0xC0)
      the UTF-8 is a 2 byte sequence.
   2. The four byte UCS-4 character code is produced by (((0xD7 - 0xC0)
      * 0x40) + (0x95 -0x80)) = 0x000005D5.

   Finally, the UCS-4 character code is converted to ISO/IEC 8859-8
   character code (using the mapping table which matches ISO/IEC 8859-8
   to UCS-4 ) to produce the original 0xE4 code for the Hebrew letter
   "VAV".

B.2.4 Vendor Codepage Example

   This example demonstrates the mapping of a codepage to UTF-8 and back
   to a vendor codepage. Mapping between vendor codepages can be done in
   a very similar manner as described above. For instance both the PC
   and Mac codepages reflect the character set from the Thai standard
   TIS 620-2533. The character code on both platforms for the Thai
   letter "SO SO" is 0xAB. This character can then be mapped into the
   UCS-4 by way of a conversion/mapping file to produce the UCS-4 code
   of 0x0E0B.

   The UCS-4 character code is transformed into UTF-8 using the
   ucs4_to_utf8 routine described earlier by:

   1. Because the UCS-4 character is between 0x0800 and 0xFFFF it will
      map to a 3 byte UTF-8 sequence.
   2. The first byte is defined by (0xE0 + (0x00000E0B / 0x1000) = 0xE0.

3. The second byte is defined by (0x80 + ((0x00000E0B / 0x40) %
0x40))) = 0xB8.
4. The third byte is defined by (0x80 + (0x00000E0B % 0x40)) = 0x8B.

The UTF-8 encoding is transferred back to UCS-4 by using the
utf8_to_ucs4 routine described earlier by:

1. Because the first byte of the sequence, when the '&' operator with
a value of 0xF0 is applied, will produce 0xE0 (0xE0 & 0xF0 = 0xE0)
the UTF-8 is a 3 byte sequence.
2. The four byte UCS-4 character code is produced by (((0xE0 - 0xE0)
* 0x1000) + ((0xB8 - 0x80) * 0x40) + (0x8B -0x80) = 0x0000E0B.

Finally, the UCS-4 character code is converted to either the PC or
MAC codepage character code (using the mapping table which matches
codepage to UCS-4 ) to produce the original 0xAB code for the Thai
letter "SO SO".

B.3 Pseudo Code for a High-Quality Translating Server

```
if utf8_valid(fn)
  {
  attempt to convert fn to the local charset, producing localfn
  if (conversion fails temporarily) return error
  if (conversion succeeds)
  {
    attempt to open localfn
    if (open fails temporarily) return error
    if (open succeeds) return success
  }
  }
attempt to open fn
if (open fails temporarily) return error
if (open succeeds) return success
return permanent error
```

Full Copyright Statement

Acknowledgement

Funding for the RFC Editor function is currently provided by the
Internet Society.

# Index

ABORT (ABOR), 959:31–32, 1415:22, 24
ABORT message and format, ETFTP, 1986:9
Access, restricted, 2577:3–4
Access controls
  commands, 959:25–27, 2228:5–11
  defined, 959:3
ACCOUNT (ACCT), 959:26, 1415:22, 24–25
ADAT (authentication/security data), 2228:1, 7–8
Address Resolution Protocol (ARP), bootstrap
  loading and, 906:2
Allen, Larry, 1350:1
Allman, Mark, 2428:1, 2577:1
  address for, 2428:7, 2577:7
ALLOCATE (ALLO), 959:30–31, 1415:22, 25
Anonymous FTP
  *See also* RFC 1635
  defined, 1635:2
  security problems, 2577:5
APPEND (APPE), 959:30, 1415:22, 25–26
application/pkix-cert, 2585:4, 5
application/pkix-crl, 2585:4, 5–6
Archive site, defined, 1635:2
arc/unarc, 1635:8
ASA, 959:14
ASCII
  data types, 959:11
  defined, 959:3
Association Control Service Element (ACSE),
  1415:19
atob/btoa, 1635:7
atox/xtoa, 1635:8
AUTH (authentication/security mechanism),
  2228:1, 6

Background File Transfer Program (BFTP).
  *See* RFC 1068
Baldwin, Bob, 1350:1
Balk, Karri, 2228:22

Base 64 encoding, 2228:21–22
Baudrate, 1986:14
Baushke, Mark, 1635:1
Bellovin, Steven M., 1579:1
  address for, 1579:4
Bernstein, D. J., 2640:12
bftpd, 1068:15
bftptool, 1068:14–15
binhex, 1635:9
Block mode, 959:21–22
Blocksize option, TFTP
  performance issues, 2348:2–4
  role of, xvii, 2348:1
  security issues, 2348:4
  specification, 2348:1–2
Booter, 906:2
Bootstrap loading using TFTP
  example of implementing, 906:3–4
  network protocols used by, 906:2–3
  role of, xv, 906:1–2
Bounce attack, 2577:2–3
Braden, R., 1068:1
Brashear, Derrick, 2228:22
Brown, Jordan, 2228:22
Bufferblock, 1986:14
Burstsize, 1986:14
Byte size
  defined, 959:3
  logical versus transfer, 959:11

Carriage control, 959:14
CCC (clear command channel), 2228:1, 9–10
CDUP (CHANGE TO PARENT DIRECTORY),
  959:3, 26–27, 1415:22, 26
Certificate revocation lists (CRLs), 2585:3
Chiappa, Noel, 1350:1
Clark, Dave, 1350:1
Clear command, 1068:16

Colella, Rich, 1639:1
Commands
 *See also under name of*
 access control, 959:25–27
 arguments, 959:48
 BFTP, 1068:16–23
 directory, 959:62–65
 FTP new, 2228:5–11
 FTP service, 959:29–35
 list of, 959:47
 optional, 959:3
 sequencing, 959:49–53
 syntax, 959:45–48
 transfer parameter, 959:27–29
Compressed mode, 959:23–24
compress/uncompress, 1635:7, 10–11
CONF (confidentiality protected command), 2228:1,
 10–11
Connections, 959:44–45
 *See also* Data connections
 establishing, 959:59
Control connection, defined, 959:4
CONTROL messages and format, ETFTP,
 1986:11–12
Cooney, Robert, 1415:1
Cooper, Geoff, 1350:1
Curran, John, 1635:1
Curtin, Bill, 2640:1
 address for, 2640:15
CWD (CHANGE WORKING DIRECTORY),
 959:26, 1415:23, 26–27

Data channel encapsulation, 2228:14–15
Data connections
 defined, 959:4
 establishing, 959:18–19
 managing, 959:19–20
DATA message and format, ETFTP, 1986:9–10
Data port, defined, 959:4
DATA PORT (PORT), 959:28
Data representation and storage, 959:10–18
Data structures, 959:15–18
Data transfer
 ETFTP, 1986:13–14
 TFTP multicast option, 2090:3–5
Data transfer process (DTP), defined, 959:4
Data types
 ASCII, 959:11
 EBCDIC, 959:12
 format control, 959:13–14
 image, 959:12
 local, 959:12–13
Debug code, 2577:5–6
DELETE (DELE), 959:32, 1415:23, 27
Delivery, BFTP and reliable, 1068:8–9
DeSchon, A., 1068:1
Destination commands, 1068:16
Deutsch, Peter, 1635:1
 address for, 1635:13
DONE message and format, ETFTP, 1986:8–9
Duerst, Martin J., 2640:12

EBCDIC data type, 959:12
Edguer, Aydin, 1635:1
Elz, Robert, 2389:1
 address for, 2389:8
Emberson, A. Thomas, 2090:1
 address for, 2090:6
Emtage, Alan, 1635:1
 address for, 1635:13
ENC (privacy protected command), 2228:1, 10–11
End-of-file (EOF), 959:4, 20
End-of-line, 959:4, 12, 20
End-of-record (EOR), 959:4
Enhanced Trivial File Transfer Protocol (ETFTP).
 *See* RFC 1986
EPRT command, 2428:2–3
EPSV command, 2428:4–5
Error recovery
 defined, 959:4
 and restart, 959:24–25
Explain command, 1068:17

F-BEGIN-GROUP, 1415:39, 40
F-CANCEL, 1415:39, 40–41
F-CHANGE-ATTRIBUTE, 1415:39, 41
F-CHECK, 1415:39, 41
F-CLOSE, 1415:39, 41
F-CREATE, 1415:39, 41
F-DATA, 1415:39, 42
F-DATA-END, 1415:39, 42
F-DELETE, 1415:39, 42
F-DESELECT, 1415:39, 42
FEAT command, 2389:3
 LANG command and, 2640:11–12
 rationale for, 2389:6
 responses, 2389:4–6
 syntax, 2389:4
F-END-GROUP, 1415:39, 42–43
F-ERASE, 1415:39, 43
File
 defined, 959:5
 structure, 959:15, 16
FILE STRUCTURE (STRU), 959:29, 1415:24, 37
File Transfer, Access, and Management (FTAM)
 *See also* RFC 1415 (FTP-FTAM gateway
  specification)
 initiated gateway service, 1415:4, 6, 11–12, 16–17,
  38–47
 parameters to FTP reply codes, 1415:50–54
 state variables and transitions, 1415:16–17
File Transfer Protocol (FTP), xiii
 *See also under* RFCs
 commands, 959:5
 defined, 1635:1–2
 importance of, xiii–xiv
 initiated gateway service, 1415:4, 5, 9–11, 14–16,
  22–38
 reply codes to FTAM parameters, 1415:48–50
 state variables and transitions, 1415:14–16
File transfer service (fts), 1068:15
Find command, 1068:17–17
F-INITIALIZE, 1415:39, 43–44

Finlayson, Rosa, 906:1
Firewalls, 1579:1–4
F-LOCATE, 1415:39, 44
F-OPEN, 1415:40, 44
Format control
    carriage control, 959:14
    nonprint, 959:13–14
    Telnet, 959:14
F-P-ABORT, 1415:40, 46–47
F-READ, 1415:40, 44–45
F-READ-ATTRIBUTE, 1415:40, 45
F-RECOVER, 1415:40, 45
F-RESTART, 1415:40, 45–46
F-SELECT, 1415:40, 46
FTAM. *See* File Transfer, Access, and Management
F-TERMINATE, 1415:40, 46
FTP. *See* File Transfer Protocol
F-TRANSFER, 1415:40, 46
F-U-ABORT, 1415:40, 47
F-WRITE, 1415:40, 47

Gateway architecture, 1415:6–8
Gateway state variables and transitions, 1415:13–17
Graham, James, 1415:1
Greenwald, Mike, 1350:1
GSSAPI, 2228:24–25
gzip/gunzip, 1635:10

Harkin, Art, 1785:1, 2347:1, 2348:1, 2349:1
    address for, 1785:2, 2347:6, 2348:4, 2349:4
Harris, Mark, 2640:12
HELP, 959:34, 1415:23, 27–28
    for BFTP, 1068:18
Hethmon, Paul, 2389:1, 2640:12
    address for, 2389:8
Hoffman, Paul, 2585:1
    address for, 2585:7
Horowitz, Marc, 2228:1
    address for, 2228:23
Housley, Russell, 2585:1
    address for, 2585:7
Hypertext Transfer Protocol (HTTP). *See* RFC 2585

Image data type, 959:12
International character set, 2640:3–4
Internationalization. *See* RFC 2640
Internet Engineering Task Force (IETF), xiii
Internet Protocol (IP), bootstrap loading and, 906:2
IPv6, FTP extensions for
    command usage, 2428:5
    EPRT command, 2428:2–3
    EPSV command, 2428:4–5
    role of, xviii, 2428:1–2
    security issues, 2428:6
ISO
    8571, 1415:3, 20
    8859, 2640:2, 25
    10646, 2640:2, 3, 4, 20, 25
Israel, Jay, 1639:1

Jones, Alun, 2640:12

KEEPALIVE message and format, ETFTP, 1986:8–9
Kerberos, version 4, 2228:25–26
Kogut, Michael, 2228:22

Langan, Russ, 1986:1
    address for, 1986:20
LANG command, 2640:8–11
Lavender, R. Greg, 1415:1
LDATA message and format, ETFTP, 1986:9–10
Linn, John, 2228:22
LIST, 959:32–33, 1415:23, 28–29
Local data type, 959:12–13
Login authorization, 2228:11–12
LOGOUT (QUIT), 959:27
LPRT (long port) command, 1639:1, 2–3
LPSV (long passive) command, 1639:1, 3
Lundberg, Gregory, 2640:12
Lunt, Steve, 1639:1, 2228:1

Malkin, Gary Scott, 1785:1, 2347:1, 2348:1, 2349:1
    address for, 1785:2, 2347:6, 2348:4, 2349:4
Marine, April N., 1635:1
    address for, 1635:13
Martin, Liza, 1350:1
Maszkowski, Rafal, 1635:1
Matthews, James, 2640:12
Message types and formats, ETFTP, 1986:7–12
Metz, Craig, 2428:7
    address for, 2428:7
MIC (integrity protected command), 2228:1, 10–11
MILNET, 1415:3
MIME registrations, 2585:4–6
Mindel, Joshua L., 1415:1
    address for, 1415:58
MKD (MAKE DIRECTORY), 959:3, 32, 1415:23, 29
MODE, 1415:23, 29
Mode, defined, 959:5
Mogul, Jeff, 906:4
Moore, Keith, 2640:12
Multicast option, TFTP
    data transfer, 2090:3–5
    role of, xvii, 2090:1
    specifications, 2090:1–2
Myers, John Gardiner, 2228:22

NAME LIST (NLST), 959:33, 1415:23, 29–30
National Imagery Transmission Format Standard, 1986:1
National Institute of Standards and Technology (NIST), 1415:3
NBS-9, 1415:18
Network Address Translators (NATs), FTP extensions for
    command usage, 2428:5
    EPRT command, 2428:2–3
    EPSV command, 2428:4–5
    role of, xviii, 2428:1–2
    security issues, 2428:6
NETwork BLock Transfer Protocol (NETBLT), 1986:1, 4, 6, 16
Network naming and addressing, FTP-FTAM, 1415:8

Network Virtual File System (NVFS), defined, 959:5
Network Virtual Terminal (NVT), defined, 959:5
Nonprint format control, 959:13–14
NOOP, 959:34, 1415:23, 30
Notification message, 1068:26–27
NULL-ACK message and format, ETFTP, 1986:10

O'Donnell, Sandra, 2640:12
OPEN message and format, ETFTP, 1986:7–8
Option Acknowledgment (OACK), 2347:1–4, 2348:2, 2349:2
Option negotiation analysis, TFTP, xvi–xvii, 1785:1–2
OPTS (options) command, 2389:6–7
Ostermann, Shawn, 1639:1, 2428:1, 2577:1
    address for, 2428:7, 2577:7

Packets
    ETFTP, 1986:5
    TFTP, 1350:5–8, 2347:1–3
Packetsize, 1986:14
Padlipsky, Mike, 949:1
Page
    defined, 959:5
    structure, 959:15, 16–18, 60–61
PASS (PASSWORD), 959:26, 1415:23, 30
Passwords, protecting, 2577:4
PASV (PASSIVE), 959:28, 1415:23, 30, 1579:1–4
Pathname, defined, 959:5
Pathnames, FTP internationalization and
    clients compliance, 2640:7
    general compliance, 2640:5–6
    servers compliance, 2640:6–7
PBSZ (protection buffer size), 2228:1, 8
Perrott, Marsha, 1635:1
Peterson, Bob, 1635:1
Pinkas, Denis, 2228:22
Piscitello, David M., 1639:1
    address for, 1639:5
Polites, William J., 1986:1
    address for, 1986:20
PORT, 959:28, 1415:23, 30, 1639:1, 2
Port stealing, 2577:5
POSIX file naming and organization, 1415:55
Postel, Jon, 959:1, 1639:1
Privacy issues, 2577:4
Prompt command, 1068:18–19
PROT (data channel protection level), 2228:1, 8–9
Protected replies, 2228:13–14
Protocol interpreter (PI), defined, 959:5
Public key infrastructure (PKI). See RFC 2585
PWD (PRINT WORKING DIRECTORY), 959:3, 32, 1415:23, 31

QUIT, 959:27, 1415:23, 31
    for BFTP, 1068:18
QUITACK message and format, ETFTP, 1986:8–9
QUIT message and format, ETFTP, 1986:9

Radiodelay, 1986:15
Record
    defined, 959:6
    structure, 959:15, 16
Reed, David, 1350:1
REFUSED message and format, ETFTP, 1986:9
REIN (REINITIALIZE), 959:27, 1415:23, 31–32
Remote command execution, 2577:5
Reply(ies)
    defined, 959:6
    description of, 959:35–43
    FTP security extensions and new, 2228:12–13
    function groupings, 959:38, 39–41
    numeric order, 959:41–43
    protected, 2228:13–14
    sequencing, 959:49–53
    values, 959:37–38
Reply codes
    FTAM parameters and FTP, 1415:47–54
    negative completion, 1639:4
REPRESENTATION TYPE (TYPE), 959:28–29
Request commands, 1068:20
Requests for Comments. See RFCs
RESPONSE message and format, ETFTP, 1986:7–8
Restart, 959:24–25
RESTART (REST), 959:31, 1415:23, 32
Restricted access, 2577:3–4
RETRIEVE (RETR), 959:30, 1415:23, 32–33
Reverse Address Resolution Protocol (RARP), bootstrap loading and, 906:2
Reynolds, Joyce, 959:1
RFCs
    online, xiv, xviii–xix
    role and list of, xiv–xviii
RFC 114, 959:2
RFC 141, 959:2
RFC 172, 959:2
RFC 264, 959:2
RFC 265, 959:2
RFC 281, 959:2
RFC 294, 959:2
RFC 354, 959:2
RFC 385, 959:2
RFC 414, 959:2
RFC 430, 959:2
RFC 454, 959:2
RFC 505, 949:2
RFC 542, 959:2
RFC 601, 959:2
RFC 614, 959:2
RFC 624, 959:2
RFC 686, 959:2
RFC 691, 959:2
RFC 765, 959:2
RFC 768, 1986:1
RFC 854, 2640:5
RFC 906 (bootstrap loading using TFTP)
    example of implementing, 906:3–4
    network protocols used by, 906:2–3
    role of, xv, 906:1–2

RFC 949 (FTP unique named store command),
    description of, xv, 949:1–2
RFC 959 (File Transfer Protocol), 1068:4, 5, 8,
    1415:3, 20, 1639:1, 2228:1, 2585:3, 2640:1, 9
  commands, access control, 959:25–27
  commands, directory, 959:62–65
  commands, FTP service, 959:29–35
  commands, optional, 959:3
  commands, sequencing, 959:49–53
  commands, syntax, 959:45–48
  commands, transfer parameter, 959:27–29
  connections, 959:44–45
  connections, establishing, 959:59
  data connections, establishing, 959:18–19
  data connections, managing, 959:19–20
  data representation and storage, 959:10–18
  error recovery and restart, 959:24–25
  history of, 959:2–3
  minimum implementation requirements, 959:43
  model for, 959:8–10
  page structure, 959:60–61
  replies, 959:35–43
  replies, sequencing, 959:49–53
  RFCs related to, 959:66–68
  role of, xv, 959:1
  state diagrams, 959:54–58
  terminology, 959:3–7
  transmission modes, 959:20–24
  typical scenario, 959:59
RFC 998, 1986:1, 12
RFC 1030, 1986:16
RFC 1068 (Background File Transfer Program-
    BFTP)
  advantages of, 1068:2, 12
  commands for, 1068:16–23
  conclusions and experiences with, 1068:12–13
  control characters, 1068:10, 16
  disadvantages of, 1068:12
  example of notification message, 1068:26–27
  example of user script, 1068:24–25
  file transfer mechanics for, 1068:4–8
  general model, 1068:3–4
  implementation structure, 1068:14–15
  Internet server program, 1068:15
  reliable delivery, 1068:8–9
  role of, xv, 1068:1–3
  server daemon, 1068:15
  user interface, 1068:9–11, 13, 14–15
RFC 1101, 1415:8
RFC 1123, 1579:2, 2228:3, 2640:1
RFC 1340, 1639:2
RFC 1350 (TFTP Protocol revision 2), 1986:1
  error conditions, 1350:2–3
  headers, 1350:3–4, 9–10
  initial connection, 1350:4–5
  overview of, 1350:2–3
  packets, 1350:5–8
  relationship to other protocols, 1350:3–4
  role of, xv–xvi, 1350:1–2
  security issues, 1350:11

termination, normal, 1350:8
termination, premature, 1350:8
RFC 1415 (FTP-FTAM gateway specification)
  comparison between FTP and FTAM,
    1415:19–20
  document type support, 1415:18
  error conditions, 1415:13–14
  error handling, 1415:54
  FTAM-initiated gateway service, 1415:4, 6, 11–12,
    16–17, 38–47
  FTAM parameters to FTP reply codes, 1415:50–54
  FTP-initiated gateway service, 1415:4, 5, 9–11,
    14–16, 22–38
  FTP reply codes to FTAM parameters, 1415:48–50
  functionality losses, 1415:20
  functions and representations, mapping of,
    1415:20–47
  gateway architecture, 1415:6–8
  gateway state variables and transitions,
    1415:13–17
  implementation and configuration guidelines,
    1415:54–55
  network naming and addressing, 1415:8
  overview of, 1415:4–6
  role of, xvi, 1415:1, 2–6
  security issues, 1415:55–56
  services provided, 1415:4–6
RFC 1421, 2228:21
RFC 1579 (firewall friendly FTP), 2428:5
  implementation, 1579:3
  role of, xvi, 1579:1–3
  security issues, 1579:3–4
RFC 1635 (anonymous use of FTP)
  commands, 1635:5–6
  etiquette, 1635:11–12
  example session, 1635:3–5
  friendly servers, 1635:5
  naming of files, 1635:7–12
  role of, xvi, 1635:1
  terminology, 1635:1–3
RFC 1639 (FTP operation over Big Address
    Records-FOOBAR), 2428:1
  LPRT (long port) command, 1639:1, 2–3
  LPSV (long passive) command, 1639:1, 3
  negative completion reply codes, 1639:4
  rationale for, 1639:4
  role of, xvi, 1639:1, 2
RFC 1766, 2640:8, 9
RFC 1785 (TFTP option negotiation analysis),
    xvi–xvii, 1785:1–2
RFC 1986 (Enhanced Trivial File Transfer Protocol-
    ETFTP)
  backoffs, 1986:5
  command set, 1986:12–13
  data encapsulation, 1986:6–7
  data transfer and flow control, 1986:13–14
  delays, 1986:3–4, 15–16
  link quality, 1986:3
  message types and formats, 1986:7–12
  packet size, 1986:5

performance issues, 1986:18
protocol stack, 1986:6
role of, xvii, 1986:1–3, 5–7
security issues, 1986:19
test results, 1986:16–18
timers, 1986:15–16
transfer rates, 1986:2
tunable parameters, 1986:14–15
RFC 2068, 2585:3
RFC 2090 (TFTP multicast option)
  data transfer, 2090:3–5
  role of, xvii, 2090:1
  specifications, 2090:1–2
RFC 2119, 2428:1
RFC 2130, 2640:7
RFC 2228 (FTP security extensions)
  base 64 encoding, 2228:21–22
  commands, new, 2228:511
  commands, optional, 2228:1
  data channel encapsulation, 2228:14–15
  declarative specifications, 2228:16–18
  login authorization, 2228:11–12
  overview of, 2228:3–5
  recommendations, 2228:16
  replies, new, 2228:12–14
  role of, xvii, 2228:1, 2–3
  security issues, 2228:22
  state diagrams, 2228:19–20
RFC 2277, 2640:2, 8
RFC 2279, 2640:3
RFC 2347 (TFTP option extension)
  negotiation protocol, 2347:3–5
  packet formats, 2347:1–3
  role of, xvii, 2347:1
  security issues, 2347:5
RFC 2348 (TFTP blocksize option)
  performance issues, 2348:2–4
  role of, xvii, 2348:1
  security issues, 2348:4
  specification, 2348:1–2
RFC 2349 (TFTP timeout interval and transfer size
      options)
  role of, xvii–xviii, 2349:1
  security issues, 2349:3
  timeout interval specifications, 2349:1–2
  transfer size specifications, 2349:2–3
RFC 2389 (feature negotiation mechanism), 2640:6,
    9, 11
  basic tokens, 2389:3
  document conventions, 2389:2
  FEAT command, 2389:3–6
  OPTS (options) command, 2389:6–7
  role of, xviii, 2389:1, 2
  security issues, 2389:7
  server replies, 2389:3
RFC 2428 (FTP extensions for IPv6 and NATs)
  command usage, 2428:5
  EPRT command, 2428:2–3
  EPSV command, 2428:4–5
  role of, xviii, 2428:1–2
  security issues, 2428:6

RFC 2577 (FTP security issues)
  bounce attack, 2577:2–3
  passwords, protecting, 2577:4
  port stealing, 2577:5
  privacy issues, 2577:4
  restricted access, 2577:3–4
  role of, xviii, 2577:1–2
  software-base security problems, 2577:5–6
  usernames, protecting, 2577:4–5
RFC 2585 (Internet Public Key Infrastructure
      operational protocols)
  certificate and CRL repository, 2585:3
  FTP conventions, 2585:3–4
  HTTP conventions, 2585:4
  MIME registrations, 2585:4–6
  model, 2585:2–3
  role of xviii, 2585:1
  security issues, 2585:6–7
RFC 2640 (internationalization of FTP)
  FEAT command, 2640:11–12
  implementation issues, 2640:16–17
  international character set, 2640:3–4
  LANG command, 2640:8–11
  language support, 2640:7–12
  pathnames, 2640:5–7
  role of, xviii, 2640:1, 2
  sample code and examples, 2640:19–26
  security issues, 2640:12
  terminology, 2640:2
  transfer encoding, 2640:4–5
  transition issues, 2640:18
Riefenstahl, Benjamin, 2640:12
RMD (REMOVE DIRECTORY), 959:3, 32,
    1415:23, 33
RNFR (RENAME FROM), 959:31, 1415:23, 33
RNTO (RENAME TO), 959:31, 1415:23, 34
Rogers, Craig Milo, 1350:1
Rose, Marshall, 1415:1

Scott, John, 1415:1, 20
Security issues
  See also RFC 2228 (FTP security extensions); RFC
      2577 (FTP security issues)
  enhanced TFTP and, 1986:19
  extensions for IPv6 and NATs and, 2428:6
  feature negotiation mechanism and, 2389:7
  firewall friendly FTP and, 1579:3–4
  FTP-FTAM and, 1415:55–56
  internationalization of FTP and, 2640:12
  public key infrastructure and, 2585:6–7
  TFTP blocksize option and, 2348:4
  TFTP option extension and, 2347:5
  TFTP revision 2 and, 1350:11
  TFTP timeout interval and transfer size options
      and, 2349:3
Server-DTP, defined, 959:6
Server-FTP, defined, 959:6
Server-PI, defined, 959:6
Service commands, 959:29–35
Set commands, 1068:20–21
shar, 1635:9

Simple File Transfer Protocol (SFTP), xiii
SITE PARAMETERS (SITE), 959:33, 1415:23, 34
Sjogren, Sam, 2228:22
Slaski, Robert L., 1415:1
    address for, 1415:58
SMNT (STRUCTURE MOUNT), 959:3, 27,
    1415:23, 35
Software-base security problems, 2577:5–6
Sollins, Karen R., 1350:1
    address for, 1350:11
Song, Tae Kyong, 1639:1
Source commands, 1068:22
Spoof attacks, 2577:3–4
State diagrams, 959:54–58, 2228:19–20
STATUS (STAT), 959:33–34, 1415:24, 35
    for BFTP, 1068:22
STORE (STOR), 959:30, 1415:24, 35–36
    Store command (RFC 949), description of unique
        named, xv, 949:1–2
STORE UNIQUE (STOU), 959:3, 30, 1415:24, 36–37
Stream mode, 959:21
STRU. See FILE STRUCTURE (STRU)
Submit command, 1068:22
SYSTEM (SYST), 959:3, 33, 1415:37
Szymanski, Steve, 1350:1

tat/untar, 1635:8, 10–11
TCP/IP port, 1415:55
Telnet, 1415:19
    format controls, 959:14
    relationship between FTP and, 959:9–10
Tihor, Stephen, 1635:1, 2640:12
Time command, 1068:22
Timeout interval and transfer size options, TFTP
    role of, xvii–xviii, 2349:1
    security issues, 2349:3
    timeout interval specifications, 2349:1–2
    transfer size specifications, 2349:2–3
Timers, ETFTP, 1986:15–16
Torkington, Nathan, 1635:1
Transfer command, 1068:22
Transfer encoding, 2640:4–5
Transfer mechanics for BFTP, 1068:4–8
TRANSFER MODE (MODE), 959:29
Transfer modes for TFTP revision 2, 1350:2
Transfer parameter commands, 959:27–29
Transmission Control Protocol (TCP), 2577:2
Transmission modes, 959:20
    block, 959:21–22

compressed, 959:23–24
    stream, 959:21
Trivial File Transfer Protocol (TFTP), xiii
    See also RFC 906 (bootstrap loading using TFTP);
        RFC 1350 (TFTP Protocol revision 2); RFC
        1785 (TFTP option negotiation analysis);RFC
        1986 (Enhanced Trivial File Transfer Protocol-
        ETFTP); RFC 2090 (TFTP multicast option);
        RFC 2347 (TFTP option extension); RFC 2348
        (TFTP blocksize option); RFC 2349 (TFTP
        timeout interval and transfer size options)
Ts'o, Ted, 2228:22
Tunable parameters, 1986:14–15
Type, defined, 959:6
TYPE, 959:28–29, 1415:24, 37–38

Ullmann, Bob, 1639:1
unencode/uudecode, 1635:8
Universal Character Set (UCS), 2640:3
    transformation format (UTF-8), 2640:4–5, 19,
        20–24
User, defined, 959:7
USER (USER NAME), 959:25, 1415:24, 38
User Datagram Protocol (UDP), 1986:1
    bootstrap loading and, 906:2
    TFTP and, 1350:3
User-DTP, defined, 959:7
User-FTP, defined, 959:7
User interface, BFTP, 1068:9–11, 13, 14–15
Usernames, protecting, 2577:4–5
User-PI, defined, 959:7
User script, BFTP, 1068:24–25

Verify command, 1068:23
VMS_SHARE, 1635:9

Wallace, M. A., 1415:3, 20
Wollman, William, 1986:1
    address for, 1986:20
Woo, David, 1986:1
    address for, 1986:20

x.509 public key infrastructure. See RFC 2585

Yellick, Kathy, 1350:1

zip/unzip, 1635:8
zoo, 1635:9